INFLUENCE AND AUTONOMY IN PSYCHOANALYSIS

Stephen A. Mitchell

TAP THE ANALYTIC PRESS

1997   Hillsdale, NJ   London

RELATIONAL PERSPECTIVES BOOK SERIES

STEPHEN A. MITCHELL AND LEWIS ARON
Series Editors

"It seems to be the fear of moulding the patient in one's own image that has prevented analysts from coming to grips with the dimension of the future in analytic theory and practice, a strange omission considering the fact that growth and development are at the center of all psychoanalytic concern."

— *Hans Loewald, 1960, p. 230*

"We can exert no influence on what most resembles our own experience; in what bears our own imprint we are unable to recognize ourselves."

— *Italo Calvino, 1983*

"The road to interiority passes through the other."

— *Williams, 1992, p. 151*

Published by The Analytic Press, Inc.
Editorial Offices: 101 West Street, Hillsdale, NJ 07642

Typeset in Bulmer MT by Compudesign, Jackson Hts., NY

LIBRARY OF CONGRESS CATALOGING-IN-PUBLICATION DATA

Mitchell, S. A. 1946-
  Influence and autonomy in psychoanalysis / Stephen A. Mitchell

    p. c.m
  Includes bibliographical references and index.
  ISBN 0-88163-240-6
  1. Psychotherapist and patient. 2. Psychoanalysis—Methodology.
I. Title
RC480.8.M58   1997
616.89'17—dc21   97-40014
                                                          CIP

Printed in the United States of America
10 9 8 7 6 5 4 3 2 1

CONTENTS

PROLOGUE
Interaction and the Problem
of Technique

T he concept of technique in psychoanalysis is generally associated with the three fundamental pillars of classical American
orthodoxy: neutrality, anonymity, and abstinence. Although
they have been put into practice in a wide variety of ways, these principles are generally understood as injunctions against the analyst's ill-
advised participation in the analytic process. They caution restraint:
remain calm and nonpartisan; stay hidden; do not gratify.

With the broad movement in the direction of a two-person, interactive view of the analytic process, these principles have fallen into dis-
repute. Even in the most conservative quarters, they are being
radically transformed. Most of us now seem to regard the analyst as
inevitably and usefully embedded in the process. Because there is
nowhere to hide, gratification and the analyst's partisanship, in one
form or another, are inescapable. With the fading of the classical
model, the very concept of technique itself has also fallen into disre-
pute. The emphasis now is on interaction, enactment, spontaneity,
mutuality, and authenticity; technique is associated with what is
regarded as the anachronistic illusion that the analyst can remain

outside the process by maintaining a wooden, mechanical demeanor. In the current analytic milieu, the term technique itself has become almost a term of abuse. Technicians are people who clean teeth, run electrocardiogram machines, and fix computer hardware. Technique in psychoanalysis is associated with precisely the impersonal, scientistic model of psychoanalytic practice many of us were trained in, found inadequate, and left behind.

But the great value of classical technique was that it helped the clinician make choices. Perhaps the most frequently asked question by beginning clinicians these days is, "How do I know what to do?" Most experienced analysts who identify themselves in one fashion or another as relational have a hard time responding with any degree of specificity to this question. When the analyst was envisioned as outside the process, it was easy to develop consistent and generally applicable guidelines for her participation. Proper technique insured replicability of good work. Now that the analyst is envisioned as embedded, to one degree or another, in the process, general guidelines are difficult to imagine. Because each analytic dyad and each situation is, in some sense, a unique configuration, we don't want to prescribe or proscribe the analyst's responses.

In the traditional approach to technique, there were clear injunctions: "Maintain the analytic frame." "Never ask questions." "Never answer questions." But these kinds of rules don't work well anymore. We assume that the analysand often sees through the analyst's posturing, and we want the analytic clinician to behave in ways that are personally authentic for him or her. Many of us now believe that *what* one does is less important than how openly what does happen is *processed* with the analysand. That is all well and good, but, still, we *do* have to decide what to do.

The analytic clinician necessarily makes clinical judgments all the time. She is constantly struggling with questions like: What *sort* of frame should be maintained? Should I express my countertransferential experiences? Should I answer the analyeand's inquiries? In response to such questions, most contemporary relational analysts would probably answer, "It depends." The recent analytic literature is full of inspirational examples of great success when the analyst did one thing or another, usually something contrary to the automatic application of classical injunctions, but there is little focus on what the analyst's response depends *on*.

Throughout this book I demonstrate that current psychoanalytic concepts like interaction (or dyadic or two-person perspectives) have a long history, have been developed broadly and differently in different theoretical traditions, and are applied quite variously by contemporary analytic writers and clinicians. We will see that viewing the analytic process in interactive terms does not translate directly into a particular course of action, a particular analytic stance, a particular set of directions to the clinician about what to do.

Because classical principles of technique were so closely tied to restraints on the analyst's potential emotional and behavioral overinvolvement with the patient, the fading of these principles has been accompanied by fears that now "anything goes." Of course, there are no authors declaring that anything *should* go, but the fear is that the abandonment of technical principles like neutrality, anonymity, and abstinence will lead us down a steep and slippery slope to irresponsible, reckless abandon.

In fact, as I demonstrate in this book, psychoanalysis is practiced today with just as much discipline and responsibility as in the days when classical theory of technique served as a framework. But discipline, or technique, in contemporary psychoanalytic work operates in a different way. The emphasis is not on behaviors but on rigorous thinking, not on constraints but on self-reflective emotional involvement, not on the application of general truths but on imaginative participation. This suggests a very different sort of "technique." The discipline is not in the procedures, but in the sensibility through which the analyst participates.

Technique in contemporary psychoanalytic practice, with its wide array of participatory options, operates in a fashion similar to technique in sports like tennis, or in arts like painting or music making, where technique is not a bad word. There is a sense that one cannot practice a complex craft without absorbing and mastering technical principles and component skills. Eventually, the technique dissolves into an individual style or statement. Artists or athletes who are merely good technicians are uninspired and limited in their potential. But great artists and athletes could never get where they are going without mastering technique.

What are the component skills that constitute good psychoanalytic technique? I suggest throughout this book that practicing psychoanalysis entails *a special kind of experiencing and thinking*. Sullivan's term participant observation provides a good start for describing the analyst's activity, but only a start, because one can be a participant observer in many different kinds of activities. The kind of participation required of the analyst is a complex blend of listening; silently responding; giving oneself over to the explicit and subtle interactional gambits offered by the patient; observing the impact on the patient of one's own ideas and emotional commitments; and giving oneself over to a range of states of mind that allow a broad array of one's own feelings and imaginings, past and present, fantastic and realistic, to come alive. The kind of observation required of the analyst is a complex form of self-reflection, with shifting foci, sometimes on the patient, sometimes on the analyst, sometimes on the patient and analyst as a unit. And the kind of hard thinking required of the analyst is grounded in her responsibility for keeping the process psychoanalytic, in which the patient's ultimate welfare is always the first priority, no matter how difficult it is at times to know precisely how to do that.

I have discussed the complex problems of teaching psychoanalysis, both didactically and in supervision, with many different analysts in many different contexts. One common view is that the best way for beginning clinicians to learn restraint is to be taught classical principles and injunctions at the start. Later on, they should be taken aside and informed that traditional principles and taboos are only guidelines and are not to be taken as absolute. Although appealing, this view seems to me to be ultimately wrongheaded and wasteful of time and energy. There is much to be learned from classical principles and concepts (I virtually always begin every course I teach with Freud), but I believe that beginning clinicians can and should grapple from the start with the ambiguity of the analytic situation and the cocreation of its meanings in the interaction of its two participants. Ultimately, rote behaviors and prohibitions are no substitute for serious thinking.

The ideas provided by psychoanalytic theories are an important component of good technique. Theories help the analyst think. They provide <u>ideas of interaction</u> that offer the clinician various options to consider in the middle of the <u>affective density that saturates the analytic situation</u>. They suggest possibilities; they provide considerations; they are tools to disentangle complexities; they warn of dangers. It is my hope that this book, while certainly not a how-to manual, will contribute to good analytic "technique" by bringing together, explicating, and offering for consideration a variety of different ways of thinking about the interactive nature of the psychoanalytic situation.

It is fitting to recognize in this book on influence the impossibility of fully acknowledging the many influences on the development of my ideas on these matters. The contemporary psychoanalytic scene is abuzz with fresh ideas, cross-fertilization, and controversy. So much of what I read sets lines of thought going for me; remembering what comes from where is just impossible. Where I have remembered, I noted in citations. Where I have not, I beg the author's forgiveness.

I am most endebted to Lewis Aron, who has reciprocated a previous collaboration between us and served as editor for this book. A better, more effective, and more gracious editor could not be found. I am deeply grateful for his encouragement, enthusiasm, and sage advice over the past decade or so and, especially, on this project. I am also grateful for the ongoing support of Paul Stepansky, Managing Director of The Analytic Press, who has played a unique, very special role in contemporary psychoanalysis, as a publisher with a rich grasp of the history of ideas and the place of psychoanalysis within that history.

Various friends and colleagues read parts and versions of this book, and I have benefited greatly from their feedback. They include Neil Altman, Anthony Bass, Margaret Black, Philip Bromberg, Steven Cooper, Jody Davies, David Engel, John Fiscalini, Jay Greenberg, Charles Spezzano, Donnel Stern, and Timothy Zeddes. As always, I am deeply grateful to the members of ongoing reading groups and candidates at the William Alanson White Institute and the New York University Postdoctoral Program, with whom I have discussed and worked through so many of the ideas found in these pages. Finally, the deepest gratitude is the one whose expression is, necessarily, the most constrained and unnamed, the appreciation of those patients who have shared aspects of their deepest experiences with me and from whom I have learned so much.

Thanks to *Contemporary Psychoanalysis* for permission to reprint sections of Chapters 3 and 4, which appeared in 1995, Volume 31, No. 1. A version of Chapter 2 appeared as as chapter in *Understanding Therapeutic Action*, edited by L. Lifson (The Analytic Press, 1996.) And thanks to the publishers of *Gender and Psychoanalysis* for permission to reprint Chapter 8, which first appeared in 1996, Volume 1, No. 1.

CHAPTER 1

INTRODUCTION

From Heresy to Reformation

Over the course of its century-long history, psychoanalysis has generated many different psychological understandings of the workings of the human mind. Of these, there are two understandings that are most important, most foundational to the entire psychoanalytic enterprise. The first, which we owe to Freud's earliest clinical explorations, is that the mind of an individual is extraordinarily complex, that there is much more going on in the mind of each of us than we are even dimly aware of. This is generally referred to as the discovery of the unconscious. The second, which was developed extensively in the second generation of psychoanalytic theorizing, particularly in the work of Harry Stack Sullivan and the American interpersonal school and Melanie Klein and her intellectual descendants, is that the apparent boundaries between individuals are much more permeable than they appear to be and that everyone handles threatening, disturbing fragments of mental complexity by locating and experiencing them in other people.

Analytic experience has taught us that people often employ a kind of externalization as an unconscious strategy for diverting attention from and controlling conflictual aspects of their own experience. That which is perceived everywhere outside a person actually originates within him. Klein (1946) called this externalizing process "projective identification"; that is, we unconsciously locate a repressed segment of the ego, a sector of self, in others, whom we then struggle to control or to avoid. Harry Stack Sullivan (1956) called this externalizing process the dynamism of "specious ideals"; that is, whatever we do not want to experience in ourselves becomes something we are preoccupied with discerning and condemning in others (pp. 101–105). Thus, someone having difficulty experiencing himself as having sexual desires might very well perpetually bemoan the sinking sexual mores of our youth; someone having difficulty experiencing herself as having aggressive thoughts might join the crusade against violence in movies or even in diet. (I once heard a vegetarian describe himself as a "non-flesh-eater.") The perception of pervasive external badness and threat generally reflects, decades of psychoanalytic experience has taught us, an inability to deal with conflictual internal processes that are difficult to accept, to come to terms with, to integrate with the rest of the personality.

Whatever contributions psychoanalysis has made to understanding group processes (beginning with Freud's, 1921, classic study, "Group Psychology and the Analysis of the Ego") have been based on the principle that groups often display the same dynamics that we find in individuals, but writ large. If we consider the psychoanalytic community as a group, and if we look back on the history of psychoanalytic ideas from our current vantage point, it becomes apparent that a massive process of externalization has for many decades been a central feature within the mainstream of psychoanalytic thought.

The Heresy of Interactionism

There has been a largely unacknowledged feature at the heart of clinical psychoanalysis from its very inception, a feature that has been difficult to come to terms with, to integrate with other analytic principles; a feature that has been dealt with through externalization, so that it is detected as the telltale, sinister feature of many nonanalytic or discredited analytic treatments. This central, largely unacknowledged feature of psychoanalysis is its fundamentally *interactive* nature. Over and over across the history of psychoanalytic ideas, theorists and clinicians who have pointed to the importance of the analyst's participation in the analytic process, to the intersubjective nature of the analytic situation, have been isolated, as if with garlic cloves or fingers forming the sign of the cross. The debased form through which interaction is externalized and then detected in "fallen" analytic approaches is established through the incantation of the dreaded words: "suggestion," "reassurance," "interpersonal," "environmentalist" and "corrective emotional experience" (see, for example, Rangel, 1982; Kohut, 1984; Rothstein, 1983; Sugarman and Wilson, 1995; and Michaels, 1996). Until very recently, and still occasionally, this externalization process has been completed with the ultimate and final dismissal: "This is not really psychoanalysis." But, like all suppressed and projected mental content, the interactive nature of the psychoanalytic relationship keeps returning.

Consider the following clinical vignette.

Dr. Green, an experienced and skilled female analyst, has been working with Helen, a very difficult, easily bruised, quickly insulted patient for about a year. Dr. Green is also a mother, and her eight-year-old daughter is in a class that goes on trips every couple of weeks or so. The parents are strongly encouraged to go on at least one of these trips, and the analyst feels that it is important to her daughter that she go on one soon. Like that of most working parents, Dr. Green's life is full of these conflicts. She decides that an upcoming trip a few weeks hence will be the one she will go on, and so Dr. Green notifies the patients she would normally see on that day and offers them alternative times.

All the patients accommodate to this change with no apparent problem, except Helen, who feels that she has been profoundly betrayed. Dr. Green simply cannot do this, she argues. It reflects a fundamental lack of caring for her and a professional irresponsibility to boot. Dr. Green patiently tries to explore Helen's fantasies about the reasons for this change. The reasons do not matter, Helen insists; it is a betrayal simply on the face of it. "Can't you imagine reasons that I would have to cancel?" Dr. Green asks, "Reasons that don't reflect a lack of caring or irresponsibility." "No," Helen insists. "It is obviously not a dire emergency, since it is planned three weeks ahead. Anything else, including medical appointments, should simply be scheduled at some other time."

Caught off-guard and feeling defensive, Dr. Green feels that there is a characteristically imperious, self-absorbed quality to Helen's perspective. She begins thinking in terms of primal-scene fantasies, oedipal rivalries, and so on and suggests to Helen that her intense reaction seems not commensurate with the situation. This interpretive judgment enflames Helen even more, adding insult (accusation) to injury (the clear betrayal). Luckily for Dr. Green, time is up, and she has a chance to collect herself and reconsider her approach.

Before the next session, Dr. Green took the opportunity to consult with a colleague about this situation. They discussed the year's analytic work: this patient had been severely traumatized as a child; it had been very difficult and risky for the patient to trust the analyst at all; important ground had been gained; and it was at just this point that the canceled appointment arose.

Thinking along developmental arrest lines (a la Winnicott and Kohut), Dr. Green shifted her stance in the next session and empathized with what she took to be Helen's experience of abandonment just at the point of increased trust and risk. This empathic response calmed the situation considerably, and this analytic couple was able to ride through the rescheduled appointment with no lasting damage. Everything seemed to be resolved, except for one problem. The stabilization of the situation allowed Dr. Green enough breathing room to reflect on these events, and she began to feel an increasing sense of bad faith on her part. The more she thought about it, the more she began to realize that Helen was right—Dr. Green had betrayed her. I do not mean "right" according to a trendy, leveling relativism, the frequently heard notion that whatever the patient feels is right within the patient's subjective reality and therefore that all convictions have the same truth value. Dr. Green began to realize that there was something in her decision to go on that trip at that time that did have to do with Helen (along with many other factors having nothing to do with her).

She realized that she had begun to feel extremely crowded by Helen and fearful of her demandingness. Dr. Green felt uncomfort-

ably responsible for Helen; she wished she could be the good ana-
lyst/mother that the patient longed for and felt entitled to. But she felt,
understandably, that she would never be able to be that. She felt grati-
fied by the recent successes of their work, but fearful of the increased
expectations that went along with that success. She was struggling,
out of awareness, with various claims on her and with her own conflicts about responding to those claims. There was, therefore, an element of satisfaction in scheduling the trip at this point. She realized
retrospectively that it was as if she were telling Helen that the latter
was not, in fact, her real daughter; she had another daughter, a real
daughter, to whom she would grant priority. She was, perhaps more
significantly, also demonstrating this priority to herself. So, while
Helen's conviction that Dr. Green's actions constituted a betrayal and
abandonment of her was not the simple, singular truth, neither was it
simply wrong and a transferencial distortion.[1]

Is this moment in this treatment representative of analytic work in
general? Any honest presentation of clinical material becomes an easy
target for critics, not operating in the heat of the moment, to point to
technical lapses, overinvolvement, another, more "correct" interpretation that could have been delivered, and so on. But at heart, I believe
that each critic knows that his or her work with each analytic patient
contains the same stresses, the same interactive complexity, the same
challenges found here.

If analytic work is deeply engaged, the patient always gets under

---

1. Inderbitzen and Levy (1994) point to what they consider to be a logical
inconsistency, a paradox, in the position of authors like Hoffman and me, who
have emphasized an interactional perspective. (It is a little difficult to respond to
their critique since they cite one work of mine as published in 1992 with the
title of a book that was published in 1988 and offer small quotes with no page
references.) They seem to find it contradictory that I argue that analyst (or anyone else) has no legitimate claim to an objective reality, unmediated through his
own subjectivity and theoretical framework, while at the same time emphasizing
the importance of the analyst's real contributions to the transference. The terms
real and reality are being used in two different senses: the first refers to an
impossible, unique, objective rendering of interpersonal events, and the second
to actual interactions and reciprocal influence, the nature of which can be
described only through some interpretive framework. There is neither contradiction nor paradox here.

the analyst's skin. (For a recent study of analysands' deeply personal impact on their analysts, see Kantrowitz, 1996.) As Heinrich Racker (1968) demonstrated more than 30 years ago, a patient's dynamics inevitably resonate with the analyst's dynamics; the patient's struggles with universal, human conflicts resurrect the analyst's struggles with those same conflicts; the patient's internal world becomes tangled up with the analyst's internal world; and the therapeutic action is located in the dyadic, interactive field that they constitute together. As Lawrence Friedman (1988) has put it,

> If treatment as written about seems so discursive and intellectual and neat and cool, perhaps treatment as it happens really works on the basis of what every psychotherapist feels daily: personal push and pull; nameless, theory-less, shapeless, swarming interaction (p. 12).

The challenge for every analytic pair is to find a way for the analyst to establish a different sort of presence in the analytic situation, proferring neither remote interpretations nor unconditionally empathic acceptance. In the dyad in question, Dr. Green needs to be able to find a way to get the patient interested in the impact of her demands on others and the way it destroys virtually all her important relationships. To find a voice to speak about these issues in a way the patient can hear, Dr. Green has to struggle through her own conflicts over responsibility and fear, her desire to repair and her guilt about disappointing, the part of herself that is deeply needful and longing, and her conflicts between career and motherhood.

Interpretations are central to the therapeutic action, but it is not the content of the interpretations alone that is crucial. It is the voice in which they are spoken, the countertransferential context that makes it possible for the patient's characteristic patterns of integrating relationships with others to be stretched and enriched. To find the right voice, the analyst has to recognize which conflictual features of her own internal world have been activated in the interaction with the patient, to struggle through her own internal conflicts to arrive at a position in which she may be able to interest the patient in recognizing and struggling with her own (the patient's) conflictual participation. This makes the work, inevitably, deeply personal and deeply interpersonal.

Scientific Objectivity, Negative Identity, and Boundaries

The conceptual tools that psychoanalytic theory has had available for understanding the interactive heart of clinical work have, until recently, been woefully inadequate. This is largely because it has seemed very important to think about the analytic process precisely in a noninteractive way. There are several important historical reasons for this commitment.

First, in the world in which Freud fought to establish psychoanalysis as a new discipline, it was essential to present psychoanalytic theory and therapy as a science among other sciences. Like many progressive intellectuals of his day, Freud saw human understanding as falling into two broad classifications: science and religion. The latter, in Freud's view, was pervaded by fantasy and illusion. Beliefs were generated and adhered to because they were appealing to the believer. Science, Freud and his contemporaries thought, was different. Science operates according to rationality and reality. Scientific beliefs describe the world as it really is, regardless of what is appealing or frightening to the believer.

Scientific disciplines of Freud's day were based on the strict separation between the subject matter of scientific study and the detached, scientific observer studying that subject matter. If psychoanalysis was to be a science, it was necessary for the analyst to remain outside the field of study, the patient's mind. Hence, the psychoanalytic situation, Freud believed, is composed of the mind of one person being studied objectively by a detached observer.

Whether or not it is still useful to regard psychoanalysis as a science proper (as opposed, for example, to a hermeneutic discipline) has recently become a hotly debated question. But even if one wants to regard psychoanalysis as a science, the implications of that claim today are very different from the implications in Freud's time (see Mayer, 1985) Contemporary philosophers of science regard the scientist/observer as more or less embedded in, and partially constructing, his understandings of the objects he is studying. The scientist/observer himself has now become part of the field of study. And whether or not one prefers to regard psychoanalysis as a science, it is now generally agreed on that there is no way for one person to study the mind of another without taking both minds and their interactive effects on each other into account. Of course, Freud cannot be faulted for assuming, like most others in his day, that science provides an objective, unedited access to reality. As Hans Loewald (1974) put it:

> Freud does not appear to have recognized that the objective reality of science is itself a sort of reality organized (although not created in a solipsistic sense) by the human mind and does not necessarily manifest the culmination of mental development or represent any absolute standard of truth, as he assumed [p. 364].

A second important reason for the powerful commitment, both conscious and unconscious, to suppress the interactive nature of the analytic relationship was that psychoanalysis was born of hypnotism. Just as persons develop counteridentifications with their parents to make room for a new, personal self, it was crucial for psychoanalysis to differentiate itself from its ancestor, hypnotism, and its reliance on the personal power and influence of the therapist.

The hypnotist cures through suggestion; the analyst cures through interpretation. Where hypnotism added influence, psychoanalysis removed historical influences; where hypnotism directed and shaped, psychoanalysis liberated and released. In Freud's (1905) compelling analogy, hypnotism operates like painting, adding pigment to canvas, whereas psychoanalysis operates like sculpture, removing unwanted material to reveal forms that had always existed beneath.

One of Freud's great teachers and heroes was Charcot, the brilliant, highly influential, and theatrical neurologist at the Salpêtrière in Paris, with whom Freud studied prior to his first psychoanalytic publications with Joseph Breuer. Freud admired Charcot's daring explorations, through the use of hypnotism, into the symptomatology of hysteria, and he named one of his children after his mentor. It is worth noting that by the time of his death in 1893, the same year of Freud's first specifically psychoanalytic publications, Charcot was widely discredited, and the charge was none other than "suggestion." It was discovered that the women patients whom Charcot used to demonstrate the flamboyant symptoms of grande hysteria had been coached prior to their performances. The symptoms that seemed to emerge spontaneously were, retrospectively, revealed to have been, at least in part, planted in the patients' minds through the doctor's suggestive influence.

Perhaps Charcot's fate served, for Freud, as a cautionary tale.[2] The problem of influence is at the heart of the struggles psychoanalysis has had with coming to terms with the centrality of the analyst's participation. Psychoanalysis has always placed fundamental value on guarding the patient's autonomy and self-direction throughout the analytic process. The use the patient makes of analytic exploration must, ultimately, be up to the patient. The use of hypnotism as a counteridentification has been comforting in this regard. It has allowed analysts to feel that their very methodology, unlike hypnotism, protects their patients from the problem of influence. It is as if the analysts' sitting behind the analytic couch rendered the patients invisible, much as the helmet Athena gave to Perseus made it possible for him to battle Medusa unseen. Analytic authors and clinicians who emphasize the interactive nature of the analytic relationship must quickly and necessarily confront the problem of influence, and, as we shall see in subsequent chapters, it is a bedeviling problem indeed. This is why these authors have quickly and summarily been branded "nonanalytic" and have been accused of practicing the black art of "suggestion." To acknowledge the two-person, interactive nature of the analytic relationship is to undermine the counteridentification with hypnotism through which psychoanalysis as a discipline was born.

The third important historical reason for the traditional psychoanalytic commitment to a noninteractive understanding of the nature of the psychoanalytic relationship is one that analytic clinicians and writers have come to appreciate only recently. The psychoanalytic process is, by its very nature, so intensely interactional that it poses grave dangers to the constructive constraints of the analyst's participation. From the days of its inception to the present, psychoanalytic clinicians have struggled with the intense passions aroused by the analytic

---

2. I am grateful to Lewis Aron (personal communication) for alerting me to the circumstances of Charcot's fate and its possible relevance to Freud.

situation, and appropriate boundaries between analyst and patient have not infrequently been crossed.

Freud noted privately early on, in a warning to Jung, who was having complex problems in an analytic/romantic relationship with Sebina Spielrein[3] that intense sexual and romantic feelings in the countertransference are inevitable.

> Such experiences, though painful, are necessary and hard to avoid. Without them we cannot really know life and what we are dealing with. I myself have never been taken in quite so badly, but I have come very close to it a number of times and had a *narrow escape*. I believe that only grim necessities weighing on my work, and the fact that I was 10 years older than yourself when I came to PA have saved me from similar experiences. But no lasting harm is done. They help us to develop the thick skin we need to dominate "counter transference," which is after all a permanent problem for us; they teach us to displace our own affects to best advantage. They are a "blessing in disguise." The way these women manage to charm us with every conceivable psychic perfection until they have attained their purpose is one of nature's greatest spectacles. Once that has been done or the contrary has become a certainty, the constellation changes amazingly [letter of 7 January, 1909, McGuire, 1974, pp. 230–231].

This communication from Freud is interesting on two counts. First, he had come to regard passionate countertransference involvements as a matter of course and, perhaps, inevitable. Second, although he regarded these as transformable into constructive learning experiences for analysts, he seems not to have been at all concerned about the consequences for patients.

A later, equally remarkable letter from Freud to Jung concerned another patient, Frau C, whom Freud had been describing to Jung for years as "my chief tormenter."[4] Frau C, who complained bitterly

---

3. See Kerr (1993) for a fascinating and insightful discussion of this relationship and its larger historical implications for psychoanalysis.

4. See Kerr (1993, p. 391) for an account of the exchange between Freud and Jung about his patient and its role in the collapse of their relationship. I am indebted to Steven Cooper (personal communication) for pointing out this piece of the Freud–Jung correspondence to me.

about Freud's "remote and uncaring" attitude toward her, consulted Pfister and Jung for advice and solace. Freud scolded Jung
gently:

> I gather that neither of you has yet acquired the necessary objectivity
> in your practice, that you still get involved, giving a good deal of your-
> selves and expecting the patient to give something in return. Permit
> me, speaking as the venerable old master, to say that this technique is
> invariably ill-advised and that it is best to remain reserved and purely
> receptive. We must never let our poor neurotics drive us crazy. I
> believe an article on 'counter-transference' is sorely needed; of course
> we could not publish it, we should have to circulate copies among our-
> selves [Letter of 31 December, McGuire, 1974, pp. 475–476].

It has taken many years for such contributions to surface, and their
full implications are just beginning to be worked out.

In their ground-breaking exploration, Jody Messler Davies and
Mary Gail Frawley (1994) have demonstrated the ways in which powerful memories and anguished features of early childhood relationships inevitably emerge in the intensity of feelings and reenactments
in both the transference and the countertransference. And in an
important recent book, the first honest and direct effort to address
this subject, Glen Gabbard and Eva Lester (1995) argue that the history of psychoanalysis is studded with transgressions stemming from
overinvolvement by the analyst.

In both of these recent, important studies, the point is made that
the traditional theory of psychoanalytic technique, with its emphasis
on the analyst's neutral, detached noninvolvement, seems designed to
deny, through fiat, the complex, constructive/destructive potentials of
the analyst's participation in work with traumatized patients. Rather
than dealing with these issues head-on, traditional psychoanalytic theorizing, by declaring the analytic situation a one-person field, rendered them invisible. Transgressions of professional boundaries that
became public could then be regarded as pathological aberrations, to
be hushed over; and individual analysts generally dealt with their own
passions toward patients secretly and privately, often with a great
sense of shame (Abend, 1986). Or, worse, such experiences with
"these women" patients whom Freud referred to were dissociated,

projected, and then pathologized through the diagnostic conclusion that the patient was particularly seductive and disturbed. From our current perspective, this partially projective use of interpretation resulted in a particular kind of boundary violation because the analyst, unconscious of his own participation, was making devastating charges against the patient masked as medical diagnosis. As the grip of this commitment to silence and denial has weakened in recent years, it has become increasingly possible to speak and write about just how difficult and anguished the analytic engagement can be for both patient and analyst.

It is a commonplace in analytic work with individuals that suppressed feelings and thoughts are much more powerful and dangerous than those same feelings and thoughts after they have been brought to light and confronted. The boundary problem at the heart of clinical psychoanalysis has suffered from the suppression generated by the noninteractive framework in which the analytic process has been understood.

Thus, the denial of the interactive features of the analytic process has served many important purposes: it has upheld the 19th-century philosophy of science principles Freud was bound by; it has sustained the counteridentification to hypnotism around which psychoanalysis defined itself early on as a discipline; and it has allowed analytic clinicians to preserve the illusion that it is possible to avoid the tangled emotional mess that emerges in the analytic relationship as the process engages the patient's deepest, most central issues.

The Myth of the Generic Analyst

The central device through which an appreciation of the interactive nature of the analytic process has been avoided throughout the history of psychoanalytic ideas is the myth of the generic analyst. If the analytic process is to free the patient's previously repressed material through interpretation, the personal characteristics, subjectivity, and idiosyncrasies of the analyst must not matter. The ideals of neutrality, abstinence, and anonymity—pillars of classical technique—reinforce this myth by making it seem possible for the analyst not to be really present and visible. These principles then came to operate very much as Sullivan's (1956) "specious ideals"; it is the nonanalytic therapists who become visible and make themselves known, not real analysts. The ideal of the generic analyst, armed with Perseus' helmet, made it possible to think of good analytic technique as "standard," that is, as rendering the personal characteristics and dynamics of the analyst invisible.

Many years ago I consulted with a woman who was extremely bitter about a six-year analysis she had undergone but from which she felt she had derived little. She complained about the analyst's withholding stance, about his telling her nothing about what he thought or felt and turning all questions back onto the patient with the rationale that doing so kept the analysis purely on the patient's experience. This woman told me that she had become very focused on her analyst's squeaky chair, which, she decided (probably with some degree of accuracy), betrayed discomfort on the analyst's part. The patient used the squeaks to guide her productions (either associations or silences), sometimes changing what she was doing when a squeak occurred or, alternatively, defiantly continuing. She had never told the analyst about the squeaks because she was convinced that the analyst would either have oiled the chair or held himself even more stiffly. These wasted years of analytic stand-off seemed both ironic and tragic: the analyst was apparently convinced that he was protecting the patient's autonomy by not interacting, while that very denial created a secret, bizarre interaction that likely included some actual features of what the analyst thought and felt, expressed in an unintended fashion.

I have come to think of this piece of a single analysis as paradigmatic of the problems generated for classical psychoanalysis by the denial of interaction. If awareness of the presence of the analyst as person is suppressed, the analyst's participation cannot be eliminated but only driven underground. It emerged as the squeaks of this particular analyst's chair, and the patient's relationship to those squeaks were given voice only in her second analysis. In a broader sense, the history of psychoanalysis has been laced through with squeaks, and it is only in the recent engagement of the phenomenon of interaction in the analytic relationship that those squeaks are now being heard and deciphered.

Counterideal: The "Corrective Emotional Experience"

Myths and ideals are often sustained through the creation of counterideals, and the most persistent counterideal in psychoanalytic history, the perpetual villain in the piece whenever orthodoxy is defended, is the concept of the "corrective emotional experience," introduced, to his eternal perfidy, by Franz Alexander (Alexander and French, 1946). Merton Gill (1994) noted that "the term corrective emotional experience ... has long been considered with scorn by most psychoanalysts" (p. 107). And Lawrence Friedman (1988) suggests that "the 'bad' example of Franz Alexander, with his 'corrective emotional experience,' is held up as a warning to theorists who talk about nonconceptual, discursive, noninterpretational elements in therapy" (p. 521).[5]

Alexander's discredited concept was introduced in the 1950s in the context of his concern with clinical efficacy and expediency. This problem by no means originated with Alexander. In the 1920s Sandor Ferenczi and Otto Rank became concerned with the increasing time analysis seemed to take. (Little did they imagine how much analyses would become extended in later decades.) Surely there must be a way to speed up the process, to make interpretations more effective, more quickly. Ferenczi and Rank (1924) emphasized the importance of the repetition of the patient's early conflicts in the present analytic relationship. They argued for a more active role for the analyst in addition to his or her interpretive function. And in their later writings, both Rank and Ferenczi explored more interventionist models of the analyst's participation (Aron, 1996, chapter 6). What if the analyst assumes a more encouraging, validating approach to the development of the patient's will and creativity (Rank's "Will

---

5. Attacks on Kohut in the early 1980s illustrate this use of Alexander's concept for the purposes of dismissal: "There are no longer unconscious conflicts to be understood and an analytic stance to reach them, but a corrective emotional experience - not called that - to bring the patient up again as he was not brought up before" (Rangell, 1982, p. 863).

"Many colleagues, including this author, suggest that despite his disavowal, Kohut is increasingly advocating a variety of a corrective emotional experience" (Rothstein, 1983, p. 24).

therapy")? What if the patient was prohibited from any gratifications to force his conflicts to an earlier boiling point (Ferenczi's "active" technique)? What if the analyst were to gratify the patient, to some extent, to undo effects of early deprivation and trauma (Ferenczi's relaxation technique)? In due time, partly because of their emphasis on interactive features of the analytic relationship, Ferenczi and Rank were both condemned to the psychoanalytic Gulag, the world of not-psychoanalysis.

Alexander's contributions[6] were aimed at similar clinical innovation. He argued that analysis works not just because of the intellectual value of the analyst's interpretations but because patients find, in the analytic situation, a different sort of experience in response to their deepest desires than they encountered in their childhood. Because this is such a central feature of the therapeutic impact of the analytic process, Alexander argued, the analyst should go about providing it more knowingly and deliberately than the principles of "neutrality" and "abstinence" implied. Alexander recommended that the analyst actively address the patient's need for an emotional experience with a different sort of object than the original pathogenic parent, which he thought the analyst could provide by correct diagnosis and a kind of analytic role playing.

Wallerstein (1990) has provided a fascinating account of the crisis for American psychoanalysis generated by Alexander's position, the threat it seemed to pose of splitting the American psychoanalytic community apart, and the two panels of the American Psychoanalytic Association that were convened to expose and condemn Alexander's heresy as "outside the realm of analysis proper" (p. 296). Alexander was dismissed as offering a manipulative interactionalism, his technical innovations branded with the curse of "suggestion." By using Alexander as a foil, "classical" psychoanalytic technique was reshaped and reaffirmed as the unique standard methodology for several decades to come. Psychoanalysis and proper analytic technique were

---

6. It is fascinating to note that Alexander was one of the most vociferous critics of Ferenczi's experiments with analytic technique, despite his own adoption of Ferenczi's concerns and many of his innovative strategies not too many years later. The criticism of authors emphasizing the interactive features of the analytic relationship often serves purposes of projective disclaimer.

preserved as noninteractional and nonsuggestive, as offering a unique situation within which the inner dynamics of the patient simply emerge in their pure form, uncontaminated by external influence.

The problem with the debate about Alexander's "corrective emotional experience" has always been that the term has conflated two distinctly different dimensions of Alexander's position. The first dimension was descriptive: Alexander understood the analytic process as affective and interactive. The patient's emotional experience and its historical constraints are entwined with the analyst's affective participation. Character change is facilitated not only through insight generated by interpretation but also through affectively charged interaction. The second dimension was prescriptive: Alexander recommended a specific technique for providing the deepest emotional corrective, a custom-designed posturing opposite to the emotional style of the parents.

Alexander's technique was rightly challenged and criticized as contrived and manipulative. But in the antiheretical fervor that characterized the response to his work, two deeper issues were missed. They were understood neither by Alexander nor by his critics, but are possible for us to see from our current historical vantage point.

First, the analyst's interpretive activity and a deeply affective interaction are not alternatives but often are different ways of describing the same event. Interpretations are always personally expressive of the analyst's own subjectivity (Aron, 1996); they are never the application of some abstract knowledge from a generic analyst, but are always an action by a particular sort of new object, different from early parental objects. Interpretations are never merely informational events; they are always relational events; they transform relationships (Mitchell, 1988; Oremland, 1991; Gill, 1994; Greenberg, 1996). Conversely, actions and interactions always contain implicit interpretative statements and concepts (Ogden, 1994). They reflect presuppositions and ideas. Interactions are never devoid of conceptual content; they open up or close off different avenues of understanding. We do not have to choose between interpretations and corrective emotional experiences; they go together. The traditional notion that interpretation is a nonaction, simply generating insight and therefore free of suggestive influence, is an illusion. Rather, our choice is among different forms of participation and the interpretive understandings and emotional experiences they offer.

Second, while the call for analytic posturing was surely contrived and grandiose, Alexander was not alone in his grandiosity. Alexander thought he could diagnose the problem and determine an emotionally corrective position; to our contemporary ears, this entails a stunning oversimplification of the complexity of the patient's conflicts and their meanings on different developmental levels. Those who dismissed Alexander, however, thought they could provide, for all analysands, a purely neutral position; this diagnostic claim entails an equally stunning oversimplification of the very different meanings that an analyst's stance can have to different patients. The analyst may think she is being neutral, yet the patient may plausibly experience the analyst's activity as seductive, withholding, sadistic, and so on. In Merton Gill's (1994) final book, he pointed to the crucial distinction between intended and unintended features of the analyst's participation. The analyst's activity and nonactivity have all sorts of impact on the patient and vice versa. What makes any particular analytic intervention manipulative is an intentional action, the impact of which remains unexplored and unspoken. It is not the content of what the analyst does, Gill argued, that makes his or her participation analytic; it is the curiosity and openness to explore the impact of one's participation. In this sense, Gill wrote, the deliberate, laconic style of the sort recommended by Charles Brenner (1969) (and Gill [1954] himself in the 1950s, as one of Alexander's most incisive critics) manipulates the transference in just the same manner Alexander was accused of using.

> Brenner's conceptualization of the situation implies a gratification-frustration index whereby the patient may respond to the analyst's stance with either gratification or frustration. His position suggests that the safe thing to do is to frustrate. . . . I would argue that he thereby violates the central psychoanalytic tenet that one should not manipulate the transference. . . . Deliberate frustration without the intention to analyze it is a manipulation. And how can one be sure of what the effect of an interpersonal manipulation will be? [Gill, 1994, p. 46].

Neutrality, defined not in concrete behavioral terms or with respect to the analyst's intention, but in terms personally meaningful to the patient, cannot be established a priori, but can be arrived at only in the interactive work with each patient (Greenberg, 1991, 1995). Thus, the deeper problem with Alexander's position, an over-valuation of what Irwin Z. Hoffman (1991) has termed the analyst's "technical rationality," was a problem that did not at all set him apart from the mainstream of his day. What sets off contemporary analytic theorists of our day from both Alexander and his critics is the growing realization that the analyst, assuming one position or another, does not stand outside the patient's dynamics. The analyst is embedded within the interaction with the patient, and the analyst's interpretive activity provides corrective emotional experiences that transform them both.

Because of the conflation of these issues in discussions of the concept of "corrective emotional experience," that term became a tool for denigrating any approach that placed some degree of primary therapeutic importance on the analytic relationship. The corrective emotional experience has come to stand for a debased form of interactionalism, and it is invoked to suggest something fundamentally nonanalytic whenever efforts have been made to deal with the interactional core of the analytic process. But the problem of interaction has not gone away.

Interaction: Coping with or Addressing the Problem?

The American Psychoanalytic Association has had for many years a Committee on Psychoanalytic Education (COPE). In 1984 this committee established a group to study the nature of the psychoanalytic process, in an attempt to arrive at a consensus within the framework of what Abend (1990) called "mainstream traditional theory" (p. 526). Arriving at a consensus proved difficult, and the stumbling block was, once again, the centrality of interaction. As Boesky (1990) put it, the problem was a "confusion about how to account for the interactional aspect of the psychoanalytic situation in a manner consistent with a one-person psychology . . ." (p. 550).

One can feel the strain in the very language chosen to describe this problem; accounting for interaction within the framework of a one-person psychology is a contradiction in terms. It is like trying to account for the process of photosynthesis in plants by limiting one's frame of reference to the earth and eliminating the sun. The laborious and problematic efforts expended in this direction are themselves evidence of the importance of the broad shift toward a two-person framework for psychoanalytic theorizing and practice that places interaction at the center of concern rather than at the periphery. But actually to let the second person in—the person of the analyst, has enormous implications for the very identity of psychoanalysis as a methodology devoid of personal influence that, above all else, safeguards the autonomy of the patient. It can only be a disinclination to deal with those implications and complexities that is responsible for the continual reassertion that an acknowledgment of interaction in the analytic relationship necessarily diverts attention from the true focus of the analytic process—the patient's unconscious conflicts and fantasies (for example, see Inderbitzin and Levy, 1994). As we shall see in the chapters that follow, what has been revealed over and over, in many different psychoanalytic traditions and languages, is that the patient's unconscious conflicts and fantasies come alive in the interactive play between the analysand's experience and the analyst's experience. One does not have to choose. Attention paid to interaction in the analytic relationship does not diminish or distract from the exploration of the patient's unconscious; it potentiates and vitalizes it.

Obligations toward the philosophy of science of his time and the early differentiation of psychoanalysis from hypnotism were compelling reasons for Freud and his contemporaries to avoid dealing with the interactive nature of the analytic process. Those obligations should no longer be of concern to us. We noted earlier a third reason for the traditional minimization of interaction through the myth of the generic analyst: the messy problem of boundaries, constraints, and influence in the intense passions of the transference–countertransference matrix. Maintaining boundaries was a real problem in Freud's day and is still a real problem for us. The verbal magic of the myth of the generic analyst did not solve the problem, and the erosion of that myth leaves it exposed for contemporary theorists and clinicians to grapple with.

Psychoanalysts have always placed great importance on the autonomy of the patient. The analyst has been portrayed as providing value-free insight, which the patient employs in the service of his or her own aims. In fact, many analysts in the early decades of this century were also social critics and regarded psychoanalysis in liberationist terms, as freeing individuals from external, social control.

But for several decades, this psychoanalytic ideal has become increasingly difficult to maintain in its original form. Erich Fromm (1960) advanced the argument that the early revolutionary significance of psychoanalysis in freeing individuals to serve as the vanguard of society had been subverted. The emphasis in Freudian ego psychology on "adaptation," Fromm argued, signaled a coopting of psychoanalysis by conservatism and establishment values. For Fromm, it was still possible for psychoanalysis to preserve the autonomy of the individual; only degraded, coopted psychoanalysis had fallen away from this fundamental ideal.

But the major trends in philosophy over the past several decades have raised considerable doubt about the plausibility of the glorification of the individual that placing such importance on autonomy seems to imply. The two philosophers with perhaps the greatest impact on contemporary philosophy, Heidegger and Wittgenstein, both complicated our notions of what it means to be an autonomous individual. Heidegger challenged the very notion of the Subject in ways that have been extended by Foucault and other postmodern writers, and Wittgenstein explored the relationship between mind and language, subverting even the possibility of a private language or, for that matter, a private mind.[7]

For Freud, the drives constituted the core of the individual, a core that was distinct and, in some sense, sheltered from social influence

---

7. Philip Cushman (1995) has developed an extensive critique of the autonomous, "bounded, masterful self" which traditional psychoanalytic theory has borrowed from the dominant trends in western culture, and Charles Taylor (1991) has noted that both Heidegger and Wittgenstein view the individual as capable of an "engaged agency," in contrast to the pseudo-autonomous, disengaged agency presumed by more rationalistic thinkers such as Decartes and Kant.

(Rapaport, 1957, p. 727). Yet, for the most influential contemporary Freudian authors (Kernberg, Loewald), the drives themselves have become relational, shaped in early interactive experiences with significant others. Some regard the body as the core of the autonomous individual; but the body as a psychological entity, the *experience* of the body, is itself a construction, shaped by language and social context (Butler, 1993). Other candidates have been proposed to fill in the missing core of the autonomous individual, the "true self" (Winnicott), "destiny" (Kohut), and "idiom" (Bollas). Yet, as late 20th-century thought has located the individual increasingly within a social, linguistic, ecological context, it is more and more difficult to imagine any of these as truly sheltered from the influence of others, as residing in the individual from the start and emerging in the analytic process.

The concept of personal "authenticity" has similarly become problematic in the light of broad philosophical movements that locate the individual in an intersubjective, social, linguistic field. The distinction between the authentic and the inauthentic has customarily been employed in relation to a fixed reference point, a core, or true, self. Yet there has been a strong trend in the psychoanalytic literature of the past several years in the direction of regarding self-experience as comprising multiple and shifting self-organizations and self-states generated in interpersonal and social fields (see, for example: Ogden, 1994; Mitchell, 1993, chapter 5; Pizer, 1992; Bromberg, 1993, 1994, 1996; Harris, 1991 and Davies, 1996.) If self-organization is contextual, how can what is authentically me be distinguished from you? And how can I determine which of the variable "me's" that emerge in different interactive contexts is the true or authentic me? Don't the very concepts of social embeddedness and multiplicity of self-organizations and self-states render the notion of authenticity meaningless?

Are the ideals of autonomy and authenticity worth saving? I would argue that they are, but not in their customary, simplified form. Personal autonomy is not something that antedates interaction with others, but an emergent property of interactive processes, not something that can be sheltered from influence, but something that grows *through* influence. In this sense, the kind of autonomy worth having is not something separable from the analytic experience and the influence of the analyst, but an important dimension of the analytic experience. Similarly, a concept of authenticity congruent with current philosophical developments would locate authenticity not with respect to specific content, a fixed reference point, but with respect to process, the manner in which experience is generated. When theorists of meditation (Epstein, 1995) look to meditative states as deepening experience by emptying it of shallow, ruminative thoughts, they are grounding a sense of the authentic in features of interiority, focus, and self-origination, not in a particular self with a consistent content, outline, or stylistic qualities. As the philosopher Charles Taylor (1991) has put it,

> each of our voices has something of its own to say. Not only should I not fit my life to the demands of external conformity; I can't even find the model to live by outside myself. I can find it only within. Being true to myself means being true to my own originality, and that is something only I can articulate and discover. In articulating it, I am also defining myself. I am realizing a potentiality that is properly my own [p. 29].

Accepting a multiplicity of self-organizations (Bromberg, 1993, 1994, 1996; Harris, 1996; Davies, 1996) does not necessitate the abandonment of the distinction between self-organizations that are shallow and conformistic and self-organizations that have a long history and reflect deep affective commitments. Consistent with current modes of analytic theorizing, it is possible to imagine the autonomy the patient emerges with from the analytic situation as an autonomy that has absorbed or "survived" (in a Winnicottian sense) the analyst's influence (or multiple influences of the analyst's multiple selves). To define autonomy anachronistically as apart from the impact of the field and reciprocal influences is to confuse autonomy with a kind of omnipotent narcissistic defense against dependency and attachment. Carlos Strenger (in press) has argued similarly that there has been a now-anachronistic ideal of autonomy central to the western tradition from the beginnings of contemporary psychoanalysis: "The essence of the Cartesian project is the liberation of the individual into total epistemic autonomy. It is an expression of the protest of human subjectivity against having been formed by factors outside itself . . . conditioned by the particular family he was born itnto, the culture that has fashioned his thought, and the historical circumstance determining his fate." For the analysand and ex-analysand, we need to add to this list the particular analyst(s) with whom he experienced the analytic process. The recently renewed interest in Erik Erikson's concept of "identity" that emerges in a rich psychological/interpersonal/cultural context reflects in part the current struggle to find ways of conceptualizing different kinds and different depths of identifications and self-organizations (Seligman and Shanok, 1995; Wallerstein, 1990). One of the major projects of this book is a reworking of the traditional psychoanalytic ideal of autonomy by confronting the problem of the analyst's influence head-on, rather than through the customary devices that have helped us avoid it.

Critics of postclassical psychoanalytic thought frequently argue that what defines psychoanalysis *as* psychoanalysis is a particular kind of objective understanding based on drives and early bodily experience; to take the interactive, two-person features of the analytic process fully into account is to make psychoanalysis indistinguishable from reassurance or, even worse, religion (Michels, 1996). Yet, even a cursory study of contemporary psychoanalysis suggests an increasing independence from any single specific ideology, any one single particular system of content. Psychoanalysts are at this point extraordinarily heterogeneous, from country to country and from individual to individual. What they have in common is not an adherence to a set of dogmas, but a commitment to certain common forms of generating experience.

In Freud's day, it made sense to define psychoanalysis in connection with a particular set of beliefs about "deep" unconscious motivation, because there was a consensus, more or less, about what was *in* the depths, what was *in* the unconscious. Today there is not. The Kleinian unconscious is quite different from the self-psychological unconscious, which is quite different from the unconscious of interpersonal psychoanalysis, which is quite different from various forms of object relational unconscious (Greenberg, 1991). How can we account for this diversity?

Historically, as we have already noted in relation to Alexander and others tarred with the brush designed for him, psychoanalysts have dealt with diversity in their ranks by a particularly heinous form of fratricide: "Only my tradition knows what is really in the unconscious; the others are not real psychoanalysts." Or "Anyone who does not subscribe to my ideas about what is unconscious is denying the unconscious." As the heterogeneity of psychoanalytic theorizing has expanded, this approach appears increasingly futile and silly. A more serious grappling with this problem would have to tease out from the diversity of analytic concepts what it is that psychoanalysts have in common, what makes it meaningful to think of all of them *as* psychoanalysts.

In my view, psychoanalysis has become a method for generating a certain kind of meaning, for fostering certain forms of experience and living. There are many, many forms of human experience, and contemporary psychoanalysis promotes and facilitates only one of them, a particularly Western, late 20th-century form. The way of life promoted by psychoanalysis operates in a matrix of dialectical tensions between conscious and unconscious thoughts and feelings; private sensations and public engagements; language and affect; past and present; actuality and imagination; verbal and nonverbal; bodily and psychical processes; social embeddedness and autonomous self-definition. These categories are not taken as polarities, as if fully separable from and antithetical to each other, but rather as interpenetrating and, in some sense, as mutually creating each other (see Ogden, 1994, and Hoffman, 1994, on the use of the concept of dialectics in psychoanalysis).

Defining psychoanalysis as a method for generating meaning within the matrix constituted by these dialectical tensions makes it possible to account for both what analysts have in common and their enormous diversity. Different schools of analytic thought and different national forms of psychoanalysis differ greatly in the relative emphases they place on these various dimensions. Freudians tend to weight the past vis-à-vis the present, while interpersonalists tend to weight the present vis-à-vis the past. The Kleinians tend to stress the fantastic, while the self psychologists tend to stress the actual. The Lacanians emphasize the importance of language, while many object relations theorists emphasize the importance of preverbal experience. British writers place great weight on the private and ineffable, while American writers place great weight on relationship and mutuality.

These differences are not inconsequential; they constitute very different visions of human nature and lead to very different forms of analytic experience. But they share a common matrix for the generation of meaning, despite their variable emphases, and that common matrix makes psychoanalytic meaning different from meaning generated by moral, aesthetic, or religious systems. Traditional authors (e.g., Michels, 1996) who believe that the credibility of psychoanalysis rests on its scientific status assume that defining psychoanalysis in terms of meaning-making makes it indistinguishable from moral, aesthetic, or religious philosophies. What they miss is that the kinds of meaning generated by the analytic process are distinct (although overlapping) from the kinds of meaning generated by other systems. Moral systems ground meaning in virtuous action; aesthetic philosophies find meaning in the interesting and diverting; religious traditions locate meaning in relation to a prime mover or designer of the universe. Psychoanalysis grounds meaning in the rich tapestry of experience generated in the dialectics between past and present, the conscious and the unconscious, the fantastic and the real, the given and the constructed.

The analyst inevitably has, and strives to have, a profound influence on the patient because he is trying to interest the patient in the advantages of a particular (his or her) form of life. One of the key dimensions of this form of life is self-reflection, a search for meaning and significance in the tensions between past and present, internal and external, actual and fantastic, conscious and unconscious. The analyst's influence is necessary—it is the only way the patient can arrive there. As Renik (1996) has put it, "the analyst's affectively driven intention toward personal influence is inextricable from our clinical method" (p. 515). The patient's autonomy is not something to be protected from the analyst's influence. The patient's autonomy, a particularly psychoanalytic form of autonomy, emerges as the patient absorbs and is increasingly able to reflect on, deconstruct, and reconstruct his analyst's influence. (See Aron, 1996, p. 151, for similar formulations along these lines.) The traditional psychoanalytic denial of the analyst's personal influence has always masked the deep wish to influence (and make reparation) on which the work depends and that, to some degree, draws individuals to the work.

The counterpart to the ability to influence constructively is the capacity to make oneself available to influence, to make oneself open to transformation through the impact of another. Of course, there are many ways to allow oneself to be influenced, and some, like compliance, are problematic and become themselves subjects of analytic inquiry. Emmanuel Ghent (1990) has explored the difference between authentic "surrender," which he regards as an essential feature of deep, authentic healing and personal transformation, and "submission," as a perversion of surrender. (See also Maroda's, 1991, discussion, building on Searles's work, of the place of surrender to a therapeutic regression on the part of both analysand and analyst.) One of the best-kept secrets of the psychoanalytic profession is the extent to which analysts often grow (in corrective emotional experiences) through a surrender to the influence of patients whose life experience, talents, and resources may be different from their own.

Thus, the traditional ideal of autonomy, redefined as an emergent rather than a preexisting property, can be reconciled with an understanding of the psychoanalytic process as fundamentally dyadic, as requiring the transformation of two people in their engagement with each other. This reconciliation entails a deepening of our understanding of the analytic relationship and its lasting residues that acknowledges rather than denies its deeply interactive nature.

What is the fate of the analytic object? If the analytic relationship is understood as essentially interactive, termination must result in important internalizations of and identifications with the analyst as an internal object. But if the patient's autonomy is to be preserved, these identifications must allow and nourish personal freedom and creativity rather than binding the patient through unconscious loyalties. What is the nature of such an ongoing, constructive internalization of the analytic process?

There is less useful literature on the termination of analysis than on any other major feature of the work.[8] The ideal of individual autonomy has led to a vision of a "complete analysis" in which all

---

8. An exception is Bergmann (1988), who understands termination along lines similar to those developed here.

transferences are resolved. The patient leaves her last session, presumably with a feeling of gratitude and perhaps fondness for someone who has been extraordinarily important but whom she does not know in any meaningfully personal sense at all!

Yet we all have a deep, intuitive sense of the importance of the lasting internal presence of and identifications with one's analyst(s) that is difficult to reconcile with the myth of the generic analyst and the perfectionistic ideal of a "complete analysis." This presence derives not just from the analysts' interpretations or their professional or work ethic or their supportive understanding, but to their subjective way of being, a sense of what they are like, their feel for life. We come to know only the version of the analyst that comes alive through his role in the analytic process. (The implications of that role are explored in Chapters 3, 4, and 6). Yet, that version is deeply personal. We can sense the presence of the analyst in the being of those we know intimately and continually rediscover it in ourselves, in our lives and in our work, in a fashion similar to the continual rediscovery and reworking of parental identifications.

In fact, the denial of the analytic object is, in some respects, very much like the denial of parental objects. There are few more shocking moments in adulthood than those in which both words and intonations of one's parents, the very words and intonations that one suffered as a child, emerge from one's own mouth (not infrequently in interacting with one's own children). The patient who cannot recognize parental presences in his or her experience is often someone whose life is organized around either unconscious identifications with parental ambitions or counteridentifications as defiant and desperate bulwarks against feared mergers with parental presences. The denial of the analytic object similarly leads to a blindness to the ways in which the former analysand is constrained by loyalties to the internalized presence of the analyst, is defying the continued influence of that presence through rigid counteridentifications, or both. Thus, Taylor (1991), drawing on the work of Michail Bakhtin, suggests that we define our identity

> always in dialogue with, sometimes in struggle against, the identities our significant others want to recognize in us. And when we outgrow some of the latter—our parents, for instance - and they disappear from

our lives, the conversation with them continues within us as long as we
live [p. 33].

It is ironic that analytic writers and teachers most concerned with
protecting the patient's autonomy from the analyst's influence are
often those around whom the most intense psychoanalytic cults
developed. Thus, Bion and Lacan both seemed to employ a carefully
crafted obscurity and elusiveness to protect their students and
patients from establishing the analyst as "the one who is supposed to
know." Yet that very stance seems to have fostered a devotional fealty.
Analytic objects, like parental objects, are most nourishing when
freely contained, where they are continually destroyed and restored in
a perpetual process of transcendence, betrayal, and reconciliation
(Loewald).

The reasons Freud and his contemporaries avoided recognizing
the interactive nature of the analytic process are for us now merely historical artifacts. But the protection of the ideal of individual autonomy
and personal authenticity is very much with us still and at the heart
of psychoanalysis as a discipline. Recent developments in all schools
of analytic theorizing suggest that we are ready to address more
directly the tension between that ideal and the interactive nature of
the process, not as something with which to cope, but as a central feature of the analytic situation. By so doing, we will learn about the best
ways for analysands to fashion out of the interactive mix in the analytic situation something that becomes most fully and richly their
own. The most constructive safeguard of the autonomy of the patient
is not the denial of the personal impact of the analyst but the acknowledgment, both in our theoretical concepts and in our clinical work,
of the interactive nature of the analytic process.

The Framework for this Book

There has been a striking convergence over the past decade in all the
major schools of analytic thought in the broad-scale, dramatic shift
from a view of mind as monadic, a separable, individual entity, to a
view of mind as dyadic, emerging from and inevitably embedded

within a relational field. (Those writers who have charted and helped work out the implications of this broad movement most systematically include Aron, 1996; Greenberg, 1991, 1996; Hoffman, 1983, 1991, 1994, 1996; Ogden, 1986, 1989, 1994; Stolorow, Brandchaft, and Atwood, 1986; Renik, 1993, 1996; and Stolorow and Atwood, 1992.) This shift has had a major impact on theorizing about the analytic situation, classically conceived as a neutral medium within which the mind of one person, the patient, emerged, unraveled, and gradually displayed itself. It is difficult to find this traditional model employed in its original, pristine form by any current school of analytic thought, including the contemporary Freudian. Even the most conservative authors now regard the analyst as having some impact on the analytic process. The blank screen, like the eight millimeter movie projector, seems on its way to becoming an antique, and analytic neutrality and anonymity are regularly described as, at best, ideals; at worst, illusions. The analytic process is often now generally understood to represent not simply an unfolding of the contents of the patient's mind, but an interaction between two people, each of whom brings to that interaction his or her own dynamics, passions, ideas, and general subjectivity.

If all analytic schools regard the analytic process as interactive to some extent, one might expect a high degree of consensus about clinical problems and technical issues among analytic authors and clinicians. This is not the case, because analytic interaction, the engagement between analyst and analysand, can be thought about in many different ways and on many different levels. It is no longer meaningful simply to characterize a particular approach as "interactive," because all approaches are interactive (Greenberg, 1996). A defense of oneself as more interactive "than thou" is pointless. The more interesting question has shifted to the *way* in which analytic interaction is understood.

In approaching clinical interaction, each tradition brings its own history to the problem, and each of these histories offers unique advantages and disadvantages. For reasons I have elaborated elsewhere (Greenberg and Mitchell, 1983; Mitchell, 1988), I do not think it is helpful simply to pick and choose pieces of theories, extracting them from their conceptual context and joining them willy-nilly. The contradictions and differences among various theories often point to important conceptual problems that need to be thought through, not skipped over. Therefore, one of our most pressing needs, at this point, is for a comprehensive framework for thinking about analytic interaction, a synthetic two-person or relational model encompassing both intrapsychic and interpersonal dimensions, housing the contributions of each tradition while eliminating their limitations and artifactual constraints. This book is intended as a contribution to this project by exploring various facets of the phenomenon of interaction in the analytic relationship from a number of different angles.

Chapter 2 continues the exploration of analytic interaction begun in this chapter with a consideration of the classical model of the therapeutic action of psychoanalysis and the logical inconsistency at the heart of it. We will see how, by omitting the centrality of the analyst's participation, the classical model divested itself of the very platform needed to explain how analysis can possibly work.

Chapters 3 and 4 explore the complex development of concepts of interaction in the two analytic traditions that have addressed this phenomenon most directly: interpersonal psychoanalysis and Kleinian and post-Kleinian theory.

For several decades, the interpersonal tradition has been on the cutting edge of thinking about the implications of analytic interaction. Unburdened by the struggle to preserve a one-person framework, interpersonal authors from Sullivan onward have emphasized the importance of here-and-now enactments and various dimensions of the analyst's participation in the analytic process. Critics (Bachant, Lynch, and Richards, 1995; Sugarman and Wilson, 1995; Wilson, 1995) have misread interpersonal psychoanalysis as a kind of shallow environmentalism and it is one of the purposes of Chapter 3 to demonstrate the ways in which interpersonal theorists, on the contrary, have struggled with the complexities of analytic interaction in the mingling of past and present, internal and interpersonal, actual and fantastic.

But the interpersonal tradition, like all traditions of theorizing, has been hampered by certain constraints. Sullivan's early, dialectical reaction to the Freudian intrapsychic model led to an operationalist methodology in which he avoided developing a systematic study of the patterns of subjective experience, the structures of the internal object world, and the ways in which they bridge past and present. This avoidance left interpersonal authors with a poverty of concepts for linking interaction with its intrapsychic roots. Too much emphasis was placed on the analyst's immediate affective reaction, as if one could quickly and easily decide what in the experience of both analysand and analyst was truly authentic. These constraints within the interpersonal tradition are part of what has interested many contemporary interpersonal authors and clinicians in object relations theories, because the latter provide a palette of concepts for painting a vision of an inner world much richer than Sullivan's cautious sketches, a new palette structured not out of drives and defenses but from the internalization of interpersonal interaction.

In Chapter 4, we consider the ironic evolution of the richly creative focus on interaction in the Kleinian tradition, which began with an extreme version of intrapsychic theorizing about the "deep" unconscious buried in a one-person frame. Because the Klein school has been one of the most cultlike of analytic traditions, Kleinian concepts tend to be presented in highly technical terms, adhered to by the converted and ignored by outsiders. It is one of the purposes of Chapter 4 to demonstrate the broad applicability of contemporary Kleinian notions of interaction and the ways in which they can be related to and integrated with interactional concepts from other traditions.

Recent Kleinian authors have made important contributions to the study of interaction in the development of the concept of projective identification and in the exploration of the patient's "relations" with interpretations. Projective identification points to the importance of both the analyst's emotional experience of the patient in the here-and-now and the patient's awareness of the analyst's affectivity. But "projective identification" is often used in a fashion that suggests that the analyst functions as a smooth or clean container for the projected features of the patient's experience. What is most often unaddressed is precisely the complex, often indeterminate mix between the patient's issues and affective experience and those of the analyst.

Chapter 5 presents an extended example of clinical interaction as a device for comparing and contrasting ideas of interaction that I have found particularly helpful. Mainstream Freudian thought brings to the problem of interaction a deep appreciation of personal history. Thus, the archaeological model of transference in the patient has been applied, by writers like Theodore Jacobs, to the historical depths of countertransference in the analyst. I compare Jacob's exploration of ghosts from the past with Darlene Ehrenberg's interpersonal emphasis on here-and-now encounters and with Thomas Ogden's recent formulation of the "analytic third" from contemporary Kleinian notions of projective identification and Winnicottian concepts of "potential space."

Chapter 6 begins with the observation that the movement toward a fully two-person, interactional framework renders obsolete all traditional notions of the analyst's intentions. If meaning is cocreated in the analytic situation, if the analyst's ideas about his own participation are not considered definitive with regard to their significance to the patient, traditional aspirations to analytic stances like "neutrality," "empathy," and "authenticity" are all called into question. In fact, the recent literature seems to demonstrate over and over that whatever analysts thought they were doing, they really cannot possibly actually do. Recent authors have emphasized that what the analyst does is less important than the ways in which analyst and patient process their interaction. Nevertheless, analytic clinicians have to do something and in fact are making continual clinical choices all the time. How ought those choices be made?

Chapter 7 explores the recent controversies surrounding the nature of the analyst's knowledge and authority, a crisis created both by two-person, interactional revolutions within psychoanalysis and by the crisis in authority and other postmodern developments in the culture at large. I suggest that both the kind of knowledge the analyst offers and the kind of authority the analyst can legitimately claim are in need of radical revision to fit with contemporary clinical theorizing and practice.

Chapter 8 brings together many of the themes of the previous chapters in the crucible of clinical work in two of the most hotly contested and controversial areas of contemporary life—gender and sexual orientation.

CHAPTER 2

THE THERAPEUTIC ACTION

A New Look

O ne of the most distinctive and fascinating features of psychoanalysis as a field is the centrality and perpetual presence of
its founder. There are few intellectual, empirical, or clinical
disciplines in which the ideas of one person have held sway for so
long. Freud's position vis-à-vis psychoanalysis in some sense sur-
passes Newton's in physics or Darwin's in biology. They made extraordinary, but more circumscribed contributions; physics and biology
have absorbed their impact and moved on. Their disciplines have
grown past them.

The relationship between Freud and psychoanalysis has been
different. Freud's ideas, his vision, the entire package of theory, technique, and understanding that constituted Freud's psychoanalysis
has had remarkable staying power—inspiring generations of analysts, serving as a perpetual take-off point and frame of reference for
virtually every dimension of the subsequent history of psychoanalytic ideas. One has only to look at the photographs of Freud and his
contemporaries to be aware of how much time has passed, how
much else has changed from Freud's day to ours. Yet his concepts
are very much alive. Why has the relationship between Freud and

the discipline he founded been so totalistic?

Surely, one reason for Freud's durability is precisely that, unlike Newton or Darwin, he founded his discipline. Physics existed prior to Newton; biology existed prior to Darwin. There was no psychoanalysis before Freud. There had been protopsychoanalytic forays into unconscious phenomena, expanded notions of sexuality, symbolic processes, and so on. But until Freud put it all together, nothing remotely like psychoanalysis existed as a system of ideas, a methodology for psychological exploration, a technique for treating mental disorders. And, because psychoanalysis, in its early decades, was so distinctively and thoroughly "Freudian," it is difficult to imagine a psychoanalysis that is wholly post-Freudian.

But there is more to it than that. Systems of thought, even the richest and most powerful, ordinarily have a life span. Think of the intellectual fashions that have illuminated and then faded from recent Western culture: Marxism, existentialism, structuralism, deconstructionism. What is different about psychoanalysis is that, in addition to being a system of thought, it is a treatment, a powerful treatment. Of course, there had been other treatments for so-called nervous disorders; but psychoanalysis was something different—a sustained, in-depth, intensive exploration of the structure of the patient's mind, the complex tapestry of the psyche.

By inventing psychoanalysis, Freud created not just a treatment, but *a kind of experience* that had never existed before. Symptomatic treatments, like hypnosis, were highly focal and time limited. A more radical cure required that the understructure of symptomatic outcroppings be traced and delineated, and that exploration led Freud into the depths of unconscious motivation and the residues of childhood.

It does not diminish Freud's achievement to suggest that he stumbled into something the power of which he had scarcely imagined. In his necessarily naive early associative tracing of symptoms to their original contexts, Freud soon encountered the phenomena of transference and resistance in all their passionate intensity. The tracing of neurotic symptoms led step-by-step into the deepest recesses of personal experience, into the remote past, the most horrifying impulses and fantasies, the most dreaded fears, the most poignant and delicate hopes and longings. Like a river explorer sucked into a whirlpool,

Freud repeatedly found himself in the grip of forces beyond his comprehension, and classical psychoanalytic theory, as a system of thought, carried him through. The theory of infantile sexuality, drive theory, technical recommendations regarding interpretation—these all became crucial parts of the conceptual craft that Freud developed to navigate the treacherous waters of the psychoanalytic experience.

The widespread interest in psychoanalysis today, so many years after Freud's original efforts, suggests that clinical psychoanalysis works, both for analysands and for analysts. Patients' lives often get better; under the best of circumstances, they get better in ways more remarkable than Freud could possibly have envisioned. They get better in ways the patients themselves could scarcely have envisioned. At its best, psychoanalysis can assuage painful residues of childhood, release thwarted creative potentials, heal fragmentation, and bridge islands of isolation and despair. And not only is psychoanalysis a powerful, transformative experience for the patient, it also provides an extraordinary experience for the analyst. It is only in recent years, with the increasing openness in writing about countertransference, that it has been possible to acknowledge how absorbing, personally touching, and potentially transformative the practice of psychoanalysis can often be for the analyst.

Thus, perhaps the most distinctive feature of psychoanalysis as a field is not just that Freud created a set of ideas or a treatment, but that Freud invented a unique, extremely powerful, personally transformative experience for both parties. Since many of us have been both analysand and analyst, we have lived that experience from both sides, and it has been compelling enough to want more and to want to offer more to other people.

To return to our original question, I would argue that one of the most important reasons for the durability of Freud's ideas over the history of psychoanalysis is that his system has made it possible for us to think that we really understand what happens in the analytic process, really understand why people change in the often profound ways that they do. It is the central purpose of this chapter to demonstrate that, whereas Freud's explanation worked persuasively in his day, it can no longer work for us and that we have had great difficulty fully coming to terms with this.

The Traditional Model:
Interpretation and Insight

Freud's explanation, stripped down to its bare essentials, goes something like this: Psychopathology results from repression, a blocking from awareness of disturbing impulses, memories, thoughts, and feelings. Repression is undone through insight, which opens up a linkage between conscious ideas and the unconscious impulses, memories, thoughts, and feelings. The analyst's correct and well-timed interpretations generate insight by creating the necessary bridges. Transferences and resistances, correctly understood, express the central unconscious conflicts with great intensity, so the competent analyst can always find just the right material to interpret.

This is a wonderful model—interpretation leads to insight and insight changes psychic structures. It must have been extraordinarily persuasive for analysts of Freud's day. The whole feel of it was so consistent with the stunning developments and new technologies in the rest of science. Microscopy was enabling scientists to look into the subvisual world and view the underlying structure of both organic and inorganic matter. (It was only shortly before Freud entered neurology that the neuron had been isolated in the study of brain function.) Telescopes were enabling scientists look into outer space and see planets, moons, stars never viewed before. Freud too had invented a methodology for entering a previously invisible realm—the psychological structure of the human mind. Free association and the other features of the analytic setting revealed the underlying patterning and fragmentation of psychic life, and interpretation seemed to be a wonderfully precise tool for excising and reworking faulty patterns and rejoining fragments.

Many things have changed since Freud's day, and these changes have rendered this model no longer very workable for us. For our purposes here, I would like to note a few salient, quite profound shifts. (For a fuller discussion of cultural changes from Freud's day to our's and their implications for psychoanalysis, see Mitchell, 1993.)

1. Scientists of Freud's time could well believe that they stood outside of what they were studying, observing its nature. Scientists of our

time believe that to study something is to interact with it, that one's methodology partly creates the object of study. So, any analytic theory today—drive theory, object relations theories, self psychology—needs to be regarded as offering not a blueprint of mind but a framework partially imposed by the analyst to order data that could be organized in many other ways.

2. The hopes of scientists of Freud's time that they would soon be able to grasp the smallest particles of matter or chart the broadest patterns of the universe seem, from our perspective, understandably naive. Considering the ever-expanding complexities of particle physics, astronomy, and cosmology, and considering that the human brain is the most complex natural phenomenon we have yet encountered, the confidence of Freud and his contemporaries that psychoanalytic theory provided a comprehensive, ultimate blueprint of mind seems wildly overoptimistic, if not fundamentally misguided.

3. An analyst's giving an interpretation to a patient in Freud's day was a very different event from an analyst's giving a patient the same interpretation in our day because the whole social context of our experience of authority is so different. In Freud's day, everyone invested the analyst with considerable authority; it made sense to do so. Thus, Freud regarded what he termed the "unobjectionable positive transference" based on childhood belief in authority as a basic ingredient in the power of the analyst's interpretations. The patient grants the analyst a certain expertise, a certain power, even a kind of magic—but that's OK, because it helps the patient really to consider the interpretation, creating the bridges that release repressions from their internal exile.

In our day, anyone who initially invests the analyst with that kind of authority has a serious problem. In our post-Watergate, post-Iran/Contra world, with all we know about the abuse of authority by political leaders, doctors, lawyers, priests, and so on, it makes no sense to grant the analyst the kind of authority Freud was granted by his patients. Or, rather, it makes a different kind of sense. The same behavior means something different in our time than it did then. Anyone approaching me with that kind of deference at the beginning of a treatment starts me thinking about the possible reasons for a brittle idealization, or a kind of obsequious handling, or perhaps both.

That sort of transference today *is* "objectionable," not in a moral sense, but in that it requires one to object, or to raise questions, because an interpretation accepted in such a mode is an act of submission. It is less likely to lead to insight than to the perpetuation of sadomasochistic object relations.

4. Since Freud's day there has developed a hefty literature on outcome of analytic and other treatments. This literature is complex, confusing, and hotly contested. But I think any fair overview would have to take account of two predictably recurrent findings that pose difficulties for the traditional model of therapeutic action—interpretation leading to insight: 1) patients, even in highly successful analyses, tend not to remember or put much weight on interpretations given to them, and 2) the particular theory or ideology of the therapist, his or her repertoire of interpretations, has little impact on outcome, whereas his or her personality or emotional presence has great impact. Now, I know that such findings can be explained. But what we do when we do this is explain away, rather than really explain, because it is bothersome, very bothersome, to think that analysis may not work on the basis of interpretation leading to intrapsychic insight.

Because of these developments since Freud's time, it is no longer compelling to think of the analyst as standing outside the patient's material, organizing it in some neutral, objective way. It is understandable that Freud and his patients saw it that way; it is no longer possible for us. Patients who today accept and internalize analytic interpretations the way Freud's patients did are not helping themselves get better; they are enacting their pathology. No matter how fond we are of our theories and interpretations—and I, for one, am exceedingly fond of mine—we must deal with the fact that something else is going on.

There is a strong tradition in psychoanalytic thinking and writing that makes it very difficult to deal directly with this problem—a tradition that enshrines Freud's model of therapeutic action as a kind of holy relic, a relic that needs to be preserved untouched, rather than reworked and revitalized. Even some of the most progressive thinkers of our time add their contributions around the traditional model of therapeutic action as a credo. Thus, Fred Pine (1993) begins an article by proclaiming, "Arlow and Brenner see analyzing as the essence of the psychoanalytic process, and I certainly concur" (p. 186). Despite Pine's recent assimilation of the contributions of object relations theories and self psychology, he makes a point of distinguishing his approach from the work of more radical thinkers like Kohut on the basis of his loyalty to the credo. The doctrinal allegiance is particularly striking in statements like this, because Pine repeats words like analyzing as if contributions from object relations theories and self psychology had not added new dimensions to and greatly enriched our understanding of what happens when the analyst makes an interpretation to a patient, as if the word analyzing today had the same meaning that it did in Freud's day.

> Although Kohut has quite a different view of the change process, in principle, I believe, one need not shift the view of the process even if one were to shift or expand the view of the significant mental contents that analysis addresses [p. 187].

Otto Kernberg, who has broadened the content about which interpretations should be made to include early object relations, also preserves the traditional model of the therapeutic action—interpretation leading to insight—as if it were still serviceable in its pristine form. Thus, Kernberg (1992) has reaffirmed interpretation as "the basic instrument of psychoanalytic technique . . . the concept and testing of changes in conflictual equilibrium is central to psychoanalytic technique as well as to its theory of outcome" (p. 121).

The Transference–Countertransference Web

As an illustration of why I believe the classical model of therapeutic action, interpretation leading to insight, can no longer serve us well in its original form, consider a moment in the beginning of the treatment of a very disturbed young man. George had been in several nonanalytic treatments before, mostly centered around problems with drug addiction. He was the son of an emotionally absent, workaholic, celebrity father who had an almost unimaginable amount of money.

George's sense of self was remarkably merged, first with his father and secondarily with his wife, whom he had married as an antidote to the power his father had over him, but with whom he had a similar, merged relationship, a blend of adoration and submission. He would recite aphorisms from both his father and wife (who were, incidentally, both devotees of psychoanalysis), as if they had been handed down on Mt. Sinai. The father had for many years been the patient of a famous analytic researcher to whose research efforts he had donated great amounts of money. I do not know if the father's analysis did him any good, but there was no evidence of it in terms of his relationship with his son.

After several weeks of his not being sure what to talk about and my not being sure what to say to him, George began filling me in on characteristic details of his problematic negotiations with his wife. He liked to spend one or two evenings a week out with his male friends, at sporting events or playing poker, but that meant leaving her alone with their two children, because she was a devout believer in the ideological principle that small children should never be left without a parent. He felt he was never in any position to decide what would be fair, because he had demonstrated his unreliability in earlier years by his drug excesses. Further, he did not want to be the kind of absentee father and husband that his own father had been. So he had to leave it up to his wife to decide when he had the right to spend an evening out. When he did go out, however, he tended to stay out longer than she was comfortable with, drink too much, and arrive home in a state that seemed to confirm his judgment that he was unable to make these kinds of decisions for himself.

I felt I might be able to say something useful here and commented on his turning over to her a great deal of power over him in a way that, I imagined, might have made him angry and resentful; I could understand how he might defiantly abuse his privileges on his evening pass. He acknowledged that this was precisely how he often felt. I tried to get him interested in the vicious-circle aspect of this interaction, how his submission made him angry, his anger made him self-destructively defiant, and his self-destructiveness convinced him further of his need for submission (Wachtel, 1987). I did not say this all at once; I felt he was with me point by point. At the end of the session, however, he asked me to summarize everything I had said. He felt that, being lazy and forgetful, he had a tendency to misuse therapy, and this seemed important. He wanted to get it clear. I repeated what I had said. Then he wanted to repeat it back to me so he could repeat it again to his wife when he returned home.

I had a progressively sinking feeling, as I imagined my interpretive description hanging, embroidered, on their wall, with little flowers around it. I tried to say something to him about his doing with me precisely what we had been talking about his doing with his wife—treating my ideas as if they were some kind of precious, supernatural guide to living rather than something he and I were working on together. He became confused and obviously felt I was both criticizing and abandoning him. I backpedaled and, I think, was able to regain the sense that we had understood something important, although clearly on his adorational terms. I reflected on his need to believe that I had all the answers but decided not to challenge that belief now and expressed instead a curiosity about his need for that belief and the lengths he seemed prepared to go to maintain it. It seemed to me that my choice was between repeating one or the other feature of his relationship with his father: sticking to my interpretation of the transference and thereby abandoning him like the "bad" father, or allowing him, with a gentle invitation to self-reflection, to use me as the overly idealized magical father. The latter, I thought, might eventually offer more opportunities for growth.

What is happening in this interaction? I think I see something in the material the patient provides that is worth commenting on interpretively. This is what I have been taught to do. The same material surely could be described interpretively in other ways—as a wish and a defense, a developmental longing, and so on. I don't really think it would have mattered. Because what happened was that George did not really hear the interpretation as an interpretation; he heard it as something else, something familiar, something recognizable within the basic categories of his own frame of reference. I might have thought I was offering an interpretation; George thought I was handing down the 11th commandment.

Is this transference of George's "unobjectionable"? In Freud's day, it might have been defensible to think of it that way, but I do not think we can really get away with that now. It seems fairly clear that George is relating to my interpretation much as to one of his father's aphorisms rather than to my idea of what an interpretation is supposed to be about.

The contemporary Kleinians (e.g., Betty Joseph, 1989) have a solution to this problem, which concerns what they call the patient's "relationship to the interpretation."[1] Make another interpretation, this time of the patient's relationship to the interpretation. This is, in effect, what I did, calling George's attention to the way in which he was doing with me what I was describing his doing with his father and wife. The content of all other possible interpretations is irrelevant, the Kleinians argue, because of the way the patient relates to interpretations. *Interpreting this mode of processing interpretations* is the only way to get through. I find this a useful way of thinking, and it sometimes works. But most often it does not really solve the problem. You will remember that when I made such a second-level interpretation to George, he became confused and disoriented. I think it was clear that he was unable to reflect on the way in which he attributed oracular status to my statements and instead felt that I was delivering yet another, a 12th, commandment, raising questions, in an obscure and critical fashion, about his failure to defer properly to the previous commandment. Trying to interpret the patient's relationship to each interpretation can create an infinite regress from which the analyst can never disentangle himself.

Because Freud could assume that the analyst, when making interpretations, stood outside the web of these kinds of sticky, repetitive transference–countertransference configurations, he never had to deal with this problem as such. Whatever other transference there was to the analyst's interpretations, the dimension of the "unobjectionable positive transference" was, as I noted earlier, considered an aid. The closest Freud came to dealing with the kinds of problems we are faced with today was when he discovered the importance of time, long periods of time, in effecting analytic change. Recall that Freud's early analyses lasted only several months. It seemed reasonable to assume that for curative insight to occur, the analyst needed merely to arrive at

---

1. This strategy is explored at length in Chapter 4.

the correct interpretive understanding and convince the patient of its correctness. Freud and subsequent analysts discovered that useful interpretations were not a one-shot deal. They take time, lots of time. One makes the same or closely related interpretations over and over again. How can this be understood within the traditional model of therapeutic action? If the conflictual material is released from repression by the interpretation, why does it have to happen over and over?

Freud developed the notion of "working through" to try to account for the temporal dimension of the analytic process—the work takes time. I have always found this the most elusive, the murkiest of all Freud's major technical concepts. Laplanche and Pontalis (1973) noted that working through takes place "especially during certain phases where progress seems to have come to a halt and where a resistance persists despite its having been interpreted" (p. 488). What does the analyst do to facilitate working through? Laplanche and Pontalis say that "working through is expedited by interpretations from the analyst which consist chiefly in showing how the meanings in question may be recognised in different contexts" (p. 488). This seems to amount to saying that during stagnant times, when interpretations seem to fail, something useful sometimes happens when the analyst continues to make them. Can this be persuasively explained in the classical model?

Picture working through in terms of the spatial metaphors Freud relied on. Even after the original conflict is uncovered through interpretation, its derivatives need to be traced and eradicated, like the troublesome shoots of a complex weed system in a garden. Once the central roots are pulled up, one needs to follow the many shoots to prevent a reemergence of the plant. But this way of thinking about working through over time does not really explain how patients like George change. George could not really use more interpretations; George seems to need some different way of grasping and internalizing interpretations. My interpretation seemed to compound the problem, not to cure it. In pulling up each root, the analyst is scattering seeds of the same weed; the very activity designed to deal with the problem perpetuates the problem. From our contemporary point of view, the analyst seems less like the surgeon Freud asked us to imagine and more like the Sorcerer's Apprentice.

Is this just a problem that comes up in the beginning of analyses? Or in especially difficult cases? I don't think so. We become most aware of the limitations of the therapeutic impact of interpretations when they fail dramatically, as with George, but the very same processes may be operating even when things seem to be going well.

Bootstraps and a Missing Platform

A vivid demonstration of the limits of interpretation in everyday analytic work and therefore of the explanatory insufficiency of the traditional model of therapeutic action is to be found in an excellent paper by William Grossman and Walter Stewart (1976). This paper points to the way in which the common (perhaps it would be fair to say the traditional) interpretation of penis envy presumes, following Freud, that penis envy is a concrete, biologically based fact rather than a metaphor to be interpreted like any other piece of manifest content. The authors thoughtfully demonstrate that, for two women who sought a second analysis, the penis envy interpretation from the first analysis had an antitherapeutic effect of gratifying various masochistic and narcissistic dynamics. In discussing one patient, they note that

> since admiration always led to rivalry and envy, and sexual interest to aggression, the only permanent tie to the object was of a sado-masochistic nature. She chose the masochistic role and the defense of a mild paranoid attitude. Indeed, the "helpless acceptance" of the penis envy interpretation in the first analysis seemed masochistically gratifying [pp. 197–198].

Here is a very interesting situation. Grossman and Stewart are suggesting that, while the content of the analyst's interpretation may or may not have been correct or relevant in one sense or another, what was most important was the way in which the patient experienced and internalized the interpretation (the patient's relationship to the interpretation). While the analyst thought he was offering an interpretation, the patient experienced it as a kind of sadistic attack or beating to which she was submitting, thereby enacting her central dynamics. While it looked as though something new was happening—an interpretation that should create insight and effect psychic change—actually the patient was reenacting her same old masochistic surrender to men, this time by submitting to the analyst and his interpretation.

Second analyses are always wonderfully privileged vantage points to observe what went wrong in the previous analysis. But in this case, the realization Grossman and Stewart arrived at, that the first analyst's interpretations had had no real analytic impact because they had been processed through the patient's masochistic dynamics, did not help the second analyst very much.

> Even to interpret her masochism posed the threat that the interpretation would be experienced as a "put down" and gratify her masochistic impulse; all interpretations, if not narcissistically gratifying, gratified masochistic wishes. They were felt as attacks in which her worthlessness, her defectiveness, and her aggression were unmasked. The analysis threatened to become interminable, one in which the relationship to the analyst was maintained, but only at the price of an analytic stalemate [p. 198].

This is a wonderful example of the central problem at the heart of every analysis. The analyst arrives at a way of understanding the patterns through which the patient organizes her subjective world and perpetuates her central dynamic conflicts. The analyst delivers this understanding in the form of an interpretation. But the patient can hear the interpretation only as something else—it is slotted into the very categories the analyst is trying to get the patient to think about and understand. The analyst makes an interpretation about the way in which the patient eroticizes interactions, and the patient experiences the interpretation itself as a seduction. The analyst makes an interpretation about the way in which the patient transforms every interaction into a battle, and the patient experiences the interpretation itself as a power operation. Or, in this case, the analyst makes an interpretation about the patient's masochism, and the patient experiences the interpretation as a put-down to be agreed to and feel humiliated by.

It is very common for the analyst not to realize that this is happening, but, as in the cases discussed by Grossman and Stewart, it often becomes quite apparent to the next analyst. Why? The patient and the analyst, as long as the analysis is ongoing, both have a great investment in thinking that the analyst's interpretations are something different, something new, part of the solution and not part of the problem. It is very easy for the patient unconsciously to organize her experience in analysis in her familiar, characteristic fashion while hoping and believing that something quite new and transformative is happening. It is often very difficult for patients to let their analysts know that they are beginning to feel that the analyst, even in offering interpretations, is only the latest in a long line of those from whom they have suffered seduction, betrayal, abandonment, torture, pathetic disappointments.

It is also very difficult for the analyst to pick up and hear the patient's hints in these directions, because the analyst wants so much to feel that the analysis is going well and that interpretations are truly analytic events rather than reenactments of chronic disasters. But it is often more complicated still. Generally speaking, the analyst, despite his best intentions, is likely to become entangled in the very same web he is trying to get the patient to explore. So, the analyst making an interpretation of the patient's tendency to erotize interactions is likely to be speaking from an erotized countertransferential position in his own experience. The analyst making an interpretation of the patient's tendency to transform all encounters into battles is likely to be feeling embattled himself and trying to use interpretations as a potent weapon in his arsenal. And the analyst making an interpretation about the patient's masochism is likely himself to have felt victimized by the patient's long-suffering misery and is speaking in a voice laced with exasperation. Thus, the analyst's experience is likely to be infused with the very same affects, dynamics, and conflicts he is trying to help the patient understand. Because analysts make their living as helpers, there is a built-in, chronic counterresistance to becoming aware themselves of precisely what they need to help their patients locate and understand in themselves. Because they try so hard to be part of the solution, it is very difficult to grasp the subtle but profound ways in which they have, in fact, become part of the problem.

When a patient, with or without the analyst's help, finally makes it unmistakably clear that he is experiencing the analyst's interpretations not as something new but as something old, there is usually a sense of great crisis in the analysis, and its value is called into question. Most often, the patient's experience of the interpretation is not fully revealed and investigated until the patient is already working with the next analyst and the new analytic pair can operate under the illusion that this problem does not really pertain to them.

Because Grossman and Stewart (1976) had laid out the issues so clearly, I was very interested to see what they would say next. Did they find a way out of this central dilemma? The next paragraph begins: "Over many years the patient was able to recognize her need to be a mistreated little girl, rather than to face her disappointments as a grown woman" (p. 198).

The first time I read this passage I was convinced that my mind must have wandered and that I had missed a paragraph. No. Perhaps the typesetter dropped the paragraph. What had happened here? The authors lay out the problem so lucidly. They show that interpretations, in themselves, can't possibly solve the problem, because the patient organizes the interpretations into another manifestation of the problem. Yet, they say that "over many years" something changed. But how? The implication is that the interpretations themselves eventually did the trick, that the traditional model of therapeutic action somehow prevailed. Yet Grossman and Stewart have shown that in itself interpretation cannot possibly have effected analytic change. There is a major bootstrapping problem here at the heart of the traditional model of therapeutic action. Something else must have happened.

Webster's says that when we describe someone as pulling oneself up by one's own bootstraps we mean that one has helped "oneself without the aid of others; use(d) one's own resources." But this definition leaves out the paradox implied by that phrase. You cannot pull yourself up by your bootstraps; try it. You are standing in them. To pull yourself up by your bootstraps, you would have to find somewhere else to rest your weight. You cannot be in them and pull yourself up by them at the same time. This seems to be precisely the problem that we have been tracing with the traditional model of the therapeutic action. Interpretations are credited with pulling patients out of their psychopathology; yet interpretations are deeply mired in the very pathology we use them to cure. There must be something else on which the analyst can rest his weight while he is tugging on his interpretive bootstraps. There is a missing platform somewhere.

When astronomers were studying the orbit of the planet Uranus, they noticed small deviations from the elliptical course they would have predicted. Even though the telescopes available at that time did not make it possible to see other planets, the astronomers realized that there must be something else out there pulling Uranus out of its predictable orbit. This reasoning made it possible for them to locate and eventually see Neptune.

We are at an analogous point in the history of psychoanalytic ideas. There is something else, some other force, that must help the analyst to pull patients out of their customary psychodynamic orbits—simply making interpretations cannot possibly be doing the job. But whatever else is out there, in the analytic situation, has been generally invisible to our available conceptual repertoire, and the preservation of Freud's now anachronistic model of therapeutic action, of interpretation leading to insight as the basic mechanism of change, lulls us into not really looking. Recent versions of this model of therapeutic action, for example, the sort of ego and defense analysis systematically and elegantly developed by Paul Gray (1994; see also Bosch, 1996), suffer from the same basic problem as earlier versions. Thus Gray stresses "an observing, listening, focus which tries to perceive, primarily via the spoken material, evidence of drive derivatives that *have reached the patient's awareness* and that have *then* developed enough conflict to stimulate the ego to a defensive/resistive solution, the outcome of which is the removal of the drive element from consciousness. At appropriate moments and with acceptable words, I invite the patient to share in observing what has taken place" (pp. 100–101). Gray maintains the traditional presumption that the observing, interpreting analyst stands outside the transference–countertransference matrix. But who is offering the invitation to share? And to whom? For Gray, the answers to these questions are simple and obvious. For me, they are complex and continually shifting, and the collaborative exploration of their intricacies are, in fact, the heart of the analytic process.

There have been several important strategies for shoring up

Freud's model, and the concept of the "working alliance," developed within American ego psychology, has been the most popular of these, particularly in this country. When interpretations fail, it is because there is no working alliance. Thus, Freud was right about how analysis works, but we have come to understand the preconditions of an effective analytic process. With more disturbed patients, rather than making interpretations, the analyst builds a working alliance. With patients who are working well, a closer look reveals an underlying working alliance. Thus, the working alliance becomes the missing platform that makes interpretive leverage possible, a place for the analyst to rest her weight when making interpretations.

But the concept of the working alliance begs all the most interesting questions of the bootstrapping problem we have been considering. Interpretations won't work unless the analyst is experienced as being outside the dynamic web of the patient's transferences. You need to have a working alliance. But how in the world does one establish a working alliance? A close reading of Greenson (1967), for example, reveals that one actually establishes the working alliance largely by interpreting the transference. But how can the patient "hear" interpretations of the transference if there is no preexisting working alliance? This concept has merely shifted the problem with the traditional model of interpretation to an earlier precondition for interpretation. (See Friedman, 1988, Chapter 2, for an extensive and extremely incisive critique of the concept of the working alliance.)

Parallel use has recently been made of many concepts borrowed from object relations theories and self psychology by writers like Pine, Kernberg, and Modell. Interpretation leading to insight is still the key process, but, in order for interpretations to work, patients must experience the analytic setting as a "holding environment" or experience the analyst as truly "empathic." When interpretations fail, holding or empathy is needed; when interpretations work, holding or empathy is presumed.

But for holding or empathy to be genuinely analytic, the patient must experience it as something quite different from anything found in her customary object relations. How is the analyst able to establish something different? To presume holding and empathy is, once again, to beg the most central questions. For the patient who has grown up in a world of dangerous and deceitful others, the analyst's offer of empathy is likely to be experienced as dangerous and deceitful, and what the analyst might feel is an empathic understanding of this problem doesn't solve the problem because the analyst's gesture, for the patient, is still embedded in a dangerous and deceitful world. Rather, it is in the long and hard struggle to establish an empathic connection that a particular patient can recognize as such and really use that the most fundamental analytic work is done, not in the effective interpretations that presuppose its achievement.

Several lines of analytic thinking have engaged the bootstrapping problem directly. Fairbairn (1952) anticipated our current struggles with this problem almost 50 years ago, when he argued that the relinquishment of the tie to the bad object is the central transformative dimension in psychoanalysis. He suggested that in order for the patient to give up, to use Freud's wonderful descriptive adjective, the "adhesive" tie to the bad object, he had to believe, through the relationship with the analyst, in the possibility of a good object relationship. Fairbairn, however, left obscure and ambiguous the questions of exactly what a good object relationship is and how one struggles through transferences to achieve it.

Important progress has been made on this problem by the interpersonalists, particularly those most influenced by Fromm. (Sullivan, although radically innovative in many areas, was quite conservative regarding therapeutic action and the analytic relationship; he considered analytic traction to rest on insight, delivered not through interpretations but through questions, from a therapist located outside the push and pull of transference and countertransference.) Fromm (1960) saw the analyst's role as more personal, and contemporary interpersonalists (e.g., Levenson, Wolstein, and Ehrenberg) locate the therapeutic action in the struggle of the analyst to find an authentic way of engaging the patient. (The decades-long struggle of interpersonal theorists with the complexities of analytic interaction are considered at length in the next chapter.)

Self psychology also has made important contributions to the bootstrap problem. Whereas Fairbairn (1952) understood the adhesiveness underlying psychopathology in terms of ties to bad objects warding off unimaginable object loss and isolation, Kohut understood adhesiveness as the need for selfobjects to ward off the experience of annihilation and disintegration of the self. In my view, Fairbairn's depiction of the untenable loss of all objects and Kohut's depiction of annihilation anxiety are two different ways of describing the same phenomenon.

Whereas Fairbairn was sketchy, Kohut was messianic; he often depicted empathy as if it were generic and easily achieved, a basic posture on the analyst's part that works for all patients. Kohut also seemed to suggest that selfobject needs are primed in the patient all the time, waiting and eager to emerge. This view (like Winnicott's notion of a prefigured "true self") is problematic, because it once again presupposes rather than explains how the analyst finds, differently with each patient, how to be that patient's analyst. The classical model circumvented the bootstrap problem by assuming that interpretations provide a direct channel between the analyst and the patient that bypass the patient's dynamics. Contemporary Kleinians (see Chapter 4) assume that only interpretations of the patient's relation to interpretations provided a direct channel. What might be called the classical self psychology of Kohut assumed that the analyst's empathic stance provides a direct channel to the patient, bypassing the patient's conflicts and reaching developmental longings poised for growth if only provided the requisite environment.

The futile search for the direct channel that has characterized so much theorizing within the various traditions of the psychoanalytic literature has been motivated partly by the hope of circumventing the messy, knotty problems of influence in analytic interaction. If the analyst has available some mode of participation for reaching the patient directly—neutral interpretations, empathic reflections, meta-interpretations of relations to interpretations—then something new can be assumed, a point of leverage taken for granted. Just as early explorers of North America were searching for a Northwest Passage linking the Atlantic and Pacific oceans to make unnecessary the endless trip around the southern tip of South America, so have psychoanalytic theorists searched for a direct passageway between analyst and patient to make unnecessary the arduous task of examining and interpreting their mutual influence on each other in the service of the patient's personal growth and development.

I am arguing that it is not useful to assume such a direct channel, but rather to understand the interactions generated between the patient and analyst in terms of the patient's dynamics as manifestations of old patterns. Meaningful analytic change, in this view, comes not from bypassing old object relations, but from expanding them from the inside out (Bromberg, 1991.) This entails new understandings and transformations of the patient's old relational patterns in the transference, as well as new understandings and transformations of the analyst's customary relational patterns in the countertransferences, including the analyst's capacity to think about analytic interactions in new and different ways. Recent developments in self psychology more directly address the bootstrap problem in their exploration of the repetitive dimensions of the transference (Lachmann and Beebe), the "dread to repeat" (Ornstein), the inevitability and utility of "empathic failures," and the fundamentally intersubjective nature of the analytic situation (Stolorow).

The point of convergence of these various lines of innovative thinking about therapeutic action, the missing planet of the analytic process, is to be found in the emotional transformation of the relationship with the analyst (Racker, Levenson, Gill, Hoffman, Greenberg, Spezzano). Interpretations fail because the patient experiences them as old and familiar modes of interaction. The reason interpretations work, when they do, is that the patient experiences them as something new and different, something not encountered before. The effective interpretation is the expression of, and sometimes the vehicle for, something deeper and more significant. The central locus of analytic change is in the analyst's struggle to find a new way to participate, both within his own experience and then with the patient. There is an enormous difference between false empathy, facile and postured, and authentic empathy, struggled toward through miscues, misunderstanding, and deeply personal work on the part of both analyst and patient.

Thus, although I find enormous value in the developmental concepts of writers like Winnicott and Kohut, I think there is a danger in the developmental perspective of assuming new growth where subtle forms of repetition may be occurring. Of course, neither of these two different interpretative approaches can be considered simply right or wrong—they are ways of organizing ambiguous data that can be organized in many ways. The more relevant question concerns not correctness, but the consequences of holding one view or the other. Looking for repetitions, if done with sensitivity and tact, has two major advantages.

First, it helps the patient appreciate how deftly old patterns can be resurrected. Since none of us ever completely outgrows such patterns, and relative mental health entails an increased capacity to refind and emerge from them, this effort serves the patient well. It conveys to the analysand the sense that authentic living is never achieved without struggle.

Second, an alertness to repetitions shapes the analytic relationship in a way that is likely to be highly beneficial. It conveys a willingness on the part of the analyst continually to question his or her own participation, an openness to criticism and self-reflection, and a dedication to patients' getting the most possible out of their analyses and, consequently, their lives.

Impasses and Outbursts

Consider a point in the second analysis of a woman named Carla, whose first analysis had come to an anguished stalemate. I use this material here because it involves a later point in work with a patient whose issues were similar to George's. I will elaborate my own struggles in the countertransference, because that is where I think a lot of the work was done.

Carla was the daughter of a brilliant, crackpot, would-be inventor who had lived in paranoid isolation, working on what he considered to be ground-breaking innovations. Carla and her siblings were forced to choose between their parents in the years preceding as well as following their divorce, and Carla felt deeply loyal to her father. She felt that she was like her father in many ways and had cultivated a deep isolation from her own peers, which was a sign of her feelings of superiority and her internal merger with her father. She was torn between her sense that her father's self-absorbed estimation of his own importance was wildly inflated and her deep need to believe in her father and her link with him. Very little ever actually happened between

Carla and her father, but, through her identification and loyalty to him, Carla felt a precious, but very shaky, fantasied sense that she was following in her father's footsteps and that her father was taking care of her.

Central to Carla's resentments against her first analyst was her feeling that she had been kind of snookered into treatment from the very beginning. She had been sent to consult with this man by a friend and really did not know what sort of treatment would be preferable. Following an extended consultation, the analyst informed her that she would be suitable for analysis and offered to see her five days a week for a token fee. (Carla later suspected, of course, that the analyst was a candidate at an institute and that she had become a training case, although this was never explicitly acknowledged.) In a certain sense, the die was cast from that initial moment, because a central feature of the transference was organized around the idea that the analyst had lured her into their analytic arrangement for the analyst's own needs.

The analyst seemed blindly devoted to psychoanalysis as a quasi-religion. Carla experienced her own devoted daily attendance as an effort to worship at the analyst/father's altar, even though she had profound doubts both about the analyst and about psychoanalysis. In return, she longed to be helped, perhaps rescued, at least talked to. Over the years, she developed a deepening sense of betrayal, abandonment, and outrage.

Carla came to see me for help in understanding what had happened in this treatment that had left her feeling so embittered. After several consultations, I had gotten enough of a sense of the features of the transference I have just recounted that I recommended that she begin a kind of trial analytic treatment with a new analyst, the purpose of which would be partly to explore what happened the first time around. We agreed it would be best for her to work with someone experienced. This meant higher fees, and, since her income was limited, only one or two sessions a week. I told her that, in my experience, working at that frequency was difficult but often quite constructive. After thinking about it a while, she asked if it would be possible to work with me, and we set up an arrangement by which I saw her once a week at a somewhat reduced fee.

Many things happened over the course of the first six months

which I will not recount here, since I will follow only the threads leading to the moment I want to describe. Generally, I felt that the work
was going quite well. She seemed deeply mired in her masochistic,
narcissistic identification with her father, but we were working well
together and I felt cautiously optimistic. Then she told me she had
found out that she actually had an insurance policy that would pay a
considerable amount toward her treatment, with a $20,000 lifetime
limit.

Given the retrenchment in third-party payments these days, I
regarded this news as roughly equivalent to a report that she had won
the lottery. I envisioned expanding to three or four times a week. I
found working with her very absorbing, but also frustrating, at once a
week. Her announcement seemed like great news. I restrained my
enthusiasm, and she herself wondered whether this meant she might
come more often. What did I think? Being well trained, I dodged the
question and asked what she thought.

Because so much reciprocal dodging ensued, I don't remember
exactly who said what, but the basic outlines were something like this:
Being a lot more frugal than I, she felt that this newly available money
needed to be spent carefully. After all, the $20,000 would last only for
several years; then it would be gone. So she really needed to be sure
that this work with me was *the* treatment for her; perhaps she would
be able to afford only one such treatment in her lifetime, and she
needed to know that this was it. And she had all kinds of doubts. Her
life certainly hadn't improved noticeably over the six months. What
did I think?

I felt increasingly uncomfortable. At first I thought that I was
doing a good job as an analyst by dodging her question and solemnly
taking the position that the decision was hers. We needed to explore
what she thought. This position did not wear well, though. As we
explored her sense that she needed to hear from me, my somewhat
righteous analytic conviction that I was not called on to venture an
opinion began to feel too easy, even a bit irresponsible. We explored
her experience of my position that my opinion was not important.
Why wasn't it, she wanted to know? After all, I was an expert to
whom she was coming for professional help. I must have an opinion;
it must be more informed than hers, or at least of some potential value

in helping her make up her mind. My withholding my thoughts from her seemed deliberately hoarding and sadistic, like her first analyst's laconic style. To ask her to believe that it was really in her best interest seemed like asking her to defer to a principle that seemed to her exceedingly abstract and dubious, and probably self-serving on my part. The more we explored her experience of my abstention, the more unfeasible it seemed to be.

Well, I thought further, what do I really think? I could imagine going two ways.

One line of association about the question of whether or not this was the best treatment for her led to the thought: "Beats the hell out of me." Most of the people I've worked with have gotten a great deal out of the work and feel it was worth it, but not all. Would it work for her? I really didn't know. She would have to decide one way or the other and take her chances: "You pays your money and you takes your choice." But that didn't feel right. It felt too facile. Did I really feel so casual about this decision? No. Maybe I should tell her to go ahead and use the money on our analytic work. That was certainly what I would do. She was in serious danger of living an enormously compromised life. If our work took, it could make a great difference in the quality of her life, much more than having the money in reserve. She should go ahead, and I should tell her so.

But that didn't feel very comfortable either. For one thing, I tend to spend money impulsively. The next $20,000 I stumble across will surely pay for the tennis court I've spent years fantasizing about. Perhaps Carla's cautiousness was valid, particularly for her. Was I so sure our work would help her? How much was that belief an extension of my narcissism? Easy for me to say. Perhaps my very passion for the work was itself dangerous to her. Further, I could imagine my clear stand on the desirability of analysis for her leading us into precisely the same sort of transference–countertransference impasse that destroyed the first analysis. Would I need to keep convincing her that the work was going well? Would I need increasingly to see it that way myself? The more confident I was that this would be good for her, the more she might need to defeat me by destroying the analysis. It began to feel as though the alternatives were either to bail out on her or to snooker her into the greater frequency of sessions by selling a product with a greater certainty than I, in fact, had.

I began to feel suffocated, a feeling I have come to regard as an invariable sign that something important is happening. This situation is set up so that there is no way for me to be my idea of an analyst. If I abstain, she feels it as an abandonment. If I encourage her, she feels it as a seduction; and there *is* something in the way our interaction develops that draws me into wanting to make claims and implied promises I have no business making. We seemed to be at an impasse.

The term impasse has been used with growing frequency in the recent literature, generally with some prescribed route out. As I suggested earlier, the contemporary Kleinians regard interpretation of the patient's relationship to the interpretation as the solution. Some interpersonalists (Cooper and Witenberg) recommend detailed inquiry into the patient's history. Other interpersonalists (Ehrenberg, 1992) regard self-disclosure of countertransferential feelings as the key. Self psychologists favor the reestablishment of an empathic stance. When things get difficult, everyone relies on what they do best.

I have not discovered any general solution to situations like these; in fact, I don't believe there are any general solutions, for reasons I will explain in a moment. But one reaction to impasses that I have found helpful sometimes is an outburst. I do not mean a countertransferential temper tantrum or a retaliatory attack. I mean a reaction that conveys a sense that I feel somehow trapped and constrained, that I feel that the analysand and I are both trapped and constrained, and that I want to burst out of the confines of options that all seem unacceptable to me.[2] So I told Carla about my sense of being stymied: I agreed with her that it did not seem fair not to say what I thought, but I could think of only two ways to respond, and neither seemed quite right. To say that I really didn't know if our work would be right for her left out my good feelings about what we had been doing and my sense of its possibilities. Yet for me to say that she ought simply to go ahead seemed to imply a certainty and a

---

2. See Symmington (1983) for a vivid account of the analyst's necessary enmeshment in the closed world of the patient's neurosis and the break for freedom that is required for the analyst to have a therapeutic impact.

promise that I couldn't make, a promise that I felt quite sure she would feel the need to defeat and feel betrayed by. As we spoke of these various options[3] I told her what I thought I would be asking myself if I were her: Did she feel the things we were talking about were at the center of what mattered to her in her life? Did she feel we were grappling with them in a way that seemed meaningful? What seemed to her to be a reasonable trial period for our efforts to bear fruit? As I spoke and she engaged some of the questions I was framing, the whole emotional tone between us shifted. I no longer felt that I was dodging her questions, stranded between unacceptable postures. She no longer felt frustrated and subtly abandoned. The treatment went on, and what seemed important was that we had found a way to work together that allowed me to function in good faith as my idea of an analyst and allowed her to begin to conceive of a way of getting something important from me that did not require a self-betraying devotion.

The way constructive analyses overcome the bootstrap problem is that the analysand and analyst struggle together to find a different kind of emotional connection. There is no general solution or technique, because each resolution, by its very nature, must be custom designed. If the patient feels that the analyst is applying a technique or displaying a generic attitude or stance, the analysis cannot possibly work. Sometimes making interpretations works analytically, not simply because of the content of the interpretation, but because the patient experiences the interpreting analyst as alive, as caring, as providing fresh ways of thinking about things, as grappling deeply with what is bothering him. Sometimes refraining from interpreting works analytically, because the patient experiences the quiet analyst as alive, as caring, as providing fresh ways to be together that don't demand what may have come to feel like the inescapable corruptions of language. Sometimes patience seems called for: a sustained involvement over time that is evidence of a kind of relationship different from past abandonments. Sometimes impatience is required: an exasperation that conveys a sense that the analyst can envision something better than the patient's perseverative patterns and cares enough not to take

---

3. See Hoffman (1992) for a discussion of a similar clinical strategy.

the easy way out and passively go along. What I am suggesting is that the central feature of the therapeutic action of psychoanalysis is the emergence of something new from something old. It cannot be there in the beginning, because you have to find yourself in the old to create the proper context for the emergence of something new. It cannot be in the application of a standard technique or posture, because then it would not really be something new and would never strike the analysand that way.

In the classical psychoanalytic literature, the concept of the "transference neurosis" referred to the central, most difficult phase of the analysis, in which the infantile neurosis reappeared in the analytic relationship itself. Whatever the patient's problems were on entering analysis, the problem had now become the analyst, who was driving the patient crazy. But, in the classical framework, the transference neurosis, like all lesser problems, could always be dealt with— through interpretation. The analyst was portrayed as *outside* the problem, and from his clear vantage point he could offer the patient illumination.

The thematic frequency of concepts like impasses and stalemates in the recent psychoanalytic literature represents an effort to describe this same central feature of the analytic process in contemporary terms. The patient is stuck; the analysis has been transformed from the solution to the problem. The patient who was imprisoned in his neurosis (see Schafer, 1983) has now become imprisoned in the analysis itself. Whatever the patient imagined were the obstacles to a more satisfying life before the analysis, those obstacles have now become the analysis and the analyst himself.

What distinguishes psychoanalysis from most other forms of psychotherapy is precisely this valuing of impasses and obstacles. As Adam Phillips (1993) has put it, "One of the aims of psychoanalytic treatment may be to enable the patient to find, or be able to tolerate, more satisfying obstacles to contend with. Poor obstacles impoverish us" (p. 86). In other forms of treatment, there is a shared agreement on getting somewhere, removing some symptom, overcoming some inhibition. In psychoanalysis, there is a similar initial contract, but the analyst knows, in a way that the patient simply cannot, that the final destination will be very different from whatever was envisioned at the beginning and that the journey itself will prove much more interesting and important than the destination arrived at. Escher's "Stairs" is an apt image for this feature of the analytic process. Just as the stair climber imagines himself rising to new heights only to emerge again and again at the beginning, so do the members of the analytic dyad discover themselves caught again and again in the same entangling interactions. In our contemporary understanding, however, the analyst is envisioned not as outside that stair system, pointing to the problems and illuminating the way through interpretations. The analyst and the patient are on the stairs together. It slowly, painfully becomes apparent that, despite the patient's arduous efforts to climb to a higher level, the patient is dedicated to just this stair system, just this imprisoned form of life with none other than the analyst as his cellmate. Paradoxically, it is precisely when the patient begins to appreciate her stair system, her impasse, not as an obstacle but as a way of life that the stairs themselves become enriched and new possibilities emerge.

> *For the beginning is assuredly*
> *the end—since we know nothing, pure*
> *and simple, beyond*
> *our own complexities.*
> — William Carlos Williams, *Paterson*

Let us imagine what happened "over the years" with the patient discussed by Grossman and Stewart (1976). It cannot be simply that the interpretations themselves gradually sunk in. There must have been something in the analyst's involvement over time—his trying over and over, refusing to give up, declining again and again the easy role as sadistic humiliator that the patient granted him—that established him as offering a different sort of relationship than the patient had encountered previously.

Coming to terms finally with the inadequacy of the classical model of therapeutic action frees us to ask the most relevant questions, questions that Grossman and Stewart did not think to explore. The analyst had begun to feel that the analysis threatened to become interminable. That's interesting to me. Did he share that fear explicitly with the patient? Did she know that the problems with the first analysis had reappeared in the second? What did she sense of the analyst's fears and frustrations? What was her sense of why he kept on trying to make something new happen when she kept organizing everything that happened in old terms?

There is no generic solution or technique. There is a great deal of disciplined thought in the skilled practice of clinical psychoanalysis, and continual, complex choices. But that thought and those choices are always taking place in the context of a unique interpersonal situation. At the heart of the work is the lived experience of constraint, discovering oneself in the confines of the patient's dynamics, which always reverberate with complementary features of the analyst's dynamics (Racker, 1968). Then analyst and analysand work together to find a way out. It can't be easy, for long, because then one has skipped over the most important part. Generally speaking, the analyst has to go first (Symmington, 1983), to break out into a different emotional state, to want more, and then to find a way to get the patient interested. It is only when that new emotional presence appears that interpretations become truly new, truly analytic events rather than disguised repetitions.

Imagine one of Freud's patients returning many decades later, seeking further analysis. Would the procedure she was familiar with work now? Could she simply free associate, awaiting interpretations as a source of enlightenment? I think not. Today's analyst would want to know a great deal more. What did the patient do with the old interpretations? What was the fate of the analyst as internal object? What were they hoping to gain by returning? Why return to this analyst at this time? What were they leaving behind? The patient's relationship to the analysis would not be taken for granted in the way it was then.[4] Analytic knowledge would not be regarded as impersonal truth, but an understanding always embedded in a relational context. Meaning would not be assumed, but would have to be invented anew.

---

4. The patient that Freud (1918) called "the Wolf Man" did in fact resurface years after Freud's death, in the offices of several later analysts, and these kinds of questions were among the ones that quickly came to the fore (see Gardiner, 1971).

In many ways, Freud's patients lived in a simpler world than our's, a world in which authentic personal meaning did not have to be so individually shaped, so hard fought. We ask more of our patients now, and, necessarily, have to ask more of ourselves.

CHAPTER 3

INTERACTION IN THE
INTERPERSONAL TRADITION

Interpersonal psychoanalysis was born of the convergence between Harry Stack Sullivan's home-grown American interpersonal psychiatry and Erich Fromm's Marxist version of Freudian psychoanalysis, which Fromm brought with him as a refugee from war-torn Europe. The person most responsible for brokering this fertile mingling of ideas was Clara Thompson, who had been trained in classical psychoanalysis and analyzed by Ferenczi. (These were the years when Ferenczi was stretching what he felt were the constraints of both Freud's theory of neurosis and classical technique.)

Thompson had a keen sense of the history of psychoanalytic ideas and recognized the strong natural affinity among Ferenczi's rediscovery of the importance of actual trauma and his emphasis on the centrality of the relationship between analyst and patient; Sullivan's innovative approach to schizophrenia as a disorder of family systems; and Fromm's relocation of Freudian libido theory into a broad Marxist perspective emphasizing the importance of culture and history ("humanistic psychoanalysis"). Thompson's vision led to the generation of an ongoing psychoanalytic tradition that emphasizes the importance of interaction from its inception.

Psychoanalytic traditions are grounded in commitments to specific theoretical principles. Spezzano (in press) has recently argued that there are, in fact, no psychoanalytic technical paradigms, in Kuhn's sense of the term, but only what Kuhn called "disciplinary matrices," which are defined solely in terms of group commitments. The two closely related commitments anchoring interpersonal psychoanalysis and developed most fully and explicitly in Sullivan's contributions are first, an ecological principle—the environment plays a crucial role in creating, shaping, and maintaining personality and its pathology; and, second, a participatory principle—the psychoanalyst is never simply an observer of the data that the patient provides but is always also a participant in cocreating that data.

Sullivan's interpersonal psychiatry emerged out of his work with schizophrenic patients and what he felt was the inadequacy of the then dominant Kraeplinian approach. Schizophrenia was understood at that time to be a deteriorative illness, with a natural, inexorable course unaffected by the human environment around it. The psychiatrist could have little impact on that deteriorative process; he could merely observe and describe it.

Sullivan's clinical experience, set within an intellectual milieu dominated by American pragmatism and the social psychology of G. H. Mead, led him to very different conclusions. (See Greenberg and Mitchell, 1983, chapter 3, and Mitchell and Black, 1995, chapter 3, for more detailed accounts of Sullivan's early work.) He saw schizophrenics not as isolated and removed from their human environment, but as exquisitely sensitive to what was going on around them. He came to regard schizophrenia not as a process emerging and evolving from within the patient, but as a reaction and adaptation to circumstances and attitudes outside the patient. In fact, Sullivan became convinced that isolating schizophrenic patients as a phenomenon to be studied destroyed the possibility of even beginning to understand the way in which schizophrenia emerged within a family system, as a response to interpersonal patterns among family members. (In addition to Sullivan's mostly indirect impact on psychoanalysis, he was one of the fathers of family systems theories approaches to family therapy.)

One of Sullivan's most powerful early impressions was the striking way in which the attitude of the psychiatrist effected the patient. Viewing the patient from a detached position, as suffering from inexorable deterioration, produced one sort of patient—one impervious and intractably damaged; viewing the patient as highly sensitive to other people, easily humiliated and terrified, produced a very different sort of patient—one responsive and accessible to change. Sullivan provided a very carefully designed therapeutic community and began to report dramatic changes in his patients' lives.

Sullivan's two principles are really specific applications of a more general concept: the environment plays a formative role in the shaping of human experience. When applied to the past, this concept translates into the ecological principle that what happened matters, that family dynamics and parental character have a powerful impact on the formation of personality and psychopathology. When applied to the present, the general concept translates into the participatory principle that what is happening matters, that the participation of the therapist plays a crucial formative role in generating the data he is struggling to understand.

These principles, which became central to the development of Sullivan's theories of motivation, development and psychic structure, were compatible with Erich Fromm's Marxist version of Freud's contribution.

Marx had derived human suffering and difficulties in living as being from larger historical and cultural forces. Human nature is not something fixed, but, rather, is formed through mankind's progressive conquest over natural forces through the historical development of human productivity. Personality, values, even ideas are shaped by necessary economic roles and functions. Conflict, within and among individuals, is generated by clashes between larger economic interests and forces. As mankind moves through the historical development of different economic structures, from tribalism to feudalism to capitalism to socialism, all conflict and tensions are resolved.

Freud approached human experience from a very different angle. In some of his earlier papers Freud (1907) was also a social critic. However, as his instinct theory became darker and more tragic (especially after 1920, with the introduction (Freud, 1920) of the dual-instinct theory and the death instinct), he placed less emphasis on social and cultural factors. Human suffering, Freud became convinced, derives from irreconcilable conflicts among the individual's own impulses. Social constraints play an inevitable and beneficial role in allowing human beings to live with each other at all and to survive as a species. The problem, as Freud saw it, was not in the environment, but in the nature of human motivation itself.

Fromm reconciled the very different visions of Freud and Marx by recontextualizing Freudian theory with an essentially Marxist view of history and culture. Fromm regarded human personality as motivated by existential needs (like the need for a "framework of orientation and devotion") that are quite malleable. Freud's theory of the dynamic unconscious was reworked as an account of the way in which the individual comes to desire not what his instincts demand, but what his culture and historical position require him to desire. The unconscious, which Freud derived from instincts, Fromm derived from social structures and pressures. Libidinal impulses, for Freud, derive from bodily tensions; libidinal impulses, for Fromm, express and maintain the socially mandated patterns through which the individual relates to the world around him.[1]

Fromm's adaptation of Freud fits very well with Sullivan's approach to schizophrenic patients. Sullivan's emphasis on disturbances in the family environment as resulting in schizophrenia in the individual fit with the general principle of Marxist analysis that individual phenomena are determined, in the last instance, by social and historical processes. *What happened matters.* Sullivan's portrait of the psychiatrist as participant observer fit well with the general Marxist principle that one's point of view (observation) or ideology is always a function of one's own vested interests or stake in the process (participation). *What is happening matters.*

---

1. Marcuse's (1955) work provides an interesting contrast to Fromm's integration of Marx and Freud. Marcuse reworked Freud's notion of a dark, bestial, instinctual human nature, in great need of control, restraint or sublimation, into a creative and constructively revolutionary human nature, oppressed by social constraints. Whereas Fromm reset Freud into a Marxist perspective, Marcuse reset Marx into a romantic version of Freud.

A point of convergence for all three major authors shaping the interpersonal tradition was the importance of establishing a veridical understanding of what really happened in the formative early years of the patient's life. What happened matters, and the analytic process can determine what that was. Veridicality was crucial to Sullivan in offering the patient a way out of her confusion about the mixed messages and mystifying hypocrisies of her early environment. Veridicality was crucial to Fromm in locating the social values and historical forces that provided the material from which the individual fashions answers to his existential needs. And veridicality was crucial to Thompson, by way of Ferenczi, in establishing an alternative to the emphasis on fantasy in classical drive theory. The *Clinical Diary* of his later years (Ferenczi, 1932) reveals how concerned Ferenczi was with establishing the accuracy of his patients' claims that they had suffered abuse as children at the hands of their caretakers. Thus, there was a shared emphasis, for the founders of the interpersonal tradition, on the importance, indeed the necessity, of arriving at an accurate reconstruction of the past, and there was a shared assumption that it was possible to do so. As we shall see, this assumption has become more complicated for the current generation of interpersonal clinicians and theorists.

Thus the concept of interaction became central, virtually definitive of interpersonal psychoanalysis from its very beginnings. The common commitment to the importance of environmental factors and the role of the analyst as participating observer made possible the convergence among the contributions of Sullivan, Fromm, Ferenczi, and Thompson. The initial mutual infatuation, however, blurred some important differences among perspectives. "Interaction" as a general principle or slogan proved to be quite different from interaction examined closely, where it lends itself to many different understandings and emphases.

Fromm wrote mostly on a sociological level. There is a rich oral history of his psychoanalytic thinking and his influence as a supervisor of interpersonal psychoanalysts was enormous, but Fromm's actual writing on the clinical level is sparse. Sullivan was much more directly concerned with interaction in actual clinical practice, and it is Sullivan's specific theoretical concepts that have shaped the thinking of most analysts identifying themselves with the interpersonal tradition. To explore the concept of interaction in this tradition, therefore, we will consider Sullivan's understanding of the experience of the patient, the analyst, and their interaction. We will see that there was considerable tension and contradiction within Sullivan's thinking itself. We will then consider the end of the honeymoon between Sullivan and Fromm, as differences in their understanding of the nature of interaction emerged, and the way in which these differences are still active in different versions of interpersonal psychoanalysis today.

Sullivan and Interaction

The Interpersonal Field

Sullivan's theory is radically ecological. The central theme in all Sullivan's contributions is the idea that a person cannot be understood, or even meaningfully thought about, except in the context of interactions with others. "All organisms live in continuous, communal existence with their necessary environment" (Sullivan, 1953, p. 31). The human environment, Sullivan stressed, includes continual interactions with others and, on a wider level, with the collective achievements of others, culture. It is folly to attempt to grasp the structure of any organism without considering the ecological niche it has become adaptively shaped to fill. Sullivan provided unusual, startling definitions of personality in his effort to push the reader beyond the ordinary yet greatly misleading tendency to think of the individual in isolation. Personality, for Sullivan (1938) "is made manifest in interpersonal situations and not otherwise" (p. 32). Personality is "the relatively enduring pattern of recurrent interpersonal situations which characterize a human life" (Sullivan, 1940, p. Xi).[2]

The personality, or self, is not something structured into the

---

2. Sullivan's provocative descriptions of the self, surprising in his day, are much more familiar to our ears, because they anticipated many features of contemporary approaches to self generally grouped under the rubric "postmodern."

person, Sullivan suggested. Personality is the patterns of what a person does when he is with other people. There are times when one is not with other people—while sleeping, fixing a car, communing with nature. From Sullivan's point of view, the personality is simply not present in those situations (unless there are prominent illusory others, as will become clear later). Personality is shaped in interaction with others and emerges in interactions with others. Personality is interaction. And psychopathology concerns disorders of personality.

Sullivan's thoroughgoing interactionism can be seen clearly in his way of defining motivation as compared with Freud's. For Freud, the basic motivational unit is the impulse, arising from bodily tensions in "erogenous zones" and becoming attached to objects only through the accidents of experience. According to Freud, the infant "turns" toward reality only reluctantly and with resignation, when the fantasies generated by the pure pleasure principle are found wanting.

For Sullivan (1940), the initial stimulus is often the environment itself: "Situations call out motivations" (p. 191). The environment evokes a response from the individual. Further, Sullivan's basic motivational units, needs for "satisfaction" and "security," are interactional from the start and in their very nature. Needs for satisfaction emerge as "integrating tendencies," drawing one into interactions with others with reciprocal needs. These needs do not arise from bodily erogenous zones but employ "zones of interaction" in their interchange with others. The need for security is the pursuit of relief from the tension of anxiety, which has been picked up through the "empathic linkage" with other people. For Freud, the primary motivational energy, the drives of the id, become secondarily retooled to allow the individual to adapt to his environment;[3] for Sullivan, the primary motivational energy is evoked by and preadapted to the environment from the start.

Consider Sullivan's (1953) portrait of the baby in the formative stages of development. The baby emits a wide range of behaviors and needs, all of which draw the child into interaction with others. The

---

3. Hartmann's (1939) theory of a prewired autonomous sphere of the ego that is preadapted to the environment added a more interactional dimension to Freud's model of an asocial id and passive ego.

personality patterns of significant others, the tendency to respond with anxiety or approval to various expressions of the baby, shape the baby's experience. As the child grows, she learns to shape her own experience according to the necessity for avoiding anxious responses in others. What the baby brings to the interactions, besides the prewired tendencies to evoke, enter into, and be shaped by those interactions, counts for very little.

> The inborn potentialities which thus mature over a term of years are remarkably labile, subject to relatively durable change by experience, and antithetic to the comparatively stable patterns to which the biological concept of instinct applies. The idea of 'human instincts' in anything like the proper rigid meaning of maturing patterns of behavior which are not labile is completely preposterous [p. 21].

Sullivan portrays the early interactions between the infant and its human environment as molding an almost infinitely malleable collection of human potentials to an interpersonal niche to which that potential becomes finely adapted and honed. Where there is conflict in a person, it has been produced by conflictual, contradictory signals and values in the environment.

Things become much more complex, however, when we consider Sullivan's view of interactions between adults, for example, the complex interaction constituting the analytic situation. There interactions with the present interpersonal environment are complicated by residues of interactions with the past interpersonal environment.

The Patient

Consider Sullivan's (1938) definition of interpersonal situations: "configurations made up of two or more people, all but one of whom may be more or less completely illusory" (p. 33). This definition seems a bit paradoxical. "Interpersonal" (e.g., in contrast to "intrapsychic") is ordinarily taken to refer to more than one person. The human environment, with which Sullivan insisted the individual is in continual interchange, must involve at least one other in addition to the subject in question. Yet Sullivan was suggesting that the other or others in the interpersonal situation can be illusory. The "correct view of personality," he suggested, concerns "the doings of people, one with another, and with more or less personified objects" (p. 33). The term interpersonal is clearly being used to refer to two very different domains: an actual behavioral sphere, in which one does things with other people; and a phenomenological sphere, experienced by the person as involving him with others even though those subjectively experienced others may have no direct relation to any actual others.

Sullivan repeatedly made the distinction between real others and "parataxic" or personified or illusory others. Parataxic experience is experience that has not been corrected by consensual validation (whereby it becomes "syntaxic" experience).[4] Illusory others, by definition, are not derived from or generated in current interaction; they are brought to the interaction by the patient. Where do these illusory personifications come from?

Sullivan did not believe illusory others are prewired (as is suggested by Jung's concept of universal archetypes, Klein's concept of a priori objects, and Bion's concept of preconceptions). Sullivan believed that all images of persons are derived from interactions with real others. Illusory personifications do not correspond to the real others in current interaction; rather, they are consolidations and transformations of real others in previous interactions. Past interactions are recorded, combined, reorganized, and reexperienced in complex relationships with real others in current interactions.

Sullivan (1938) seems to have been suggesting that there is a continuum of degrees to which one's experience of others corresponds to the way they actually are. The pathological end point of the contin-

---

4. Sullivan (1940) less typically defined parataxic somewhat differently, referring not to illusions, but to unconscious representations of others. "When, besides the interpersonal situation as defined within the awareness of the speaker, there is a concomitant interpersonal situation quite different as to its principal integrating tendencies, of which the speaker is more or less completely unaware" (p. 92). As far as I know, Sullivan never considered the interesting possibility that the image of the other in awareness is actually more illusory than the image of the other outside of awareness, which might contain disclaimed perceptions.

uum is defined by dream states and states of insecurity reaching schizophrenic proportions. In the latter,

> interpersonal phenomena are present, but the people concerned are
> largely fantastic, complexly related to real people. Characteristics of
> related real people have been magnified or minimized, moved from
> one personality to another, combined in poignantly artificial patterns.
> Experiences from long ago involving people but remotely related to
> those seemingly involved contribute elements to the fantastic person-
> alizations. The novel and unreal are created out of items of actual
> experience, but the items are combined into patterns that reveal little
> about anyone except the subject-individual ... [p. 70].

At some points, Sullivan stated that the presence of illusory others
is characteristic largely of "mental disorders" (p. 34n; see also
Sullivan, 1950, p. 222). Yet at other points Sullivan (1954) suggested
that parataxic distortion is "a feature of all interpersonal relations" (p.
25) and that all experience is laced through with illusory others. "As a
matter of brute fact," he wrote, "these bilateral parataxic interpersonal
situations are the rule rather than the exception among us, and the
average person magically stripped of his illusions about his friends
and acquaintances would find himself surrounded by strangers"
(Sullivan, 1936, p. 24).

Why are parataxic distortions, illusory others maintained? They
are crucial in maintaining security. In Sullivan's view of personality
and psychopathology, the effort to minimize anxiety is the central
motivational principle. The most important device through which the
self-system keeps anxiety at a minimum is foresight; future interpersonal threats are anticipated on the basis of recall. New situations are
organized on the basis of old categories (Sullivan calls these "me-you
patterns") so that they can be perseveratively handled in proven and
trustworthy ways. Parataxic distortions provide the patient with an
illusory sense of security by automatically transforming potentially
threatening novelty into a known, even if miserable, familiarity.

Although Sullivan put great emphasis on the importance of the
past (recall continually seeds foresight), he went out of his way to
stress that past experience is maintained because it enhances security
in the present. Sullivan was aware that this stress on the importance of

the past brought him dangerously close to elements of classical psychoanalysis that he found problematic: concepts like introjection, the superego, and the repetition compulsion. Early experience with parents, Sullivan (1956) suggested, are "interiorized":

> to become the obsessional verbal magic used to allay anxiety, to ward off the feelings of guilt and shame which represent the critical evaluation in the self. . . . This may sound a good deal like "introjection"—a term I have always boggled at. The self grows by learning techniques for . . . removing threats of anxiety from the significant people . . . a way of picking your way among the significant people so that you do not feel insecure very often. . . . Memory is a fragment of the real situation . . . he remembers, in connection with the act that brought anxiety, the really relevant elements of the significant other person concerned. Then on future occasions when the person is about to move in the direction of the same sort of act, this recollection appears in the form of a feeling of unpleasant anticipation, which, in turn, comes to be called by the name of guilt, or shame. . . . So if you wish, you can talk about the significant person having been introjected and becoming the superego, but I think you are apt to have mental indigestion [p. 232].

Why was Sullivan so touchy about the term introjection? He wanted to portray the patient as an active agent who moves through experiences doing things to keep himself less anxious, including anticipating future threats. Maintaining personifications of others is useful in this process. Sullivan wanted to avoid giving the impression that early experiences with others are "inside" the patient in any reified sense or that the patient is passively and mechanically repeating past experience in the present (as Freud's concept of the "repetition compulsion" implies).[5]

The portrait of the analysand provided by Sullivan is of someone who approaches the analytic relationship, like all relationships, with maladaptive patterns organized around personifications of illusory

---

5. Sullivan's concern about the reification and spatialization of concepts of internalization strikingly anticipated many features of Schafer's (1968, 1976) later critique and redefinition of traditional psychoanalytic concepts.

others. These illusory others are composed of reworked fragments of experiences with actual others in the past. These illusory others stand between the patient and current interpersonal reality. What the analytic situation provides is the opportunity to sort out the past from the present, the illusory from the actual. This sorting requires a highly complex set of technical skills on the part of the analyst.

The Analyst

Working with more disturbed patients, who inevitably get under one's skin, tends to force an awareness of the analyst's inevitable participation in a way that is easier to avoid with better organized, better behaved patients. In the Kleinian tradition, for example, the concept of "projective identification" to describe the patient's impact on the analyst was developed to account for analytic work with more disturbed patients and with small children, both of whom are difficult to simply observe from afar.

The concept of "participant-observation" grew out of Sullivan's work with schizophrenic patients and is the centerpiece of the portrait of the analyst within the interpersonal tradition. This concept was developed to challenge the more traditional assumption that the psychiatrist encounters, gathers, and analyzes data from a more or less detached, objective position. Sullivan suggested that the events contributing information are those in which the psychiatrist participates, not those which he looks at as though from atop an ivory tower. Sullivan repeatedly stressed the therapist's "participation in the data," and this principle is often evoked as the fundamental criterion distinguishing interpersonal analysts from more traditional Freudian analysts. But what sort of participation was Sullivan thinking about?

Sullivan (1954) portrayed the analyst as a very somber, conscientious worker. There is no fun involved in doing therapy (pp. 10–11). The work of the therapist is investigation: the eliciting of information from the patient, and the long and arduous task of sorting out the past from the present, the illusory from the real. The therapist is an expert who is continually checking and verifying the data he is eliciting.

But the working therapist is not observing the patient from a remote or invisible location, like a blind in a wildlife preserve; he gets his data only through interacting with the patient and therefore is continually influenced by and, in turn, influencing what it is he is looking at. Let us break down this mutual influence into its components.

The purposeful activity of the therapist going about his investigative work is likely to have a powerful impact on the patient. The therapist therefore needs to develop an awareness about what he is like as an investigator, what kinds of impact he tends to have on strangers (Sullivan, 1954, pp. 67–68). The patient is never responding to a neutral stimulus, a generic therapist. He is always responding to a particular therapist approaching his work in a particular fashion. So, as the therapist goes about his data collection quite purposively, he is bound to have an impact on the patient and on the data that is obtained.

The therapist, in Sullivan's view, strives for a simplicity of motivation, with an even, conscientious interest in obtaining information. Unlike the patient, the therapist does not become involved with illusory persons. The therapist, as Sullivan (1954) put it, has an "aptitude to do nothing exterior to his awareness" (p. 68).

Yet Sullivan (1965) was fully aware that this is an ideal and that all humans have a less than complete awareness of their interactions with others: "No one can hope fully to understand another. One is very fortunate if he approaches an understanding of himself" (p. 5). So, from time to time, the therapist is likely to lose his simply investigative stance and participates in unintended ways in interactions with the patient. A crucial component of Sullivan's (1954) highly disciplined approach to clinical interaction is the therapist's ability to discern quickly when the collection of relevant data has gotten derailed and to correct whatever countertransferential participation may have contributed to the derailment (p. 126).

Sullivan made it quite clear that some forms of unintended participation on the part of the therapist are quite useful and some are out of bounds. The therapist is likely to become mildly anxious from time to time. This reaction is inevitable and also potentially helpful in alerting the therapist to shifts in the patient's affective state. But very intense feelings in the therapist are neither expectable nor helpful. Genuine anger toward the patient, for example, Sullivan (1954) regarded as an indication of a "serious defect in his equipment"

(p. 127). Thus, normal features of interpersonal interactions are not appropriate to the analytic situation, where there is a "taboo . . . on trafficking in the ordinary commodities of interpersonal relations. . . . The psychiatrist . . . deals primarily in information" (p. 13).

One of the most striking features of Sullivan's portrait of the analyst is the element of control he insisted the analyst should have over his own participation with the patient. The session is a detailed inquiry provoked, directed, and titrated by the analyst, in which the patient's level of anxiety is regulated at all times. Consider Sullivan's summation of the analyst's handling of transitions, in which the analyst is portrayed with the kind of control a conductor maintains over his orchestra:

> The smooth transition is used to move gently to a new topic; the accented transition saves time and clarifies the situation; and the abrupt transition is ordinarily used either to avoid dangerous anxiety or to provoke anxiety where you can't get anywhere otherwise [p. 49].

Sometimes, Sullivan (1954) suggested, the expression of irritation" (p. 127) is useful (in contrast to genuine anger); always, "the appearance of spontaneity is desirable" (p. 128). But, despite inevitable periodic departures, the analyst is firmly in control. The analyst who is working effectively, Sullivan suggested, is never taken by surprise. "there are few things more disastrous to the therapeutic hopes of an interview than for the interviewer to be surprised at what occurs. Surprise and astonishment on the part of the interviewer are useful only when forged—when done for effect" (p. 191n).[6]

The other side of the analyst's role, in addition to participation, is observation. The observation post is not off to the side or above the field to be studied. All observation is done from the field of study itself, as the analyst is also participating in the data he is looking at. What distinguishes the analyst from other participants in interpersonal

---

6. The striking differences between Sullivan's approach and some contemporary interpersonal approaches is perhaps no more apparent than when one considers attitudes toward the analyst's being surprised (see, for example, Donnel Stern, 1990).

interactions, and significantly too, is the analyst's self-awareness. "The skill of the investigator resides not in achieving some fancied aloofness but in being free from serious inhibitions of his awareness as to the stream of events which involve him" (Sullivan, 1936, p. 15).

Sullivan felt that, by observing his own participation (whether the patient is speaking of the past, the present outside the analytic relationship, or the analytic relationship itself), the analyst can separate out the impact of the patient on him and the impact he is having on the patient. The goal of observation is progressively to eliminate illusions and distortions, omissions and obfuscations; the goal of observation is to gain a closer and closer approximation to the truth, to "what actually happened" (Sullivan, 1953, p. 275). The patient's understanding of the past is elevated, through the analyst's clarifications, to "correct recall" (1954, p.71). And the patient's understanding of himself in the present approaches the ideal of self-awareness to which the analyst strives: "the patient as known to himself is much the same person as the patient behaving with others" (Sullivan, 1940, p. 237).

One way to position Sullivan's epistemology in relation to more recent developments within the interpersonal tradition would be to say that Sullivan was half-way to Heisenberg. Sullivan put great emphasis on the importance of the analyst's participation in and impact on what he is observing. However, unlike more recent theorists (e.g., Hoffman, Greenberg, Aron, Cushman, Stern, Altman), Sullivan believed that, through self-awareness, the analyst is able to factor out that participation and apprehend reality in an objective, unmediated fashion. This is a major difference.

In discussing "personifications" of both the self and others (Sullivan's term for what, in Freudian ego psychology have been called representations), he stressed.

> I would like to make it forever clear that the relation of personifications to that which is personified is always complex and sometimes multiple; . . . personifications are not adequate descriptions of that which is personified [Sullivan, 1953, p. 167].

In Sullivan's terms, personifications are complex distortions of reality, but it is possible to represent reality in a simple, veridical way. The analyst can provide adequate descriptions of "that which is personi-fied" that serve as the standard against which the patient's manner of organizing experience is measured. The analyst's expertise lies pre-cisely in his ability to parse out reality from illusory, paratactic distor-tions. In the process of self-observation, the analyst climbs out of his participation and its impact and is able to see things as they really are. In contrast to later theorists, Sullivan failed to realize that participa-tion and observation are never separable, that in the very act of observing one is also participating and therefore arriving at a version of reality, not the undistorted vision of reality.

The Interaction

Sullivan (1954) portrayed the interaction between the analyst and the patient (more correctly the patient's "self-system," which is what the analyst is able to interact with) as initially adversarial. The analyst is the enemy, and the patient experiences the threat as coming not from something inside him (e.g., the repressed in Freud's system), but from the interpersonal field.

The analyst is a threat for two reasons. First, clarification itself is dangerous, and it is the analyst's job to clarify. The self-system uses obfuscation, confusion, mystification, and distortion to maintain secu-rity. "The interviewee's self-system is at all times, but in varying degrees, in opposition to achieving the purpose of the interview" (p. 139). The patient has a great stake in keeping things confused and obscure, and a good deal of the patient's participation in the session consists of unwitting efforts to throw the analyst off track so as to reduce the threat of clarification: "Thrusts from the environment which attempt to interest him in some other aspect of reality are dena-tured as quickly as possible, and he is back to his preoccupation" (Sullivan, 1956, p. 247).

Second, the analyst is a threat because he is experienced by the patient in illusory, paratactic ways. Although the threat is experienced as coming from the other, the representation of the other as something threatening may very well be a displacement from the past. The most difficult part of the analyst's task is the delicate process of teasing apart the distorting residues of the past from the reality of present interactions.

> Until a patient has seen clearly and unmistakably a concrete example of the way in which unresolved situations from the distant past color the perception of present situations and overcomplicate action in them, there can be ... no therapeutically satisfactory expansion of the self ... [Sullivan, 1940, p. 205].

Sullivan offered different technical approaches for accomplishing the separation of the residues of the past from present reality. He wrote of "hounding" the patient, dogged inquiry in which hard-won descriptions of security operations are worn "to a very high polish" (Sullivan, 1956, p. 279). Sometimes he suggested various kinds of posturing by the therapist to open up new possibilities for the patient.[7] At crucial points, once the discrepancy between representations of others and their actual behavior has been established, Sullivan (1956) recommended turning to history: "'Let us see where in the world these patterns begin of presuming that the other fellow is taking a slice when he is saying something that is approximately complimentary. Where did that begin?'" (p. 280). Whereas later interpersonal theorists would often minimize history, Sullivan (1940) put great emphasis on historical reconstruction as the means through which illusion and reality in current interaction are differentiated from each other: "'This impression that you have had about me must have a history, must be the recollection of some such a person who was once really important to you—perhaps you can recall someone.'" (p. 235).

Sullivan (1956) put great emphasis on the clarification of past interactions. With respect to obsessionals he said, "These people really know that their parents were not happy and that one of the parents, at least, was savagely cruel to them" (p. 268). More effective living in the present and the clarification of the past go hand in hand. It

---

7. Sullivan's technique has been presented in vastly divergent ways by different interpreters and students of Sullivan. Cooper and Witenberg (1983) present a view of Sullivan's technique that stresses the sustained and detailed inquiry; Havens (1973) stresses Sullivan's position taking as a device for provoking new experiences.

is only by gaining a clearer idea of what happened long ago that the analyst is able to help the patient separate out the residues of past interactions from the undistorted reality of present experience.

Sullivan's portrayal of interaction in the psychoanalytic process is much more complex than it may appear at first glance. It encompasses several important paradoxes or tensions that Sullivan himself never stated clearly and directly and that he was unable to resolve:

1. Because of his ecological commitment, Sullivan saw motivations as invoked in situations rather than emerging as endogenous pressures from within an individual. Yet he also felt that situations are often organized not according to present reality, but according to distorted, perseverative fragments of past experiences. The situation the patient experiences himself as being in may bear little relation to what is actually going on. If "situation" is redefined in this way, it is difficult to distinguish between motivations evoked by situations and motivations brought to situations by individuals. How can we know whether it is the past environment (an earlier interpersonal field that has now become an internal, intrapsychic presence) that is determinative or the current environment?

2. Sullivan was firmly committed to the principle of the analyst's participation in the therapeutic process. Yet Sullivan did not feel that the analyst participates through normal interpersonal processes and emotions. Self-awareness enables the analyst to separate out the effects of his participation in the interaction; he maintains considerable control over both the level of the patient's anxiety and the quality of the analyst's own participation. Yet knowledge of another and self-knowledge are always at best fragmentary and very incomplete.

3. Sullivan's ecological commitment led to his firm conviction that what actually happens matters. It is essential to sort out past from present, fact from fantasy, real others from illusory others. The analytic process, from this point of view, consists of extensive detective work, in the effort to determine what actually took place. Sullivan's participatory commitment, with its view of the analyst as participating in the process (although not as embedded as later interpersonalists portray), might raise questions about who is to do the sorting.

Sullivan's characterization of the analyst as an expert in rationality and objective observation, however, confirms the analyst's credentials for teasing apart the interwoven threads of analytic interaction. Thus, the assumption that the analyst's expertise resides in his rationality was crucial to Sullivan's view of the analytic process as a sorting out of illusory from actual integrations within the interaction that constitutes the analytic relationship. This manner of defining the therapist's expertise allowed Sullivan to circumvent the complex problems of influence implicated by the therapist's participation in the process. Because, through participant observation, the therapist could factor himself out of the interaction, the therapist could control the impact of his own participation and protect the patient's autonomous development.

Thompson: From the "Past" to "Character"

Sullivan never identified himself as a psychoanalyst and was only secondarily concerned with differentiating interpersonal psychiatry from psychoanalysis proper. It was Clara Thompson who fashioned interpersonal psychoanalysis by joining Sullivan's interpersonal psychiatry, Fromm's humanistic psychoanalysis, and concepts drawn from divergent Freudian trends like Ferenczi's. To make the interpersonal school *psychoanalytic*, it was necessary for Thompson both to provide bridges between Sullivan concepts and more traditional psychoanalytic concerns and also to distinguish interpersonal psychoanalysis as a distinct school of psychoanalytic thought, quite different from the traditional Freudian mainstream. Thompson used the concept of "character" to achieve both purposes.

Character was an increasingly important concept in psychoanalysis in the 1930s and 1940s.[8] In Freud's early writings, with their emphasis on symptom neuroses, character had been a minor background theme. With the increasing emphasis on the ego in Freud's later writings and with the development of ego psychology in the work of Anna Freud and Hartmann, the general shape and structure

---

8. See Spezzano (1993) for an interesting discussion of the concept of character and its evolution in the psychoanalytic literature.

of personality became more important. Wilhelm Reich's (1949) classic text, *Character Analysis*, played a key part in this shift in emphasis.

The concept of character offered a natural point of intersection between Sullivan's theorizing about interpersonal relations and Freudian ego psychology. Sullivan was little interested in symptoms, which he felt often diverted attention from the more important issues concerning anxiety, the overall shape of the self-system, and repetitive parataxic integrations.

Fromm's (1947) concepts played an important role here. Fromm's basic motivational foundation, to which he added Freudian and Marxist dimensions, was existential. He viewed people as struggling, most fundamentally, *in the present*, with the anxieties and vagaries of the human condition. The form of that struggle for each person was that person's character, shaped by cultural and historical forces and maintained through psychodynamics. Thus, Fromm extended Freud's descriptions of libidinal fixations (oral, anal, phallic) into culturally designed styles of meeting existential needs and relating to the world and other people (receptive, hoarding, and marketing orientations).

Thompson drew on Fromm's emphasis on character to reorient Sullivan's concepts away from Sullivan's original emphasis on the residues of the past to a greater focus on current beliefs patterns. She argued that Sullivan's concept of parataxic distortion encompassed, simultaneously, two different dimensions of Freud's clinical theory, both transference and character structure (Thompson, 1964, p. 29). In parataxic distortions, residues of the past are displaced into present situations ("transference" for Freud) and that displacement serves to organize the person's current experience and interactions with others ("character" in ego psychology). Thompson's first task, creating the bridge between Sullivan's interpersonal theory and psychoanalytic theory was thereby accomplished.

Thompson's second task was to define and shape the now interpersonal psychoanalysis as a distinct psychoanalytic point of view, sharply different from traditional Freudian theorizing. This was done in many different domains of theory and practice. For our purposes, what is important is the shaping of the interpersonal approach to interaction.

As we have noted, Sullivan himself had placed considerable

emphasis on the past: illusory personifications are shaped in early experience; they operate as an organizational grid through which present experience is filtered; it is the clarification of illusory personifications that makes it possible for a patient to discover potentially new experience in the present.

The concept of "character," as Thompson (1964) shaped it, placed less emphasis on the past. She replaced Sullivan's emphasis on personifications from past interactions with an emphasis on irrational attitudes derived from past interactions, but now functioning independently in the shaping of present interactions. In addition to "old transferred attitudes from childhood" she stressed the importance, in the analysis of character, of "habitual attitudes developed in the course of a lifetime as ways of coping with life" (p. 25).

This approach to the relationship between past and present became a key feature of the way interpersonal authors distinguished themselves from more traditional psychoanalytic theorists. Many of the concepts and much of the sensibility of traditional Freudian psychoanalysis suggest that the present is an arena wherein the infantile past is perpetually replayed: the repetition compulsion, the timelessness of the unconscious, the determinative constellation of oedipal dynamics, the archaeological metaphors, emphasis on the memory work, reconstruction, and so on. The patient only seems to live in the present; within their psychic reality, their inner world, patients are still living and struggling with the parents of their childhood, their infantile sexual and aggressive conflicts, the childhood fantasies and dreads.[9]

Interpersonal authors increasingly emphasized the embeddedness of the patient in the present. The past, memory work, reconstruction—these are unimportant as such. What is crucial is a clarification of the patient's ways of handling current anxieties, present experience. Thompson (1964) distinguished Sullivan's interest in the past *as present* from an interest in past in itself: "According to Sullivan's

---

9. This emphasis on the past at the expense of the present has been recalibrated in the writings of many contemporary Freudians. The useful distinction between the "present unconscious" and the "past unconscious" as developed by Sandler and Sandler (1984) is a case in point.

thinking . . . the repetition compulsion is not simply a compulsive reliving of the past, but a repeated re-creating of similar situations so structured that the outcome is inevitably the same" (p. 27). Techniques for managing anxieties and creating familiar outcomes were, of course, learned originally in the past, but they became honed and transformed over the course of a lifetime. It is the study of the patient's stereotyped devices for structuring his or her interpersonal relations in the present, particularly in the relationship with the analyst, that is at the center of the psychoanalytic process:

> Instead of one's emphasizing that in the analytic situation the patient relives his past, the analytic experience has come to be seen as an interpersonal situation where the ways in which the patient contributes to his current difficulties in living become manifest and clarified [Thompson, 1950, p. 237].

For Sullivan, the problem with the patient's present relationships is the residues of past relationships, which the analyst works conscientiously to uncover and reset into their original historical setting. As the emphasis in later interpersonal theory shifted away from the past, the analytic project was defined differently. Now the problem was not so much residues of the past cluttering and distorting the present, but irrational attitudes in the present interfering with more rational, healthier integrations. Thus, Thompson (1964) defined transference as consisting of "irrational attitudes toward another person" (p. 14). Countertransference is similarly defined as "the transference of irrational aspects of the analyst's personality to the relationship with his patient" (p. 162). Thus, the central feature defining the interpersonal tradition, in contrast to mainstream Freudian psychoanalysis, became an emphasis on the here-and-now rather than the there-and-then.

It is important to note that in her approach to interaction in the analytic relationship in the here-and-now, Thompson tended to grant the analyst a wider range of rational reactions and feelings than did Sullivan (1954), who warned against "trafficking in the ordinary commodities of interpersonal relations" (p. 13). But she clearly believed it possible to distinguish sharply between the analyst's rational and irrational reactions and felt it incumbent upon the analyst continually to purify her experience of the latter, contaminating influences: "Only constant self-analysis can finally weed out the last of our neurotic character trends" (Thomson, 1964, p. 166).

The importance of the analyst as stimulus in the analytic situation also became greatly expanded and particularized from Sullivan's original formulations to contemporary interpersonal authors. For Sullivan, the analyst is an investigator who needs to be aware of his impact on strangers. By 1950, Fromm-Reichmann was portraying the analyst as inevitably individuated in her manner of working, in ways that may be useful for some patients and not useful for others: "the therapist should learn to find out what type of patient responds best to his personality as it colors his type of therapeutic approach" (p. 40). In 1956, Thompson further dispelled the myth of the generic analyst who provides each patient with what is essentially the same, neutral experience:

> The analyst comes to his patient bringing his whole past, his whole life experience. This includes special interests and values. It can be hoped that prejudices and unconstructive values are at a minimum, but there are possibilities of wide variation, nevertheless [p. 174].

Thus, in this second phase of the development of the interpersonal tradition, the tension in Sullivan's (1956) model between the past environment and the current environment was replaced by a tension between the irrational and rational dimensions of the patient's character and experience.

> One might say that the patient meets the therapist and certain well-tried mechanisms in the patient automatically go into action, sometimes with very little relation to what the therapist is in reality. However, this is not entirely so—for the real personality of the analyst affects the patient, at least unconsciously, and influences him as to whether he evokes one mechanism or another [p. 15].

In the shift from the past to character, the establishment of a veridical understanding of the patient's early years was still essential. Irrational beliefs, embedded in character, derive from parental character pathology and family values; it is important to trace those beliefs back to their point of origin and separate illusory, wishful understanding from a more accurate reconstruction. But this vision of the patient suffering from irrational character traits is somewhat different from Sullivan's portrait of the patient as living in a world of illusory others. Sullivan was interested in drawing out and becoming acquainted with the illusory others, in recreating in some detail the original contexts in which they developed. As Fromm's emphasis on character became integrated into the interpersonal tradition, the past was regarded as a reservoir of illusions and false solutions to existential dilemmas. The past was less interesting in its own right; there was a greater urgency about determining the way in which the patient evades dealing more accurately and more realistically with the present.

Who is to decide what is rational and what is irrational in a patient's organization of experience?

For Thompson, Fromm, and Fromm-Reichmann, as for Sullivan, the analyst's expertise lay in her capacity to rise above her participation to a more objective, vantage point. This makes possible the sorting out of the rational from the irrational, the real from the illusory dimensions of the patient's experience. Once again, it is the rationality of the analyst that removes the analyst's personal influence from analytic interaction, transforming the analyst into a generic, objective observer whose understanding of the patient would be roughly equivalent to that of any other competent analyst.

Current Developments in the Interpersonal Tradition

Life is more complicated for the contemporary interpersonal clinician than it was for his ancestors. The major reason for this added complexity is that it is more difficult now to reconcile the two founding commitments of the interpersonal tradition (the ecological principle and the participatory principle) with each other. Why should this be so?

Adherence to the ecological principle still works pretty much the same way and has become, perhaps, even more compelling. The burgeoning field of infant research has generated considerable data and much theoretical emphasis attributing formative impact to parental character, mood, rhythms, and forms of interaction with the infant and growing child. There is now much more evidence than there was in Sullivan's day for the assumption that what happened matters.

The problem derives from the way in which the participatory principle has become transformed from Sullivan's and Thompson's day to ours.

Although early interpersonalists viewed the analyst as a participant embedded in interaction with the patient, they all regarded the analyst as capable of climbing out of the interaction (Stern, 1997) to function as an observer as well. They all wrote as if it were possible to separate the act of observation from the forms through which one is participating. Sullivan, Thompson, and Fromm, like all progressive intellectuals of their day, had a firm belief in a particular type of rationalism and located analysts' expertise, in no small part, in their capacity, through self-analysis and self-observation, to arrive at an objective, rational vantage point.

Contemporary interpersonalists have extended the participatory principle a great deal further, in ways that are consistent with more general intellectual currents of our day. Relativity theory and Heisenberg's uncertainty principle in physics, the revolution that Thomas Kuhn's (1962) work has provoked in the philosophy of science, developments in contemporary philosophy and linguistics establishing the embeddedness of all concepts in particular language systems—these and related developments have led to the view that all understandings are housed in perspectives. The analyst's point of view, even if arrived at through rational, self-reflective observation, cannot be separated from his forms of participation. Observation is never neutral. Observation is always contextual, based on assumptions, values, constructions of experience. The most important application of this more general movement in the history of ideas to the interpersonal tradition is found in Levenson (1972): "Nothing ... can be understood out of its time and place, its nexus of relationships. It is an epistemological fallacy to think that we can stand outside of what we observe, or observe without distortion, what is alien to our own experience" (p. 8).

The movement from a belief in participation-free observation to perspectivism has raised many more problems for interpersonalists than has generally been acknowledged. One of the biggest problems is how to reconcile this extension of the participatory principle with the ecological principle.

What happened in early childhood is important. This was no problem for Sullivan and Thompson because of their belief in the singularly rational perspective of the analyst. Who decides what happened? The analyst, of course.

But things become more complicated with the erosion of the analyst's position as the singular rational vantage point in contemporary perspectivism. If the analyst provides a perspective on what happened and what happens, who is to decide what, in fact, actually happened? What about veridicality? What happened is important; this principle is still central and differentiates the interpersonal position from other traditions, which put more weight on instincts and fantasy. The interpersonalist regards actual events rather than fantasy-based psychic reality as formative. Yet, with the extension of the participatory principle into perspectivism, it is not at all clear who is to decide what happened in the patient's past and what is happening now in the analytic situation.

Levenson's development of the concept of demystification, borrowed from R. D. Laing and applied to Sullivan's analysis of the confusion perpetrated on children who grow up to be obsessionals, illustrates the problems confronting contemporary interpersonal theorists.

The patient, in Levenson's (1983) account, is fundamentally confused and, consequently, interpersonally incompetent. The problem results not from conflict or deprivation, as in other analytic traditions, but from garbled communications, resulting in "half-truths, rooted in the ground of omitted information." From this perspective, "neurotic distortion emerges from the relationship between what is done and what is said about what is done" (p. 25). The patient requires demystification. But what does that mean exactly? Is there such a thing as unmystified experience, straightforward and objective? Who could possibly have access to that vantage point? Certainly not the analyst, who can experience things only within the context of his own personal experience. It is here that the veridicality of the ecological principle clashes with the perspectivism of the participatory principle.

It should be emphasized that perspectivism, in its fullest implications, does not suggest that the analyst's understanding is irrational or that rationality is no longer a meaningful value (see, for example, Nagel, 1995). Clearly, there are some perspectives that are irrational: the earth is flat; the moon is made of cheese, and the like. Perspectivism does suggest, however, that there cannot be a singular rational perspective on the complexities of human experience, that there may be many rational interpretive understandings of the same piece of experience. Irwin Z. Hoffman and Donnel Stern have explored this problem extensively in their writings on social constructivism, as has Lewis Aron (1996) in his work on the patient's experience of the analyst's subjectivity and Owen Renik (1993) in his stress on the "irreducible subjectivity" of analytic interpretations.

Levenson (1983) tries to circumvent the clash between perspectivism and the commitment to a singular veridical reality by distinguishing the Truth, which more traditional analytic theory claims to uncover, from the patterns that the interpersonal analyst struggles to articulate: "The therapist does not explain content; he expands awareness of patterning" (p. 116). Levenson suggested that the patterns underlying experience are quite manifest and unmistakable, like the repeated motifs in a patchwork quilt. He appeals to two

> very striking clinical observations. First, that these configurations are very powerful and consistent and run not only through every aspect of the patient's life, but also in the kind and sequences of material presented in the therapy. So that in a patient presenting the dreams, the transference, the recounting of early historical material, or present engagement, all will be harmonic variations on the same theme. Not only will this be true within one session, but it will carry over from session to session, with an extraordinarily persistent continuity. . . .
>
> The second observation, which is really very impressive, is that any small piece of the clinical material contains the total configuration. Both past and future. Thus the patient's opening comment in the waiting room or coming in the door or as he sits in the chair, will establish the leitmotif that runs through the entire session, picks up the last session, and will very likely continue on into the next session. Any 10 minutes of a taped session can be explicated to an entire analysis. Any dream of the patient contains *implicit* in it—literally, enfolded in it— the entire story of the patient's neurotic difficulties [pp. 19–20].

Does the distinction between content and pattern really hold? Levenson claims that the pattern is "literally enfolded" in the analytic material. This suggests not perspectives on experience, but an underlying structure in experience that can be discerned from the outside. If each element is a grain of sand containing a microcosm of the cosmos, would all analysts really see the same cosmos? To say that the entire story is enfolded in each piece of clinical material, can be found in the grain of sand, suggests they would. But this notion is hard to reconcile with the multiplicity of perspectives within the contemporary analytic world on what constitutes the most important patterns and structures within human experience. Would everyone really agree with Levenson's reading of all clinical material? When he delineates a pattern, is this really the same pattern, or a derivative of a common pattern, that other analysts would see? If that were true, there would be much less divisiveness among psychoanalytic schools! As Levenson (1991) has noted,

> as the therapist inquires into the patient's life and as the events that are reported become more complex, it becomes evident that it is possible to view them from a variety of perspectives. That is to say, anything the patient tells you is subject to an almost infinite number of observational perspectives, a veritable *Rashomon* [p. 120].

Unless one assumes a singular, raw, objective reality, "expanding awareness of patterning" is the same thing as providing an explanation of content. Levenson confounds his own extremely creative organization of clinical material with nature itself.[10]

Like all individuals in conflict over important values or principles, contemporary interpersonalists have trouble acknowledging the conflict and struggling with it directly. Adherence to the ideal of veridicality really does not allow many choices. If there is to be a singular, accurate rendering of what happened, someone has to have access to it. So we end up with rhetorically compelling but ultimately confusing claims to access the patterns. Despite his persuasive arguments in

---

10. For critiques of Levenson along similar lines, see Greenberg, 1987, and Hoffman, 1990.

favor of a perspectivist position, Levenson (1993) has tried to avoid the problems inherent in such a position by distinguishing it from what he has termed "the tarpits of constructivism" (p. 385). He seems to feel that it is possible both to accept the necessarily perspectival nature of all human knowledge and still believe one has unmediated access to the truth.

A patient's accounts cannot simply be taken at face value; that would be foolish. Further, the patient's accounts often shift around. Must we assume that the patient does know the truth of the patterns underneath his mystification? The patient thereby becomes an unrecognized seer, even unrecognized by himself. Who will demystify the patient? Who is to say what is mist and what is naked reality? We cannot appeal to the analyst's greater rationality, as our analytic ancestors could; to do so constitutes an arbitrary pulling of rank, a smuggling back in of an implicit appeal to the analyst's greater rationality, totally insupportable, as Levenson himself has shown, by contemporary epistemology. There may be times when the patient seems to know things without knowing that he knows. But it is only by a theoretical sleight of hand that the analyst can claim to show the patient what it is that the patient knows without knowing he knows. So we end up with patterns that must be assumed to be lying on the surface of experience for all to see.

Levenson's problem is the problem for *all* interpersonalists and, in a broader sense, for all analysts striving fully to come to terms with the interactive nature of the analytic situation: once the analyst has relinquished claim to an exclusively rational, impersonal perspective, we need to locate the authority to know what happened and what is happening somewhere else. It is not possible to abandon the commitment to the importance of actual, interactive events, both past and present. It is no longer apparent, however, how we might determine what, in fact, those events are.

Ehrenberg (1992) offers the most extensive elaboration of the current interpersonal approach to interaction and illustrates both its advantages and problems.[11] She puts great emphasis on the use of

11. There is a range of many different clinical approaches, all of which might be considered "interpersonal." Ehrenberg provides a rich combination of

countertransference, and particularly on the analyst's disclosure of her own experience, as the central vehicle for analytic exploration. It is easy to understand how Ehrenberg moves from interactionism to self-disclosure. If the most significant dynamic processes take place in the interplay between analysand and analyst, it might be useful to judiciously divulge some of the analyst's experience for purposes of mutual exploration.

Ehrenberg presents her approach as an antidote to fallacious claims to analytic objectivity. The patient is repeatedly confronted with "what she did interpersonally," which places the focus on the "intimate edge," the interactive boundary between patient and analyst. Ehrenberg makes "the immediate interactive experience the crucible of the work and the arena for working through" (p. 6). At that edge, the analyst can be most authentically engaged and therefore has the most opportunities for understanding and growth.

The problem is in determining where that boundary might be. Ehrenberg suggests that

> the "intimate edge" is . . . not a given, but an interactive creation . . . always unique to the moment and to the sensibilities of the specific participants in relation to each other and reflects the participants' subjective sense of what is most crucial or compelling about their interaction at that moment [p. 35].

But this presumes either that there is, in fact, an objectively locatable boundary or that there is a consensus in the subjective experience of the two participants about where the boundary is. In my experience, this is only rarely the case.

Consider this brief scenario:

A patient begins treatment. At the start of each session he lies down, exhales slowly, and sinks into what he experiences as a meditative mood conducive to free association and analytic self-reflection.

---

concepts drawn from the interpersonal tradition and various object relations theories. Among current authors, she is one of the most radical in her emphasis on countertransference disclosure, and so using her work suits my comparative purposes in this chapter. The contributions made possible through her kind of approach are taken up in Chapter 5.

After two or three minutes of silence, he begins to speak. The analyst finds himself with thoughts that seem important in those initial silences and begins to interrupt them with his own associations and reflections. The patient becomes angry; he feels interfered with and tells the analyst to be quiet, allowing the patient to create what he feels was the necessary analytic ambiance for himself. The analyst feels controlled by this ritualistic silence. He feels that to comply with it would be inauthentic on his part, destroying the necessary precondition for him to be engaged as an analyst. Eventually the patient quits.

Where was the intimate edge between them? It depends on whom you ask. From the patient's point of view, there never was an intimate edge because the analyst never allowed the patient the preconditions necessary for him to be fully in the room. From the analyst's point of view,[12] the edge was located at the point that the analyst felt constrained and told not to speak. Edges can be defined only within perspectives, and interactions, because they involve at least two parties, contain, by definition, more than one perspective. Therefore, any interaction can be described in more than one way. To place the central analytic focus on interaction is itself not enough, because what must be further considered is who is defining the interaction.

The interpersonal tradition, for decades alone among analytic approaches in maintaining a two-person point of view, has made enormous contributions to the study of analytic interaction. In the great dialectics that characterize the development of psychoanalytic ideas, the field-theory emphasis of the interpersonalists has been a precious antidote to the denial of the analyst's participation that characterized, for decades, the mainstream Freudian approach. The interpersonal emphasis on the analyst's authenticity has been like a breath of fresh air in the stultifying atmosphere created by the traditional demands to shoehorn the analyst's experience, demands that often become an overly formal, mechanical, and ultimately deeply disingenuous analytic stance. Interpersonal authors made countless contributions (e.g., Feiner and Epstein, 1979), enabling us to mine the potential uses of countertransference, the rich

---

12. I am not at all suggesting that Ehrenberg would work in the way this analyst did. I am using this example to illustrate the perspectivistic nature of defining boundaries, edges and the "here-and-now."

resources discoverable within the analyst's experience.

Now many authors from all schools try to encompass the two-person, interactive nature of the analytic situation and to take the impact of the missing second person, the analyst, more fully into account. But this is a complex project, and each author brings to it the advantages and disadvantages that her tradition offers. A major problem for contemporary interpersonal authors has been that the contradiction between veridicality and perspectivism has never been fully addressed, leading to an overly simplistic view of what authentic engagement on the part of the analyst might involve. Determining what happened and what is happening is a defining feature of the interpersonal model, and the analyst's countertransferential experience, the disclosure of her authentic response, is granted the power to determine the answers. This approach leaves the analyst open to mistaking his own experience for reality.

How does one decide to divulge one's own experience? Which features of one's own participation will be most useful as a guide to understanding the patient's experience? When is it helpful to talk about the interaction at all? In the interpersonal approach there is a tendency toward early disclosure. It is all "grist for the mill" anyway, it is argued; why not get it out in the open?

The grist-for-the-mill argument works pretty well if one assumes that the analyst's experience really is a reliable guide to an accurate and singular rendering of what is happening. If, however, one regards current as well as past interpersonal reality as in some measure ambiguous, yielding meaning and understanding only through interpretive construction, that is, if one really takes perspectivism seriously, all "grist" is really not equal. Some grist simply does not go through the mill.

While many interpersonal analysts have provided refuge for patients fleeing years of frustration and stagnation in classical analyses, many Freudian analysts have provided refuge for patients (like the man in our foregoing brief example) fleeing experiences with interpersonal analysts that they experienced as out of control and intrusive. But even in the majority of situations, when the patient stays, the grist does not simply wash through. A truly interactive methodology would have to look for traces of the grist in the resultant grain or sausage itself. I wonder if the phrase "all grist for the mill" arose in the kind of horrifying settings described by Upton Sinclair in *The Jungle*, in which pieces of the millers were, in fact, dropped into the mix and thus required the disclaimer. Thus, if the patient who liked to sigh and be silent on beginning his sessions had stayed and worked with the analyst who felt it necessary to share his initial thoughts, it would have been a different analysis, a different interaction, than if the analyst had held his tongue, making it possible to discover what might have happened next.

Current Strategies

There have been two major creative strategies in the recent interpersonal literature for dealing with the problems that have emerged in approaching interaction from within the interpersonal tradition. Both strategies are firmly anchored in the extension of the participatory principle from observation to perspectivism, and both strategies involve a reconsideration of the ecological principle (and its original assumption of veridicality), which the extension of the participatory principle demands.

The first strategy has been to center the analytic process on an articulation of the patient's own subjective experience. How does the patient organize his world? What does the patient notice about other people, particularly about the analyst? The extension of participation to perspectivism has forced an abandonment of Sullivan's emphasis on illusion and Thompson's and Fromm's emphasis on irrationality. The patient's subjective experience is not explored so that the illusory, irrational dimensions of it can be peeled back. The patient's subjective experience is not explored so that he can deal with what is more objectively "real." The patient's experience is explored so that he can become who he already is in a fuller, more expressive, and self-reflective fashion. John Fiscalini (1994) has termed this group "radical empiricists or experientialists," who

> have expanded interpersonal theory with personalistic and individualistic ideas and sensibilities and a greater clinical emphasis on immediate experience, the intrapersonal, and on what has been called the first-personal (Wolstein, 1983, 1987) or the personal self (Fiscalini, 1990, 1993) [p. 121].

This emphasis on the detailed and textured exploration of the patient's subjectivity has also been developed by some interpersonally influenced writers interested in bridging interpersonal theory with other traditions. Thus, Jay Greenberg (1991) notes that "the goal [of psychoanalysis] is not to confirm or disconfirm anything that the patient believes; the analyst's interest is in facilitating the patient's awareness of the range and richness of her experience" (p. 237).

For some writers stressing the importance of the patient's subjective experience, there has been a renewed interest in the past (see, e.g., Mitchell, 1988). If the patient is granted a plausible perspective on his experience, the historical origins and resonating textures of that perspective become more interesting in their own right. This represents a return to some essential aspects of Sullivan's original interest in early (illusory) others, but without Sullivan's anachronistic epistemology. There is a natural bridge between this dimension of current interpersonal thought and some of the concepts developed within object relations theory. It is a small step from Sullivan's "personifications" to notions like internal objects, internalized object relations, representations of self and others, and so on.

This dimension of contemporary interpersonal theorizing also has some important elements in common with both self psychology and the Independent group of the British psychoanalytic society: the emphasis on the patient's subjective experience, the cultivation of the implicit creativity in the patient's own individuality and unique experience, the role of the analyst as instrument for an expansion of the self-experience of the patient. There are also important differences. For the self psychologist, the analyst's role in locating and helping the patient express his own experience involves a suspension of the analyst's own subjective experience and an effort to listen and to empathize from what the analyst understands to be the "patient's point of view." Similarly, for some (Winnicottian) analysts of the British Independent group, the analyst functions largely as a warm yet generic "holding environment," bracketing his own idiosyncratic responses to prevent "impingement" and to allow the patient's "true" self to emerge undistorted.

In contrast, the contemporary interpersonal analyst regards her own participation as always embedded in her own subjective experience. The analyst's understanding of the patient's point of view is always mediated through the analyst's point of view. The material with which the analyst is working can never be anything other than the analyst's construction of the patient's construction of the patient's point of view.

The second strategy that has developed within the interpersonal tradition in response to perspectivism has been an emphasis on what Fiscalini (1994) describes as "the 'here-and-now" analytic situation as the center of the work, with much greater focus on the interplay of transference–countertransference patterns within the co-participant transactional field" (p. 120). This line of theorizing locates great therapeutic value in the differences between the analysand's experience and the analyst's. Earlier generations of interpersonalists could characterize differences in terms of the illusory/irrational elements in the patient's experience and the clearer, more rational vantage point of the analyst. Contemporary interpersonalists anchor the value of the analyst's perspective not in its putative rationality, but in its role in generating data.

In this line of theorizing, psychopathology is viewed not as a product of illusion or irrationality, but as a narrowness in perception, a tendency to truncate new experiences into stereotyped patterns. It is not so much that either the patient or the analyst is wrong as that both lack imagination when caught in the perseverative enactments of familiar organizations of experience. New possibilities, including new possibilities in the analytic relationship, are collapsed into repetitive patterns. Transference is less a distortion than a perseveration. The analyst's perspective, admittedly one among many possible perspectives, is valuable not because it is more correct or real, but because it is something new and potentially liberating and enriching (see Mitchell, 1988, 1993). This potential has complex cognitive and, especially, affective dimensions. An interpretation that is effective and growth enhancing creates a powerful sense of fit between remembered events, affective states, and conceptual grasp. Whereas previous generations of interpersonalists viewed the analytic process as one of clarification, current interpersonalists emphasize the dread of the new and unexpected (Stern, 1990).

Thus, contemporary interpersonalists tend to approach the

problem of protecting the patient's autonomy by emphasizing the continually interactive nature of the analytic process and the reciprocal influence, which needs to be kept under constant analytic scrutiny. Levenson (1983) has borrowed the concept of "deconstructionism" from literary criticism to suggest the need for the analyst to continue to monitor and interpret the impact of his own participation. For Levenson, the analyst's influence is not minimized through restraint but through continual reflection and explication: "unless one examines the method by which one arrives at the truth and treats that as having an independent validity, separate from the truth arrived at, then one simply is indoctrinating the patient" (pp. 91–92). Each interaction is examined, and that examination itself is examined, in a perpetual regress.

Levenson's deconstructionism is very much like the technique recommended by Gill (1994), who became increasingly interpersonal in his orientation and was probably more directly and constructively concerned with the problem of the analyst's influence than any other theorist in the history of psychoanalytic ideas. Interaction between analysand and analyst is not an occasional contaminant of an otherwise one-person analytic process, Gill argued persuasively; the process itself is fundamentally interactive. The analyst's influence cannot be eliminated by addressing some irregularity when it appears; the analyst must be considered to have a continual influence on the process. Therefore, Gill recommended a mode of analytic listening specifically designed to deal with the impact of the analyst's participation:

> It is the analyst's awareness of this unremitting influence of patient and analyst on each other and his attempt to make that influence as explicit as possible that constitute his "neutrality." . . . The neutral analyst is the analyst who continuously self-analyzes his countertransference neurosis . . . and who attempts to deal with the effect of his countertransference on the analytic situation as fully as possible [pp. 50–51].

But does talking about the analyst's influence really eliminate or reduce it? It is here that the kind of solutions offered by Levenson and Gill fall short of their hopes for it. For example, Gill's mode of listening and active, collaborative exploration of interaction is hardly just a corrective—it is a very dramatic form of participation. In earlier work, Gill (1983) sometimes seemed to suggest that a scrupulous analysis of the analyst's influence, including an analysis of the patient's reactions to the analyst's analyzing his own influence, would remove that influence, dissolving or resolving the transference. In his final book, aptly titled *Psychoanalysis in Transition*, Gill (1994) came to terms with the ways in which continually analyzing interaction in the analytic relationship is neither pragmatically possible nor always desirable. He informed the reader of an interesting difference between his own characteristic approach and a formulation he borrowed from Hoffman on this very point.

> The analyst's task is to be as aware as he can of how he is being experienced and to use that awareness as wisely as he can in conducting the analysis. I owe to Hoffman this last way of putting it; my own inclination was to say that the analyst should make that awareness as explicit as possible [p. 118–119].

Because he took so seriously the ideal of deconstructing the analyst's influence, Gill only reluctantly realized that talking continually about interaction may foreclose some forms of interaction that play an important part in the analytic process.

Thus, current interpersonalists think about what the analyst provides in terms quite different from earlier generations. The standard is not objectivity or rationality, but candor, openness and authenticity. The goal is not to circumvent influence, but continually to deconstruct or reflect on it. The analyst's contribution is important not for its transcendent correctness, but for the genuineness of its self-reflective reports on the interaction with the patient. Whereas early interpersonalists regarded the "consensual validation" that the analyst provides as the correction of distortions to arrive at the Truth, contemporary interpersonalists regard the consensual validation provided by the analyst as an agreed on version of the truth that is useful, not contradicted by other data, and potentiating new experiences and personal growth. In the interpersonal tradition, coming to terms with ways of thinking about mutual influence is a work in progress.

CHAPTER 4

INTERACTION IN THE KLEINIAN TRADITION

Along with her extraordinary contributions to psychoanalytic thought, the work of Melanie Klein has provided the analytic community with some of its most interesting ironies and unexpected turns.

Klein's vision has traditionally been understood and positioned as "id psychology" par excellence. In the great schism that split the analytic world between the Kleinians and the ego psychologists (developed in the contributions of Anna Freud, Hartmann, and Mahler), Klein saw her work as extending Freud's most radical explorations, as plumbing the instinctual depths of the psyche; while the ego psychologists veered off to explore (what the Kleinians considered) the more superficial, surface adaptation of the ego to its surround. Klein traced oral, anal, and oedipal instinctual currents to their earliest, most primitive roots. Alone among major theorists, Klein took seriously Freud's speculations about a death instinct and portrayed the earliest days of the infant's life as rent by a profound struggle between biologically rooted, instinctually driven forces of life and death. Klein understood her own work, and it has been understood by many others, as an ever-deeper exploration of the dark recesses of the instinctual core of the individual psyche.

Yet Klein's writings stimulated the extraordinarily rich, creative burst of theorizing that has become known as British object relations theories. Even though they broke off from the Kleinian group proper, the contributions of the major British Independents—Fairbairn, Balint, Winnicott, Guntrip, and Bowlby—all were in some sense rooted in, and impossible without, Klein's ideas. And, ironically, perhaps the central, most important feature of the post-Klein, British object relations theorizing is the importance it places on the environment—on the critical significance of the interactions between the infant and caretakers and of the interactions (apart from the delivery of interpretations) between the analysand and analyst.

This surprising reversal came about because of what Klein found as she plumbed the depths of the id. Instead of impulses, the directionless packets of tension Freud had depicted in his "id," Klein began to describe protorelationships between impulses and their built-in objects, passionate love and hate experienced in relation to good and bad objects and part-objects. Greenberg and I(1983) traced the ways in which Klein's theorizing about the instincts provided a conceptual bridge to later object relations theorists. The relationships Klein depicted were all in the mind of the child, prior to and largely independent of real experience with others. Fairbairn, Winnicott, and other later theorists took Klein's concepts—internal objects, internal object relations, paranoid and depressive positions—but filled in the objects with real interactions with real caregivers.

We find a similar ironic and unexpected turn when we consider the impact of Klein's work on subsequent theorizing about the nature of the analytic process. Klein herself was very traditional in this regard. She regarded the analytic situation in purely one-person terms. The patient provides free-associations (with children, the associations are offered in the form of play); the analyst listens for and interprets the conflictual psychodynamic struggles underlying the patient's conscious experience. The analyst is present purely as interpreter.

As with theory, Klein's contributions to technique can be (and often have been) regarded as extensions of the original "id psychology" of Freud. The ego psychologists picked up on a different thread in Freud's opus, following his suggestion (e.g., Freud, 1910) that interpretations should be directed only at resistances and material that had already emerged in the preconscious. The analyst must address the surface, they felt, and work her way slowly down. The id can be reached only by way of the ego, and the ego positions itself to ward off the analyst's interventions.

In contrast, Klein favored immediate, deep interpretations of instinctual conflict and psychotic anxieties. With the proper tools, the analyst can penetrate to the patient's deepest anxieties, Klein felt, and those deep interpretations are reassuring, because the patient feels deeply understood. Kleinian analysts took on the reputation for "speaking directly to the unconscious." In some respects, Klein's technical approach was the most radical extension of a one-person perspective: the sole focus is on the deepest recesses of the patient's instinctual conflicts, which the analyst interprets from a neutral perch, like a well-concealed photographic blind in the heart of the jungle.

Yet, once again, what Klein "found" in the unconscious opened up a radically different path from the direction she herself was pursuing and felt comfortable with. For what Klein discovered in tracing the unconscious phantasies[1] of her patients was a mechanism she called "projective identification," in which the patient imagines he has placed part of his own mental content into the mind of another, originally the mother, currently the analyst. The patient, in the deepest recesses of his unconscious, imagines a profound form of interaction between himself and others. It is crucial to remember that for Klein *the interaction never actually takes place*; it is fantasized. Projective identification is a defense mechanism like any other defense mechanism; it takes place in the mind of the patient, and the analyst discerns its presence by discovering its workings within the patient's associations.

It was a short step, however, from projective identification as a fantasy of interaction to projective identification as an actual form of interaction. The focus was still on uncovering the deepest contents of

---

1. I have retained the Kleinian spelling phantasy with reference to the distinctively Kleinian notion of unconscious , primitive thoughts and images.

the patient's mind, but, with the interpersonalization of the concept of projective identification, the contents of the patient's mind were now often to be found in the analyst's experience. This development was accomplished in the work of Klein's analytic descendants, and it has developed, in the past few decades, into one of the most powerful and fascinating tools for the study of interaction in the analytic situation.

Klein herself, it should be noted, remained loyal to a purely one-person perspective, even as her followers began to become interested in interaction, in the analyst's experience as providing clues to the patient's struggles. Thus, Paula Heimann's (1949) ground-breaking exploration of the useful dimensions of countertransference played a major role in the split between Klein and Heimann (see Grosskurth, 1986), and Klein always remained dubious of Bion's extension of her concept of projective identification to an exploration of the analyst's emotional states. Despite her own reservations, however, Klein's contributions have played a central role in the recent exploration of the interactive nature of the analytic process.

The Classical Kleinian Period

An understanding of transference is the centerpiece of any conceptual model of analytic process. The analyst listens to what the patient is saying and finds something problematic. The patient is bringing something to the immediate analytic situation from somewhere else. Something is being transferred. What is it? Where does it come from? Different answers to these questions create the important variations among current approaches to the way the psychoanalytic process works, its therapeutic action.

Transference for Freud is a *temporal* displacement. As Freud listened to his patient's verbalizations, he heard conflicts between instinctual impulses and defenses, and the instinctual impulses he discerned were the sexual and aggressive wishes of infantile life. The patient's experience is disjointed in time. He experiences the analyst as he experienced his oedipal objects of long ago; he wishes for gratifications from the analyst that are appropriate only in the context of early childhood.

Klein's concept of the analytic process remained traditional in fundamental respects. She viewed the analytic situation as a neutral medium within which the mind of the patient revealed itself through associations. She positioned the analyst outside the flow of the patient's dynamics, as an objective interpreter of them. The analyst makes no contribution to the content of the sessions: her own dynamics, the idiosyncrasies of her own personality, her manner and actions, these are all rendered invisible or standard in good analytic technique. For both Freud and Klein, what the analyst does is to interpret, and the material that the analyst interprets is wholly independent of the analyst herself.

Yet important innovations in Klein's understanding of the analytic process evolved slowly, and the changes in that understanding were often masked because of her identification of herself as simply an extender of Freud's vision. Her mission, as she saw it in the 1920s, was to find direct evidence in the play of children for the theories about early childhood that Freud had developed in his reconstructive analytic work with adults. However, by the early 1950s, Klein realized that, with her emphasis on unconscious phantasy, internal objects, and infantile anxieties, she had arrived at a view of the analytic situation that was new in certain major respects.

Klein considered analytic work with children to be identical in its essential nature to analytic work with adults. The patient associatively reveals the contents of her mind, within which are contained unconscious impulses and fantasies, which the analyst interprets. The only difference is that, whereas with adults thoughts are revealed verbally through free associations, with children thoughts are revealed through play. When we examine Klein's understanding of the *way* the analyst functions in the traditional role of interpreter, however, we find important differences between Freud and Klein. These concern the content of interpretations, the timing of interpretations, and the locus of interpretations. Klein's departure from Freud in all these areas derives from her very different way of understanding the nature of transference.

Transference for Klein was not primarily a temporal displacement, but a displacement from internal to external. As Klein listened to her patients' verbalizations, she heard not conflicts between discrete impulses and defenses against those impulses, but conflictual battles among larger sectors of the patient. Klein did not hear errant sexual or aggressive impulses, but more complex versions of the self organized around overwhelming and overpowering commitments to love and hate. Klein envisioned an elaborate internal object world, with different segments of the self passionately engaged with dramatically different types of objects, where issues of violence and destruction, love and redemption are continually at play. The stakes are always high; the anxiety often unbearably intense.

Thus, the *content* of Klein's interpretations became different from the content of Freud's interpretations. Klein's interpretations became more complex. They did not depict discrete impulses attached to ancient forbidden objects; they depicted ongoing, current relationships between segments of the self engaged with current phantasied internal presences, displaced into the medium of the analytic relationship. As Klein (1952) put it, "[Freud] is referring to the object of an instinctual aim, while I mean in addition to this, an object-relation involving the infant's emotions, phantasies, anxieties, and defences" (p. 51).

For Freud, the patient's past is alive in the oedipal objects of their desire; they play out early loves, fears and traumas over and over again, in what Freud called the repetition compulsion. For Klein, the patient's past is alive because it has been internalized into dynamic presences that are in active, loving, and murderous relationships with each other. For Freud, the content of interpretations takes the form: "This is what you desired and experienced then and are displacing it onto now." For Klein, the content of interpretations takes the form: "This is what you intensely desire and dread now."

The timing of interpretations also changed dramatically. Freud was dealing with what he regarded as essentially static situations. Infantile conflicts underlie the surface structures of the patient's mind, and their derivatives are discernible in the patient's free associations. Like a paleontologist slowly uncovering fossils from underlying geological strata, the analyst has all the time in the world. The infantile conflicts, like the fossils, are not going any place.

Klein was dealing with what she came to regard as much more dynamic situations, and the prototype became the child at imaginative play. The child uses the toys of the consulting room to create complex scenarios, and the action often moves at a frantic pace. Murders, dismemberments, magical restorations are packed together in a dense mix, and a continual commentary is necessary to keep track of the action. If the child is to become more in touch with the kaleidoscopic flow of phantasy, Klein became convinced, one or two carefully worded, succinct interpretations per session will not do.

Klein extended her work with children into a very different understanding of the pacing of interpretations with adults as well. Free associations, she came to believe, contain complex unconscious phantasies in which the patient moves around and continually repositions different segments of self and different sorts of objects: now they are inside the self; now they are in the outside world; now they are at war; now they are at peace. The material to be uncovered interpretively is not static and buried, but fluid and accessible. As De Bianchedi et al. (1984) have noted, there is a "dramatic point of view" inherent in Kleinian metapsychology: "The ego and its objects interact in a personified way, they assume roles, are endowed with intentions, experience sensations and personal feelings, and carry out meaningful actions (the plot). This drama takes place in different settings and always unfolds within an emotional context" (p. 395). The goal of Kleinian interpretation is not a reconstruction of the distant past, but a running commentary on current dynamic phantasy. The analyst for Klein became less like a paleontologist and more like a war correspondent. What is crucial is an up-to-date account from the front.

Along with changes in the content and timing of interpretations, there evolved in Klein's clinical method a shift in the locus of interpretations as well. Freudians had always combined interpretations of the transference (those which Strachey, 1934, for example, considered "mutative") with other kinds of necessary interpretations, of both the past and of the patient's current life outside the analytic relationship. The Kleinians became more exclusively focused on the analytic relationship itself. This was a natural extension of Klein's evolving redefinition of transference and the analytic situation.

Klein regarded the patient in the analytic situation as concerned essentially with maintaining his psychic equilibrium and managing the clashing sectors of his experience evoked by the analysis. As the goal of interpretation shifted from reconstruction to running commentary, the locus of interpretation shifted from past to present, and from outside to inside the analytic relationship. Speaking about the past can be used to avoid dealing with powerful feelings concerning the analyst in the present. "The patient may at times try to escape from the present into the past rather than realize that his emotions, anxieties, and phantasies are at the time operative in full strength and focused on the analyst" (Klein, 1952, p. 56n).

For Freud, the present is a vehicle for understanding the past, and it is by understanding the past that the patient is set free from infantile fixations. Klein's manner of understanding the relationship between past and present slowly reversed Freud's. For Klein, the past became a vehicle for understanding the present, and it is by understanding the present that the patient is set free from pathological patterns of managing anxiety.

> For the patient is bound to deal with conflict and anxieties re-experienced towards the analyst by the same methods he used in the past. That is to say, he turns away from the analyst as he attempted to turn away from his primal objects; he tries to split the relations to him, keeping him either as a good or as a bad figure: he deflects some of the feelings and attitudes experienced towards the analyst on to other people in his current life [Klein, 1952, pp. 55–56].

It is very important to keep in mind that despite the dramatic shifts in Klein's vision of the analytic process in the direction of interaction, the analytic relationship and the here-and-now, Klein always regarded the material that was interpreted as located exclusively inside the patient's mind. The phantasmagoric ways in which the patient experiences the analyst are direct products of the patient's phantasies and have nothing at all to do with anything the analyst has actually done or experienced.

There is a corollary to Klein's traditional intrapsychic focus that is crucial to understanding her theory of the analytic process. The patient is able to differentiate the analyst in his interpretive capacity from phantasied images of the analyst in the transference. Thus, there is an implicit assumption, as I noted in Chapter 2, of a channel through which the patient can hear the running commentary of the analyst's interpretations that circumvents the transference and makes them analytically usable to the patient.

The assumption of a clear separability between real objects and phantasied objects runs throughout Klein's thought and constitutes a central, self-contradicting confusion in her model.

On one hand, Klein believed that there is a continual interaction between real objects and phantasied objects. The child's world is dominated by powerful phantasied objects derived from instinctual sources; she projects these onto the outside world and then reintrojects them to form her internal objects, which are, in a perpetual cycle, reprojected onto external objects. Real objects are the repository of the child's projections, and the indestructibility of real objects are vital to the child's gradual development of reality testing and belief in his reparative capacities. (See Greenberg and Mitchell, 1983, Chapter 5, for a fuller discussion of Klein's derivation of early object relations.)

On the other hand, Klein (1932) assumed that real objects are somehow distinguishable and protected from the child's projections all along:

> The small child's super-ego and object are not identical; but it is continually endeavoring to make them interchangeable, partly so as to lessen its fear of its super-ego, partly so as to be better able to comply with the requirements of its real objects, which do not coincide with the unrealistic commands of its introjected objects . . . the ego of the small child is burdened with this difference between the standards of its super-ego and the standards of its real objects, with the result that it is constantly wavering between its introjected objects and its real ones—between its world of phantasy and its world of reality [pp. 249–250].

Consider the claim Klein is making here: the real parental objects are internalized through a channel separate from the phantasy-dominated cycles of projection and introjection. This is an odd claim. It suggests that despite internal presences with attacking, persecutory attitudes, the child sees the parents realistically as having different, more benign attitudes. She seems to assign to the small child a capacity to apprehend reality directly in a fashion difficult to imagine even in adults. The assumption of two distinct although intermingling channels between the mind of the individual and the outside world has been retained throughout Kleinian thinking and is one of its central and most determinative features. Thus, Hanna Segal (1992) has argued that the mind of the infant is wired with Chomsky-like universal grammatical images to generate both "perceptions" and delusional phantasies of early objects. These are never found in pure form and (as in Freud's notion of instinctual "fusion") inevitably intermingle, but they are generated separately and independently of each other.[2]

This understanding of the relationship between perception and fantasy, objectivity and subjectivity, contrasts with the more widely held notion that more objective, consensually valid organizations of experience are formed gradually, through interaction with others.

Perhaps this odd attribution of the capacity to discern an objective reality to the mind of the small child was important to Klein because a similar, parallel claim was essential to her model of the analytic process. As I noted in Chapter 2, Klein believed that the analyst's interpretations are generally experienced by the patient not in the context of the transference, but *as interpretations*, that they have access directly to unconscious recesses of the patient's mind. The analyst may be experienced in the transference as a killer or seducer, but at the point at which the interpretation is made, the patient is able to grasp the analyst's offering as neither an attack nor a sexual overture. Thus, the assumption is maintained throughout that at the moment an interpretation is delivered, the patient can distinguish the analytic object from other, familiar objects within his world. We shall see that a challenge to this assumption has been an important feature in the development of contemporary, neo-Kleinian thinking.

---

2. "Preconceptions or primitive phantasies are tested in perception, just as hypotheses are tested against reality. This matching of inner phantasies against external reality takes place throughout life but is interfered with if the phantasy omnipotently distorts the object and interferes with reality testing. Reality testing then fails and the wish-fulfilling phantasy is preferred to and dominates reality; but the dominance is always only partial" (Segal, 1994, p.79).

Contemporary Kleinians: Projective Identification and Countertransference

Elizabeth Bott Spillius has, among her other contributions, provided an invaluable service as a historian of the Kleinian tradition. Her commentaries and recent papers by other authors have begun to modify the unfortunate way in which Klein's work has been perceived in the United States. Mainstream American psychoanalysis has, until recently, been dominated by Freudian ego psychology, which was antagonistically pitted against the Kleinians in the internecine wars within the British Psycho-analytical Society dating back to the 1930s (see King and Steiner, 1991, Grosskurth, 1986). While Klein's contributions were widely appreciated throughout Europe and South America, her work was denigrated as either preposterous or sinister in the United States (see, for example, Greenson, 1974). There was a kind of splitting in the importing of British object relations theories, entailing an often striking idealization of Winnicott as a counterpart to a villainization of Klein.

Spillius (1988) adds a broader perspective on the negative reaction to Kleinian thinking by arguing that the Kleinian literature of the 1950s and 1960s represented a falling away from the freshness of Klein's original vision. In Spillius's view, Klein's original clinical approach contained a balance and originality that was lost when applied by her followers. Klein framed interpretations in terms of body parts and processes because this language was close to the experience of the disturbed children with whom she was working. In the hands of subsequent authors, "part-object" language became jargonized and formulaic. Klein's clinical emphasis on aggression was always balanced, Spillius argues, by an equally strong emphasis on love and reparation. In the hands of subsequent authors, however, aggression became an almost exclusive focus.

Therefore, the Kleinian theory and technique broadly rejected by the American psychoanalytic community in the 1950s and 1960s was, in Spillius's view, an essentially debased version of the Kleinian approach. A new and revitalized application of Klein's contributions has emerged in the past two decades. Although analytic authors virtually never acknowledge the validity of any critics or detractors, contemporary or neo-Kleinian contributions seem to have very much incorporated and responded to the criticisms of the Kleinian literature of the 1950s and 1960s.

The key innovation marking the transition from the classical Kleinian period to the contemporary Kleinian approach was the change in the way Klein's concept of projective identification was understood and used (see Sandler, 1987; Tansey and Burke, 1989). For Klein, as noted, projective identification is, like all defense mechanisms, a phantasy in the patient's mind. The patient imagines placing a sector of himself into another person and remains identified with (and often attempts to control) that other person, who now contains part of him. How does the analyst know that the patient has such an unconscious phantasy? The same way that the analyst discovers and is able to interpret other unconscious phantasies: by following the patient's free associations and discerning their latent meanings.

It was Bion who began to think of projective identification not just as a phantasy, but also as an event, not just as a process taking place in the mind of one person, but also as a form of interaction taking place between two people. Bion interpersonalized projective identification.

The target of projective identification, Bion suggested, feels something. The mental content that the patient is evacuating, nudging, pushing, insinuating into the mind of the analyst registers in some fashion *in the experience of the analyst*. Bion broadened the concept of projective identification into a vital developmental interaction and form of communication between the baby and mother. The baby projects the dense, intolerable, chaotic jumble of early experience, dominated by psychotic anxieties, into the mother, who, if she is appropriately receptive, receives, contains, and reorganizes that mental content in a soothing fashion, and that content is subsequently reintrojected by the baby.[3]

The analytic situation and the positions of its two participants vis-à-vis each other can be, and has been, thought about in many different

---

3. Bion's account of projective identification as a form of interaction between mother and baby bears a strong resemblance to Loewald's (1960) account of the interaction between the primary-process mentation of the baby and the secondary-process resources of the mother.

ways. Like most complex phenomena, we often try to grasp its nature through metaphors drawn from other areas of experience. Freud's favorite, recurrent metaphors for portraying the analytic situation were military; he invoked images of troop deployments, hunting wild animals, chess (a mock battle) strategies. The predominant metaphor through post-Freudian analytic theorizing, in its shift from oedipal to preoedipal dynamics, has been the baby at the breast. How that relationship is viewed varies greatly. While Winnicott evoked a playful, spontaneous, omnipotent baby, Klein portrayed a baby rent by sometimes unbearably intense greed and envy, gratitude and hatred. Bion (1962, 1963) added a new metaphor, the mind of the mother as container, and that addition has opened up an extremely rich avenue for subsequent Kleinian contributions.

The baby, unable to bear and process the intensely anxious, dense jumble of his own primitive thoughts and impulses, projects them into the mother; she contains and organizes them, and the baby reinternalizes them in a now tolerable and usable form. This developmental event became the paradigm for understanding the analytic situation in contemporary Kleinian thought. The analytic situation is no longer viewed as involving the displaying of the mind of the patient and the observing and decoding of its contents by an external observer. The analytic situation is now understood as involving the stormy and extremely intense colonizing of the mind of the analyst by the patient. The most important data for analysis are no longer found outside the analyst in the patient's associations; the most important data for analysis are now discovered within the analyst's own experience itself. The Kleinian understanding of the analytic situation became profoundly interactive. The analyst purges his mind of all mental content, all "memory and desire" and many of the experiences that show up during the session are understood as deposited there through the patient's projections. Bion (1967) wrote, "The psychoanalyst should aim at achieving a state of mind so that at every session he feels he has not seen the patient before. If he feels he has, he is treating the wrong patient" (pp.18–19).

How do the contents of the patient's mind get into the analyst's experience? This question of transmission is approached quite differently by different authors. Some authors seem to imply a kind of telepathic process. The patient has a phantasy that his own murderousness, or panic, or dread is located inside the analyst, and the analyst begins to find himself experiencing precisely that murderousness, panic, or dread. Other authors (Grinberg, 1962; Racker, 1968; Grotstein, 1981; Ogden, 1982; Tansey and Burke, 1989) suggest that the patient's fantasy about what is inside the analyst leads the patient to treat the analyst accordingly, and the analyst picks up and unconsciously identifies with the way in which the patient is treating him.

Joseph (1989), who, after Bion, has made the most important contributions to contemporary Kleinian approaches to projective identification, speaks of the pressure brought to bear on the analyst by the patient's projections. The patient's words, demeanor, and silences all have an impact on the analyst's experience, creating states of mind in the analyst that correspond to the patient's projections. Thus, Joseph argues, patients are involved in "living out experiences in the transference rather than thinking and talking about them" (p. 7). And that living out nudges the analyst into dynamically relevant experiences and states of mind. The analyst, in turn, does not simply deliver interpretations from a neutral, detached platform outside the analytic field, as portrayed by Klein. Analysts often find themselves operating from within the countertransference, from within the context of the state of mind induced in them by the patient's projections. Thus, in the innovations in Kleinian thought developed by Bion and Joseph, the analytically essential material to be understood is no longer found only in the mind of the patient, but is discovered in the mind of the analyst as well and in the complex interactions between the two participants. Spillius (1988) suggests that, although there are differences in emphasis, this new focus on projective identification and countertransference has become "part of the standard approach of every Kleinian analyst" (p. 10).

More than any other group of analysts, the Kleinians worked with children and psychotics. Merton Gill (1983, p. 213) once quipped that an analyzable patient is one with whom the analyst can maintain the illusion of neutrality. Whereas well-behaved neurotic patients often make it possible to preserve a sense of oneself as neutral and always in control, children and psychotics tend to be less well behaved and, consequently, tend to get under the analyst's skin. Bion's realization that the patients he was working with had gotten under his skin led to the development of the concept of projective identification as an effort to explain how that came about. Gradually, subsequent Kleinian authors realized that the impact of less disturbed patients on the analyst's experience is no less important in psychoanalytic work with them but merely more subtle and easy to miss.

Related to the question of transmission noted earlier (the mechanism through which the patient's projections show up inside the analyst's experience) is the question of the nature of the receptor site in the analyst that receives the patient's projections. Here, too, there is an interesting range of approaches.

Bion established a dramatic ideal that has had a powerful impact on the ways in which Kleinians tend to approach this problem. Bion (1967) argued that, in order for the analyst to receive and clearly apprehend the patient's projections, he has to rid himself of his own mental content, to transform himself into a clean and featureless container. The analyst should proceed with "neither memory nor desire," Bion suggested; the analyst encounters the patient afresh each time, remembering nothing about her, wanting nothing from her. Memories and desires can only interfere with a full experience of where the patient is today and what the patient needs the analyst for and feels about them.

At the other end of the continuum, Racker (1968)[4] portrays the analyst as able to receive and experience the patient's projections only through his own powerful identifications with them. The primitive states of mind the patient experiences as residing in the analyst correspond to very similar, primitive states of mind that constitute the analyst's internal world. All of us, Racker argues, experienced intense, enveloping anxieties as children, and those anxieties, primitive impulses, early configurations of self in relation to powerful and often

---

4. Racker is most accurately described as a neo-Kleinian. Although he employs Klein's language and basic concepts, he recontextualizes them into a framework in which aggression is derivative and reactive, not instinctual, and in which the healing power of the analyst's love (reminiscent of Ferenczi) is emphasized. Many features of Racker's approach to analytic interaction anticipated subsequent contemporary developments; in many respects he was radically ahead of his time and perhaps ours as well.

frightening objects—that whole pulsating mass of childhood longings and terrors—are alive in each of us and regularly evoked in the analyst by the patient's projections. Thus, for Racker, the patient's projections are not received by the analyst's suspending his own memories and desires; the patient's projections are received by discovering which of one's own memories and desires have been stirred up.

This central question concerns the place of the analyst's own dynamics, his own idiosyncratic subjectivity, in the interactions that constitute the analytic process. Bion's approach can be viewed as an extension of the classically Freudian concept of neutrality. For Freud, the analyst is a blank screen onto which the patient projects his transference. For Bion, the screen became a container; the projections are found not on the surface of the analyst but inside his own experience. There is an implicit anal ideal in this way of thinking about analytic interaction. The container, like the screen, needs to be blank. The analyst's own idiosyncratic subjectivity, the analyst's own dynamics and issues, are contaminants.

Racker's (1968) approach, in sharp contrast, places the analyst as her own person at the center of analytic interaction. The analyst can experience the patient's projections only through identifications made possible by similar experiences of her own. If we follow along this line, the next important question concerns the nature of those early, intensely conflictual experiences of the analyst's that make possible the reception of the patient's projections.

Racker suggested that as infants we all have certain kinds of universal experiences leading to common internalized object relations. We all began life as helpless beings, often overcome with intense needs, in the hands and at the mercy of a powerful maternal object. Therefore, we all suffered, and episodically still suffer, from intense paranoid and depressive anxiety, longing for the other who can relieve us of our profound need and fearing that she has purposely abandoned us to our suffering. From Racker's point of view, we have all felt this feeling; we all feel it. It is a kind of generic experience. Therefore, when a patient projects such neediness into the analyst (claiming for himself an illusory self-sufficiency), the experience that arises in any competent analyst ought to be roughly the same, because it is a generic, infantile state of mind that is evoked. It should not matter whether the patient is in treatment with analyst A or analyst B or C. The experience evoked in each analyst should be essentially the same, and the very same, correct interpretation of the patient's projections should emerge.[5]

Thus, even in Racker's formulations, the idiosyncratic features of the analyst's personal history and character are ultimately factored out of analytic interactions. This makes it possible for us to retain the belief that, although central to the process itself, the personal, idiosyncratic features of the analyst have no ultimate impact or influence on the product of the analysis, which is solely determined by what is brought by the patient and is merely evoked, facilitated, and actualized by a competent analyst. Although the role of the analyst in this line of contributions to understanding analytic interaction is very much a hands-on participation (metaphorically speaking), the analyst still leaves no fingerprints.

Interaction in the analytic relationship has been explored within the Kleinian tradition largely through the concept of projective identification. It should be noted that within this concept, the roles are very asymmetrical and well defined. The patient does the projecting; the analyst does the receiving and containing. This kind of role specificity with regard to projective identification has important implications for the ways in which influence and the problem of autonomy have been approached in this tradition. No matter how deeply implicated the analyst is in the process at any point, in a general sense, the patient is always understood to have "started it" (Hoffman). The patient's projections set the agenda, no matter how deeply and personally the ana-

---

5. Other authors have approached the analyst's receptor sites for the patient's projections in ways similar to Racker. Grinberg (1962) wrote about "projective counter-identification," and Money-Kyrle (1955)suggests that the analyst's understanding of the patient is based on an unconscious identification with the patient through his (the analyst's) child self. Pick (1985) argues that the patient does not project into the analyst indiscriminately, but projects into specific parts of the analyst, which is where the analyst receives the projection: "for example, ... the patient projects into the analyst's wish to be a mother, the wish to be all-knowing or to deny unpleasant knowledge, into the analyst's instinctual sadism, or into his defences against it. And above all, he projects into the analyst's guilt, or into the analyst's internal objects" [p. 41].

lyst is drawn into the dynamic turbulence. Thus, the particular analyst exerts no influence on the process and the patient's autonomy is protected.

Not considered is the extent to which the analyst might be understood to involve himself in projective identifications of his own. Are there dynamics that begin with the analyst and into which the patient is drawn? Do particular analysts draw out different dynamics in their patients? Might one consider the practice of psychoanalysis in general an extension of projected features of Freud's psychodynamics, and the particularities of the ways it varies from clinician to clinician an elaboration of their own histories and internal worlds? This theme is explored further in the next chapter.

Interactive Themes in Current Kleinian Contributions

As we noted at the beginning of this chapter, it has always been difficult to assign a place to Kleinian theory with respect to the traditional categories dividing psychoanalytic schools: drive theory versus object relations. Klein always identified herself as a loyal devotee of instinct theory. Yet Freud's instinct theory relegated objects to a secondary status. The source, the aim, the impetus were all intrinsic features of the drive; the object was found "accidentally" and was valuable only because it was useful in achieving the aim of the drive, tension reduction. Klein, on the other hand, regarded the object of the drive as an essential, a priori feature of the drive itself; oral libido does not cathect the breast as it does in Freud's theory, because the baby happens to discover through feeding that the breast is a source of pleasure. Oral libido, for Klein, is directed, inherently and fundamentally, toward the breast. Thus, despite the similarity in terms, political loyalties have masked the extent to which Klein's drive theory was always a different kind of drive theory from Freud's drive theory; for Klein, the drive is inherently directed toward and perpetually seeking its natural objects.

This relational dimension of Kleinian theorizing has been further developed by more contemporary Kleinian authors. Rather than locating mind in the individual, as Freud did, an individual that is forced through necessity (frustration) to turn toward and deal with external reality, contemporary Kleinian authors now tend to view mind as located within a field comprised of more than one individual. Thus, Pick (1985) argues that

> insofar as we take in the experience of the patient, we cannot do so without also having an experience. If there is a mouth that seeks a breast as an inborn potential, there is, I believe, a psychological equivalent, i.e., a state of mind which seeks out other states of mind [p. 35].

Here mind is conceived of as fundamentally dyadic, not seeking gratification through the use of others, but seeking out others as an end in itself. As Bion's interpersonalization of the concept of projective identification became increasingly central to Kleinian thinking, psychic life has been located increasingly in the interactive field between individuals and their reciprocal impact on each other. This trend approaches Fairbairn's concept of libido as "object-seeking."

The patient in the contemporary Kleinian literature is portrayed not as simply pursuing infantile gratifications, regressing to infantile states, or maintaining his own equilibrium, with the analyst observing from a detached and neutral perch. The patient is portrayed as intensely engaged with the analyst in the here-and-now, as hyperaware of the analyst and the details of their interaction, as desperately needing to push and pull the analyst into states of mind essential to the patient's sense of safety.

In the contemporary Kleinian literature, the best way for an analyst to learn about a patient is no longer through an interpretive examination of the patient's free associations, but through a self-reflective awareness of the patient's impact on the analyst. Thus, Joseph (1989) suggests that

> our understanding of the nature and the level of anxiety is interlinked, and depends, in large part, on our correct assessment of the use that the patient is making of us . . . frequently the guide in the transference, as to where the most important anxiety is, lies in an awareness that, in some part of oneself, one can feel an area in the patient's communications that one wishes not to attend to [p. 111].

The analyst explores her own experience for pockets of anxiety, and it is there, Joseph suggests, that the most important information about the patient's transference may lie.

In addition to the analyst's own experience in the countertransference, contemporary Kleinians also stress the importance of the patient's perceptions and fantasies about the analyst. The patient is not simply using the analyst as a projective screen for his own dynamics. The patient is deeply and intently embedded in interactions with a real person in the actual present. As Pick (1985) has put it, the patient "will take in, consciously or unconsciously, some idea of the analyst as a real person" (p. 36). For contemporary Kleinians, exploring the patient's ideas about that person are crucial to understanding what is going on:

> I would then wish to explore most carefully her picture of me, this old, supposedly lonely, rather embittered person, and her quiet conviction of what I was like, and only very slowly and over a long period, hope to explore how much of these ideas might be linked with actual observations of myself or the way I function, how much projected parts of herself, and so on. . . . To assume that all these ideas were projections from the beginning would almost certainly be inaccurate, would numb one's sensitivity as to what was going on . . . [Joseph, 1989, p. 148].

Along similar lines, Racker (1968) regards the contertransference as the analyst's most important instrument for exploring the patient's dynamics. The patient's experience is half an interactive unit; the patient's ideas about what is happening in the other half of that unit are a route into the patient's deepest hopes and fears. Thus, Racker suggests, the best way to explore the patient's transference is to explore the patient's fantasies about the countertransference.

For Racker and other contemporary Kleinian writers, the traditional exclusive focus on the intrapsychic has been broadened into a perspective in which the intrapsychic dynamics of the patient get acted out in the interpersonal field between the patient and the analyst, often surfacing in the intrapsychic experience of the analyst. The analyst's actions, interpretive and otherwise, are not divine interventions from afar, but are experienced always within the interactive context of the analytic relationship. Thus, O'Shaughnessy (1982) notes that "it is now widely held that, instead of being about the patient's intrapsychic dynamics, interpretations should be about the interaction of patient and analyst at an intrapsychic level" (p. 139).

The Centrality of Interpretation

In the intensely rivalrous analytic world of the past several decades, all-important lines of thought have been developed in the context of competing approaches. The more influential an analytic school becomes, the more scrutiny and criticism it is subjected to. Analytic authors virtually never grant any credit to their critics, yet it is apparent that theoretical positions are often stretched and enriched by responding to and, in some cases, assimilating some of the arguments of their critics. Thus, in the intense polarization between the Freudians and the Kohutians during the 1970s and 1980s in the United States, the Freudians were criticized for not grasping the importance of empathy, and the Kohutians were criticized for underemphasizing the place of aggression. In recent years, empathy has become an increasingly common term in the Freudian literature, and self psychologists struggle increasingly to develop a self-psychological approach to aggression.

The Kleinians were severely criticized during the 1950s and 1960s for overemphasizing the power of interpretation. Freud (1910) had established the technical importance of timing in the delivery of interpretations—the analyst ought to interpret only material whose derivatives were already in the preconscious. This means that one speaks only to intentions, feelings, and processes that the patient is capable of recognizing as his. Anna Freud extended this approach in her work with children, who, because of their immature egos, were regarded as incapable of using deep interpretations and requiring auxiliary support. This emphasis on timing was greatly elaborated in Freudian ego psychology (Blanck and Blanck, 1974) into an analytic technique in which interpretations were very carefully controlled and titrated. The patient's mind was envisioned (in a spatial metaphor) as complexly layered, and analytic interpretations were to be addressed only to the surface, to the active resistances. Deep interpretations were regarded as at best ineffective, at worst dangerous.

Klein's approach to interpretation was shaped in her early work with very disturbed children. In contrast to Anna Freud, Klein felt that intense anxiety was most effectively assuaged not by withholding interpretations, but by interpreting at the point of the deepest anxiety. She felt that subsequent developments in the child's play suggest that he is able to hear and use even interpretations of the most primitive and terrifying phantasies. Thus, a very different kind of interpretive activity developed in the Kleinian school. (See Grosskorth, 1986, for an account of this controversy.)

When a Freudian ego psychologist makes an interpretation, she envisions herself reaching the most adult dimension of the patient, creating an alliance with his observing ego; when the Kleinian makes an interpretation, she envisions herself as bypassing the patient's ego and making contact with the most primitive infantile wishes and dreads. The utility of an interpretation for the ego psychologist is measured in terms of its recognizability; the utility of an interpretation for the Kleinian is measured in terms of its impact on the patient's anxiety. This is why Kleinian analysts were characterized either admiringly or mockingly (depending on who was doing the characterizing) as "speaking directly to the unconscious."

In the Kleinian literature of the 1950s and 1960s, the analyst was portrayed as a whirlwind of interpretive activity.[6] Interpretations of early infantile wishes and phantasies, often of a very sadistic nature, were made very quickly (often in the beginning of the initial consultation) and with great rapidity thereafter. This was probably the most severely criticized feature of Kleinian technique and responsible for the largely negative perception of the Kleinian school in the United

---

6. There is a passage in a paper by Money-Kyrle (1955) that illustrates the classical Kleinian principle of making interpretations at all times: "I thought he (the patient) had, in phantasy, left parts of his 'good self' in me. But I was not very sure of this, or of other interpretations I began to give" (p. 27). It seems striking that not being sure of what he was talking about did not stop him from making interpretations, or of framing what he was offering as speculations rather than interpretations.

States until recently.[7] Greenson (1974), for example, contrasting his own measured, careful ego-psychological interpretations to the Kleinian approach, suggested that the latter demands of the patient a masochistic surrender to the analyst's interpretations. Better functioning patients leave immediately; more primitive, masochistic patients remain and submit.

Part of what is new in the contemporary Kleinian approach has derived from a creative response to this criticism. Racker (1968) prefigured this response in his exploration of what he termed the patient's "relationship to the interpretation," and it has been developed with great perspicacity and refinement by Joseph (1989). What is central to these new developments is a concern with the patient's capacity to *use* interpretations.

As we have noted, for Klein and her contemporaries, the patient's capacity effectively to use analytic interpretations was presumed. Klein believed that there was a channel through which the small child directly perceives the parents in a realistic fashion, bypassing severe early introjects; similarly, Klein believed that there was a channel through which the analytic patient recognizes the analyst's interpretations as benign and helpful, bypassing severe transferential anxieties and phantasies. What was presumed in early Kleinian thinking is now called into question. Thus, Joseph (1989) focuses on the patient's ability to hear, recognize, and effectively use interpretations in a fashion that has traditionally been the province of Freudian ego psychology:

> This patient S. had almost no part of her ego available for understanding—she was operating in a more primitive way, her defences being used to struggle against facing psychic reality. I would not therefore feel it to be of value to her, at that point, to do anything other than

---

7. It is this technical approach that makes Winnicott's book *Holding and Interpretation* (1986) so shocking to many American readers. Winnicott was trained as a Kleinian and remained heavily influenced by Kleinian technique throughout his career. This was not apparent in most of his writings, composed of short papers and abbreviated vignettes. In *Holding and Interpretation*, the reader is presented with an extended account of a treatment, often verbatim, and the sheer multitude and complexity of the interpretations are quite startling.

> begin to build up a picture of her unconscious defenses and the kind of person that I think she unconsciously experienced me to be [p. 121].

This kind of careful delineation of layers of resistances stems from a view of the patient in which primitive defenses dominate the transference and subsume the patient's entire experience of the analyst, including the analyst's interpretive activity. If the patient lives in a (paranoid-schizoid) world that is fundamentally split between good and evil, the analyst's interpretations themselves will be slotted into one or the other category, as divine revelation to be worshipped or poison to be dreaded.

In recent years, the concept of "pathological organizations" has been added to the classical Kleinian notions of the paranoid-schizoid and depressive positions to characterize highly defensive configurations of internal and external object relations. Rosenfeld (1965, 1987) has provided vivid descriptions of malignant, narcissistic and perverse organizations, and Steiner (1993) has explored various forms of desperate "psychic retreats." In this new literature, once again, the omnipotent power assigned to interpretation in the classical Kleinian era has been diminished. The analyst may intend his interpretation to be a set of ideas to be considered and reflected upon, but the patient has no way of doing that. As Steiner (1993) has put it, "The analyst needs to understand that in this phase there is no question of interesting the patient in understanding in the usual analytic sense since his [the patient's] priority is to find his equilibrium" (p. 215). Thus, in contemporary Kleinian thought, the capacity to use interpretations, rather than being presumed, is considered a developmental achievement, continually lost and only episodically regained.

The recent rethinking of the nature of interpretation reflects a two-person view of the interactive nature of the analytic situation. In the classical Freudian and early Kleinian view, the analyst is outside the patient's dynamics, unaffected by them and delivering interpretations about them. Now the analyst is understood as embedded in the anxieties and pressures of the patient's dynamics (often located inside the analyst through projective identification). The analyst's interpretive activity is now understood in the context of the analyst's own struggle with those anxieties and pressures.

Thus, a new kind of question has emerged with regard to the timing of the analyst's interpretations: Why is the analyst interpreting now? Rapid, early interpretations are now understood as possibly reflecting the analyst's anxiety and difficulty in containing the patient's terrors and fantasies. Interpretive activity, rather than opening up a channel to the unconscious, may enable the analyst and the intellectualizing patient collusively to distract themselves from the patient's deeper dreads. As Joseph (1989) puts it, (in contrast to Money-Kyrle, [1955]),

> if the analyst actually struggles in such situations to give detailed interpretations of the meaning of individual associations then she is living out the patient's own defensive system, making pseudo-sense of the incomprehensible, rather than trying to make contact with the patient's experience of living in an incomprehensible world. The latter can be a very disturbing experience for the analyst, too. It is more comfortable to believe that one understands 'material' than to live out the role of a mother who cannot understand her infant/patient [p. 158].

Thus, contemporary Kleinian authors emphasize the inevitable intensity of the analyst's experience in the countertransference. Strong passions, rather than being regarded as evidence of the analyst's own need for further analysis, are regarded as a constructive necessity in the analyst's efforts to know her patient deeply and help him contain and reown the pieces of his experience, which he continually fragments and projects into others. In order to help the patient contain frightening pieces of his own experience, the analyst has to be able to tolerate containing those projected pieces rather than trying to pass them back instantly, like a "hot potato," through interpretations.

The necessary "emotional closeness" of the analyst to the patient is now seen as predictably uncomfortable for the analyst (Malcolm, 1986, p.78), and there is the perpetual danger that the analyst will deal with her anxieties by making interpretations so as to regain control. Thus, in this contemporary Kleinian view, the question must always be raised whether the function of the analyst's interpretation is to convey to the patient, "You are the sick one here, and I am the analyst. These crazy anxieties and phantasies are in you, not in me." Not only is it no longer presumed that the patient has a transference-free receptor site in which to receive analytic interpretations; it is no longer presumed that the analyst has a countertransference-free source within her own experience from which to generate interpretations. Britton and Steiner (1994) have detailed the ways in which an "overvalued idea" in the form of an interpretation drawn from the analyst's doctrinal beliefs can lend a false "sense of integration to otherwise disparate and confusing experiences . . . the facts being forced to fit an hypothesis or theory which the analyst needs for defensive purposes" (p. 1070).

Thus, what is now taken into account is the function of the interpretation for the patient, the way in which the patient is able to relate to and use interpretations, and the function of the interpretation for the analyst, that is, the way in which the analyst uses her interpretive activity in the context of her inevitable countertransference struggles.

> Our healthier patients will soon be able to tell us if they feel, rightly or wrongly, that an interpretation suggests that we are on the defensive and interpreting accordingly. In our work with anxiety we not only have to maintain that we can stand our patients' projections, we actually have to do so [Joseph, 1989, p. 112].

At this point in the evolution of Kleinian thinking about interpretation and other aspects of theory and technique, we find a rich mixture of traditional principles and innovative thinking. Although Fairbairn and Winnicott are virtually never directly cited, their versions of object relations theories have had a clear impact on contemporary Kleinian thought. We can discern Fairbairn's influence in the notions of pathological organizations and psychic retreats. The depictions of the paranoid-schizoid and depressive positions, which dominated the classical Kleinian literature, were standard, generic configurations with standard, generic objects (good and bad breasts, good and bad penises, etc.). Pathological organizations and psychic retreats are much more custom designed internal worlds, drawn from experiences with real people at crucial developmental phases, very much like Fairbairn's depiction of closed internal worlds composed of attachments to internalized bad objects. There is, for example, a striking similarity between Rosenfeld's (1987) depiction of a malevolent internal "gang" in pathological, malignant narcissism and Fairbairn's (1958, p. 385) depiction of the patient's transferencial efforts to "press-gang" the analyst into pathological internal object relations.

Winnicott's influence is even more palpable. In the classical Kleinian literature, the emphasis was generally on aggression and its vicissitudes, with primitive destructiveness and envy presumably emerging spontaneously out of an excess of constitutional aggression. Increasingly in the contemporary Kleinian literature, envy and aggression are recontextualized as reactions to and flights from dependency and its attendant anxieties. It is the desperate effort to ward off depressive anxiety consequent to the dependent object relation that is regarded as the well-spring of destructiveness. Thus, Spillius (1993) has redefined envy as a defense against "acknowledging the acute pain and sense of loss, sometimes fear of psychic collapse, that would come from realizing that one wants a good object but really feels that one does not or has not had it." (p.154) And the kind of maternal functions Winnicott regarded as essential to the analyst's role have found their way increasingly into the Kleinian literature. For example, Money-Kyrle (1955) speaks of the analyst's reparative and parental functions, in taking care of an immature part of the self that needs to be protected from a sadistic part. This nurturative dimension of the analyst's activities has been extended by Pick (in very Winnicottian tone), who notes that "whether one knows it or not, the interpretation will contain some projection of our own wish to protect the baby from the sadistic part. The maintenance of a careful setting is in some way a demonstration of this care." (p. 41)

Despite the absorption of these innovations, several important principles with roots in the classical Kleinian model still hold sway in their contemporary literature and shape the distinctively Kleinian approach to interaction.

1. Although the analyst is now portrayed not as a detached observer but as affectively embedded in and struggling with the same powerful affects and conflicts as the patient, the analyst is still granted the power to discriminate the real from the fantastic and projected. As

Schafer (1997) has put it, "These Kleinians remain objectivist or realist in their phenomenology. They consistently present their material as though they are in the position of purely independent observers— even of their own countertransferences" (p. 19). Thus, the fundamental asymmetry of the traditional psychoanalytic assignment of epistemological powers is preserved: the patient is regarded as too much at the mercy of his own dynamics to know what is real, while the analyst is positioned, by the very definition of her role, with the capacity to sort out the actual from the distorted.

2. Although the analyst is now often portrayed as nudged, through the patient's transference, into subtle and unwitting enactments of countertransferential pressures (even in the very act of interpreting), the (anal) ideal of a clean, uncontaminated nonparticipation is generally still preserved. With each new set of papers by the more progressive contemporary Kleinian authors, one can sense the struggle between the new clinical awareness of interaction and an old, rigid technical posture. There is an increasing awareness of the ways in which the analyst is embedded in the patient's dynamics and the ways in which that embeddedness can be used by the analyst to understand the patient's projections and frame appropriate transference interpretations. But a valiant effort is made to preserve the classical distinction between thought (or feelings) and actions. In the countertransference, the analyst inevitably experiences the patient's conflictual emotions, including intense impulses to act. These experiences are useful, both to provide the patient with the experience of being contained and to provide the analyst with material for interpreting. But, as much as possible, the analyst should refrain from actually acting, so as to keep the transference uncontaminated.

John Steiner (1993) and Michael Feldman (1997a, b) have provided vivid descriptions of the analyst caught in the countertransference in double-binding dilemmas between choices of reenacting the roles of fantasied ideal objects or critical bad objects. They even suggest that some degree of enactment of these roles is inevitable. But, unlike their counterparts in the American relational literature (Aron, Bromberg, Davies, Hoffman, Spezzano), they regard the analyst's actual participation in such interactions as regrettable and see no value in transference-countertransference interaction followed by collaborative self-reflection. As of this writing, Pick has come closest to such a convergence with American relational theorizing:

> My stress is that, within the analyst as well, spontaneous emotional interaction with the patient's projections takes place, and that if we fully respect this and are not too dominated by the demand for impeccable neutrality, we can make better use of the experience for interpretation [p. 43].

It is noteworthy that even for Pick, despite her emphasis on the patient's search for and awareness of the analyst as a real person, the "spontaneous emotional interaction" takes place, or should take place, only inside the analyst's mind, not in actual "spontaneous emotional" interchange with the patient.

Thus, in the contemporary Kleinian literature, as in the classical Kleinian literature, the belief is preserved that in performing his traditional analytic function, the analyst rises above the patient's projected affects and conflicts and is experienced by the patient in just that way. In this sense, there is a preservation of the traditional assumption that, when the analyst acts properly analytic, he is invisible and that therefore the patient's experience of the analyst in the transference is revealed, like a bas-relief, against a neutral background. Despite the radical shifts and reconceptualizations in many features of Joseph's (1989) contributions, we can see the importance to her of maintaining this ideal:

> There is always a problem as to how to keep the transference uncontaminated—not, or minimally, contaminated by the analyst's acting out verbally, in tone or attitude, and so on. It is clear that we are demanding that the analyst should be able to feel and explore most carefully the whole range of disturbance and yet not act out and not masochistically suffer without verbalizing [p. 148].

3. Although the patient is no longer assumed to be able to hear interpretations directly, outside his own dynamics, contemporarary Kleinians tend to assume that, when the analyst makes an interpretation about the patient's relationship to interpretations, this interpretation is grasped in some direct, unmediated fashion.

Let us say that a patient who is chronically ensconced in the para-noid-schizoid organization hears the analyst's interpretations as dan-gerous attacks. Mr. X, for example, would respond to virtually anything interpretive that was said to him with, "Yes, I have thought of that, and. . . ." The analyst's experience was of having his state-ments instantly miniatured into familiar clichés. It was never possible for the analyst to have a thought that Mr. X had not already thought about for a long time. Mr. X could never be surprised. Nothing new could ever happen. Mr. X always remained in control.

In the *classical* Kleinian literature, the assumption would be made that the analyst's interpretations nevertheless are able to get through. Despite the ego's defenses and resistances, the unconscious resonates with the analyst's correct understanding. In the *contemporary* Kleinian literature, by contrast, it would be assumed that the patient's paranoid-schizoid organization, pathological organizations, and manic defenses create a wall through which the analyst's interpreta-tions cannot penetrate. The patient experiences the analyst's interpre-tations as dangerous attacks and disarms them accordingly. What is the analyst to do?

The analyst should make an interpretation about the patient's rela-tionship to the interpretations (or what Joseph, 1989, calls the "immediate situation" and what Steiner, 1993, refers to as shifts between pathological and healthier organizations). The patient should be shown that he experiences the analyst's interpretations as dangerous and how he processes them to neutralize them. The assumption is made that no interpretations will be heard by the patient as interpretations except—and this is an important excep-tion—interpretations about the patient's relationship to the interpre-tations. The assumption that in most situations the patient is likely to be able to hear interpretations about his relationship to interpretations is a central feature of the contemporary Kleinian approach to interac-tion and distinguishes that approach from other current models.

The Non-negotiability of the "Analytic Frame"

Schafer (1997), characterizing contemporary Kleinians as Kleinian Freudians, has emphasized that, in addition to their loyalty to Freud, "they rely on interpretation and scrupulously attempt to avoid other types of intervention" (p. xii). But I noted in Chapter 2 that "interpretation" is a word whose meanings have become gradually transformed over the course of the history of psychoanalytic ideas. We are not really told much when a theorist states his allegiance to the principle of interpretation. We need to know what he thinks interpretations are and what happens when the analyst delivers one.

The Kleinian understanding of "interpretation" has been almost completely transformed by the gradual but remarkably extensive elaboration of the concept of projective identification (in Bion's interpersonalized terms). Traditionally, interpretations were understood to be delivered by a largely detached analyst reading the patient's free associations. Now, interpretations are understood to be preceded by the analyst's reception and containment of the patient's projective identifications, which she discerns significantly through a self-reflective exploration of her own experience.

Originally, projective identification was understood solely as a defensive process. Increasingly, projective identification has been understood to have expressive and communicative aspects. As these latter functions have been given more weight, the containment aspect of projective identification has become increasingly significant. If the patient is regarded as unconsciously intending to rid himself of unwanted mental content by fantasizing its relocation into the mind of the analyst, a relatively rapid interpretation of that defense might be appropriate. But, if the patient is unconsciously trying to teach the analyst something about the patient's experience, or to enlist the analyst's aid in holding features of himself he is terrified of maintaining in his own mind, the analyst's rapid interpretation might very well be perceived as a rejection of the patient's need for containment, a failure of a necessary, quasi-parental function. In this sense, the contemporary Kleinian notion of "containment" is very similar to the Winnicottian notion of "holding." The analyst needs to convey not just an interpretive understanding of what is projected, but a willingness and capacity to provide experiences of "holding" necessary for the patient's security and equilibrium. As Steiner (1993) has put it,

> such containment depends on the analyst's capacity to recognize and cope with what the patient has projected and with his own counter-

transference reactions to it. Experience suggests that such containment is weakened if the analyst perseveres in interpreting or explaining to the patient what he is thinking, feeling, or doing. The patient
experiences such interpretations as a lack of containment and feels
that the analyst is pushing the projected elements back into him. The
patient has projected these precisely because he could not cope with
them, and his immediate need is for them to continue to reside in the
analyst and to be understood in their projected state [p. 373].

But *how* shall the analyst contain the patient's projections? *How* is
the analyst to convey to the patient his willingness to serve that function? It is here that the contemporary Kleinians' adherence to the
most concrete application of classical theory of technique seems
greatly to reduce their options. Analysts interpret, or they remain
silent. Steiner, Feldman, and other innovators within this tradition
regard interpretation as sometimes experienced by the patient as a
failure of the analyst's containment function. But what else can the
analyst do other than interpret or remain silent?

Steiner (1993) illustrates this problem in dramatic fashion. He
argues that, because the patient maintains his own equilibrium by dis-
tributing various fragments of his own mental content into the mind
of the analyst, the patient holds many beliefs about what is going on in
the analyst's mind that are often extremely important to explore. He
illustrates the ways in which this exploration can be accomplished
through what he calls "analyst-centered," as opposed to "patient-
centered" interpretations. Analyst-centered interpretations take the
form of statements like: "You experience me as . . ." or "You are afraid
that I . . ." or "You were relieved when I . . ." (p. 374), and so on.
Steiner presents clinical material illustrating some very interesting and
thoughtful interpretations of what he speculates are the patient's
unconscious phantasies about the analyst's experience; he gauges the
accuracy of these interpretations by what he takes to be rises and falls
of the patient's anxiety.

Two features of this approach seem remarkable to me. First,
although Steiner's intent is largely to convey to the patient his capacity to contain her projections, to let her know that he is really with her
and struggling constructively to work with her needs of him, he never

says anything about *his own* thoughts or feelings about his experience with her. Despite the effort to bring in the analyst as a second person in the process, who really is affected by and reciprocally shaping the process, everything needs to be framed in terms of interpretive presumptions about the patient's thoughts. To my ear, this locks the analyst into a strange reversal of the old joke about the narcissist who suddenly says to his conversational captive, "Enough about me. Tell me about yourself. What do you think about me?" The analyst who feels he can only either be silent or make interpretive statements struggles to signal to the patient his successful containment of the patient's projections by conveying something like: "Enough of my making interpretive statements about what is going on in your mind. Let's talk about my mind. Here's what *you* think is happening in my mind."

Second, it does not seem to have occurred to Steiner to *ask* the patient about his own experience of the analyst. Presumably such questions would represent a departure from the strictly neutral and hierachical framework within which he feels it is necessary to locate the analyst's interpretive function. This approach can be contrasted to the kind of interpersonal/relational methodology developed by Blechner (1992) and Aron (1996) who similarly regard the patient's beliefs about the analyst's experience as important, but who attempt to develop that material by questions aimed at encouraging patients to explore their conscious and unconscious fantasies.

At this point in the evolution of their clinical practice, the contemporary Kleinians' exploration of the interactive features of the analytic process seem to run into the brick wall of traditional injunctions against any behavior other than interpretations and silence as legitimate analytic functions. As Steiner (1988) puts it,

> Using all the means available, including self-observation, the observation of his actions, the responses of the patient, and the overall atmosphere of the session, the analyst can arrive at some kind of understanding of his patient and of his interaction with him. If the analyst can stand the pressure, he can use this understanding to formulate an interpretation that allows the patient to feel understood and contained [p. 385].

As we noted in the preceding chapter, the interpersonal tradition has available other "means" for exploring interaction. This marks a crucial difference with regard to the ways in which analytic interaction is understood and the technical options through which the analyst participates in the analytic relationship.

A key principle maintained throughout both classical and contemporary Kleinian thought and distinguishing the Freudians and the contemporary (or Freudian) Kleinians from major trends in relational approaches is that the analytic situation has a fixed and universal unconscious meaning for all patients. This principle is crucial to the way in which Kleinian analysts frame clinical choices in tense moments.

The analytic situation is understood within the Kleinian tradition to constitute a re-creation of the patient's relationship with the primary object, the breast. Whatever else is going on (and many other things are understood to be going on), the patient seeks the analyst's help and experiences the analyst as the breast that is necessary for sustaining life. The analyst's interpretations, whatever else they are, are also, at the deepest level, the mother's milk that the patient desperately seeks and needs. Thus, Joseph (1989) typically describes the way in which the patient's anxiety centers on the dangers she feels because of her position as the helpless, dependent recipient of the analyst/mother's ministrations.

> We can see what this movement achieves in terms of his balance. It cuts out any real relationship between the patient and myself, between analyst and patient, as mother and child, as a feeding couple. It obviates any separate existence, any relating to me as myself; any relationship in which he takes in directly from me [p. 173].

Note the assumptions and equations in this vision: there is a "real" relationship between patient and analyst, and it consists of the relationship between a mother and child—a nursing mother and child.

This is a very powerful organizing metaphor for viewing analytic interaction, and it underlies a great deal of the clinical illustration in contemporary Kleinian literature. But it is very important to grasp that within the Kleinian tradition this is not understood as a metaphor at all. The patient's relationship with the analyst is not *like* the baby's relationship with the breast; at the deepest unconscious levels, the analyst *is* the breast for the patient and the analyst's interpretations *are* good or bad milk or both.[8]

This assumption anchors the contemporary Kleinian approach to many current controversies regarding analytic technique. Should the analyst disclose her experience in the countertransference? Should the analyst ever depart from a strictly interpretive stance to meet a patient's request, respond to a patient's needs? The answer to these questions is necessarily no. All departures from the traditional analytic functions of listening (and now containing) and interpreting are, by definition, an acting out of countertransferential pressures.

The analyst, simply by virtue of being an interpreting analyst, is assumed to have a universal, generic meaning for the patient as the primary object (breast) offering potentially life-giving sustenance (interpretations/milk). Because of anxieties over his dependency on that primary object, the patient will do anything and everything to destroy its goodness. Efforts to get the analyst to depart from the traditional analytic stance by disclosing her own experience, revealing information about her own life, satisfying patient's wishes through means other than interpretations—these are all attempts to spoil the analyst as the primary object, to destroy her potential to offer the sustenance/interpretations that the patient so deeply longs for, feels so desperately dependent on and therefore is so much at the mercy of.

Thus, Kleinian thinking about these kinds of clinical situations and issues almost always centers on the injunction that the analyst "stand firm" in her analyzing function. The key assumption here is that, when the analyst is standing firm (by not disclosing or not gratifying noninterpretively), this act can be presumed to have a universal meaning to all patients. Whatever else the patient experiences (for example, that the analyst is fearfully hiding, sadistically torturing, and

---

8. Joseph (1989) provides many vivid examples of this equation: "I have had ample material to show him that words are seen as an extension of his tongue, which he feels he excitedly rubs against the analysis as the breast, hoping to excite it, me, rather than use the interpretations, nipple, and take in their contents" (p. 63).

so on), at a deep, unconscious level the patient equates the analytic situation with the primary object relation. The analyst can maintain her analytic function and her interpretive potency only by standing firm because there is a deep correspondence between the analyst's demeanor and activity (traditionally defined) and the patient's prewired, universal image of the good breast.[9]

Michael Feldman (1993) recently addressed this issue directly in an elegant argument in favor of the analyst's preserving a traditional, purely interpretive stance. In recent years, several Kleinian authors have attempted to broaden the customary emphasis on the nursing couple and build bridges to mainstream Freudian thought by reintroducing oedipal themes. Feldman argues that the analyst universally represents, in the patient's unconscious mind, not just the breast but also the oedipal couple. By attempting to draw the analyst into noninterpretive interactions, the patient is not just trying to omnipotently control the primary object (the breast), but also trying to seduce the oedipal parent into a betrayal of her spouse and an incestuous intimacy with the patient (as oedipal child).

> If the patient feels that the reassurance he seeks has been achieved by drawing the analyst into the enactment of his wishes, I suspect this *always* involves the fantasy of having separated the analyst from those objects or functions that offer him balance and perspective. This confirms the patient's belief in his omnipotence, with the accompanying anxiety and guilt. More importantly, perhaps, it confirms the presence (externally and internally) of a weak and unsupported figure from whom he is unable to actually gain reassurance. This may, of course, reinforce the need to go on using projective mechanisms, to defend against the confrontation with a weak and divided parental couple, or their representation in the analyst's mind [pp. 340–341].

---

9. See Priscilla Roth and Hanna Segal (1990) for a discussion, along just these lines, of a case in which the analyst ˌworking in a self-psychological manner, chose to answer the patient's request for reassurances regarding her fears about the analyst. "Only the analyst's survival *as a functioning analyst* can modify the persecutory guilt linked with her omnipotence.... the analyst's failure to survive her demanding attacks *as a functioning analyst* confirms in her mind her omnipotence and leaves her in despair" (p. 549).

For Feldman, there is only one genuinely analytic way of reassuring the patient—by the analyst's holding fast to her interpretive function. By acting as an interpreting analyst, traditionally defined, the analyst resonnates with and reaffirms the universal images in the patient's mind of a robust primary object (good breast) and a reliable parental couple,

> the restoration of an oedipal configuration in which both parents are allowed a relationship with one another as well as with the child. The analyst is then allowed a complex relationship with different parts of his own mind, and different versions of the patient with whom he is dealing. The internalization of this configuration enables the patient to achieve a greater degree of integration between different elements of his own personality and, ultimately, a genuine experience of reassurance [p. 341].

Epistemological controversies (traditional psychoanalytic positivism versus hermeneutics and constructivism) are often argued on a very abstract plain. But how the analyst understands the nature of her own knowledge and the claims she makes for it has an enormous, very practical impact on the way the analyst shapes her participation in the analytic relationship. The Kleinians claim to know the (universal) meaning of the analyst's activities for all patients. Whatever else the analysand is speaking about, he is, most fundamentally, positioning himself vis-à-vis the analyst as primary object and as an oedipal couple. This assumption underlies the almost exclusive focus on the here-and-now transference in contemporary Kleinian literature. As Schafer (1997) has pointed out, approvingly, this entails the treatment of all other extraanalytic features of the analysand's life, past and present, as manifest content for expressing transferential anxieties and conflicts "as an arena in which the problems of the internal world are represented and played out" (p. 3).

This is strong assumption—that analysts know what their actions mean to their patients inevitably and universally, despite whatever the patients may think they mean.[10] If you buy this assumption, it makes

---

10. This sort of approach to the analytic "frame" as essential and universal was also developed in the work of Robert Langs (1979).

perfect sense to preserve the analytic frame along traditional lines, claiming for the analyst's understanding the elevated properties of neutrality and objectivity. If you make this assumption, you operate according to what Schafer (1997) has termed a "policy of suspicion" (p. 3) with regard to whatever the patient says, thinks, and feels. If you make this assumption, you stake out a powerful position in your interactions with the patient and interpret the patient's efforts to question that position or engage you in other ways as destructively motivated resistances to your analytic function. If you make this assumption, you gauge the correctness of your interpretations not by anything the patient says in response, but by the rise or fall of anxiety, which presumably reflects the impact of the interpretation on the patient's internal object world.

It is precisely this assumption that has been challenged in the perspectivism/constructivism of contemporary relational authors, who regard the meaning of the analyst for the analysand not as given and universal (and known to the analyst) but as individually constructed, developed, and negotiated between analysand and analyst. Merton Gill's (1983b, 1994) contributions have been extremely important on this point. What the analyst *thinks* she is doing is not the same thing as the meaning to the patient of what she is doing. There is a leap between meaning in the analyst's mind and the meaning for the patient. An analyst who thinks she is warm and reassuring *might* be experienced in this way, or she might be experienced as fawning and desperate. Conversely, the analyst who is "standing firm" according to their idea of a robust primary object or a healthy oedipal couple *might* be experienced this way by a patient. But they might also be experienced, plausably, depending on the patient's history of relationships with significant others, as rigid, brittle, and sadistically uncaring.

Consider a striking example (of assuming the meaning to the patient of the analyst's participation) drawn from an extended case discussion by Herbert Rosenfeld (1987). Rosenfeld believes that the patient, Adam, was involved in various tricks to seduce the analyst away from the truth contained in the latter's interpretations.

> His only hope to be analyzed successfully was if he had an analyst who would remain firm in spite of his constant attempts at seduction. It

seemed he was angry and envious of the firmness he needed from me to enable him to give up his narcissistic omnipotence. . . . Adam did not acknowledge that I was right. But the next day he . . . told me a dream. In it a colleague of his, who is in analysis with me, had six holes drilled into his bones because I as a surgeon tried to find cysts there. No cysts could be found, but the patient, although near collapse, was very brave. There were no associations to this dream. The dream seemed another clarification to show the tricks Adam was playing at that time. The dream seemed to have involved a wishful transformation of the truth. It recognized that I had been touching very precisely on some of Adam's more serious problems, and this he wanted to deny. In the dream he was proud and brave because he was coping so well with the suffering caused for him by a bad analysis. In fact he behaved much more as if he was avoiding the pain of realizing that I was locating his problems precisely [p.69].

For Rosenfeld, whatever else the patient might transferentially experience the analyst as up to, he also experiences the analyst as a good primary object on whom he conflictually depends for substinance/interpretations of the truth. As long as Rosenfeld does not feel he is "acting in" sadistically in the countertransference (of which he assumes he is the ultimate arbiter), the patient's experience that he is having his bones drilled can only be a resistance to the truth[11]

In a relational approach, in contrast, the analyst does not minimize the importance of unconscious meanings of the analyst's actions for both the analysand and the analyst. But she does not presume to know what these are. Meaning is co-created and negotiated.[12]

---

11. Rosenfeld's papers vividly exemplify the tension in the contemporary Kleinian literature between a two-person understanding ("I want to stress again and again that the analysis is not a one-sided process but an interaction between two people," p. 272) and a one-person technique.

12. Schafer's (1997) position on these issues is particularly interesting, because, with his hermeneutic, narrative-based methodology he cannot really believe that the analyst knows, in some unmediated way, what meanings really lie in the patient's mind. Meanings and narratives are constructed, both by patient and by analyst. Yet, Schafer endorses the "policy of suspicion," in which the patient's narrative-based experience of the analyst and other features of reality are

A recent essay on envy by Elizabeth Bott Spillius (1993) sheds some interesting light on the place of envy in the patient's feelings about the analys. Spillius derives envy not, as Klein did, from an excess of constitutional aggression but from the interpersonal context in which the patient was and is given to: "One crucial factor seems to me to be the conscious and unconscious feelings of the giver about giving, and the way these feelings are perceived or misperceived, consciously and unconsciously, by the receiver" (p. 164). She explores a range of subtle but crucial differences in the ways in which being given to can be experienced. In one case, she asks the reader to "suppose that the giver gives eagerly and with pleasure, but only in order to demonstrate his superiority over the receiver" (p. 165). Although Spillius does not systematically apply this framework to the analytic relationship, it is extremely thought provoking to do so.

What kind of giver does the patient experience the analyst as being? What is the patient's sense of the analyst's attitudes, conscious and unconscious, toward giving things, including interpretations, to the patient? Relational theorists put enormous emphasis on a "mutuality" between the participants in the analytic relationship (see, especially, Aron, 1996.) Some authors (Bromberg, 1996; Slavin and Kriegman, in press) have argued that it is essential to a successful analytic process that the patient have an experience of the analyst as changing on the patient's behalf; others (Searles, 1975) have suggested that many patients need some experience of having a therapeutic impact on their analyst. In the Kleinian tradition, in contrast, it is felt to be crucial that a strict hierarchy be maintained between the roles of the two participants. Mutuality in any form is equated with a seduction of the analyst away from their analytic function as a primary feeding/oedipal object. How does the patient experience the analyst's insistence on this hierarchy? It is difficult to imagine that some patients do not experience it, correctly or incorrectly, as a power operation, an enforced superiority that makes taking and using interpretations from the analyst a form of submission, generating envious

---

treated as manifest content, and the analyst's narrative-based understandings are granted the traditional privaleges of nonnegotiability and objective truth to which the analyst is entitled to "stand firm."

spoiling. It might be that a certain portion of the destructive envy that is so prominent a feature of Kleinian case descriptions is an iatrogenic consequence of a rigid hierarchy in the definition of analytic roles.

Presuming that the analyst knows what her presence and actions mean to the patient has important political and clinical, as well as epistemological, dimensions. This issue is sometimes addressed as if it concerned merely the question of power and authority within the analytic relationship. Challenges to the more traditional analytic presumption of knowledge, like Gill's, are represented as a flight from the analyst's rational authority and the superimposition of a false egalitarianism on the analytic relationship (e.g., Schafer, 1985). Surely, the dimension of power in these issues is not unimportant (see Benjamin, 1997), but that is not our primary concern here. (Issues of epistemology and authority are taken up in Chapter 7.)

What is important to stress here is that the presumption that the analyst knows what her actions mean to the patient represents the decisive fork in the road dividing two broad, and very different, approaches to shaping interaction in the analytic relationship. In certain respects, contemporary Kleinian thinking has moved increasingly from a one-person to a two-person perspective in its understanding of mind in general and the interaction between the two participants in the analytic situation. Along with most other contemporary analytic schools, contemporary Kleinians believe that the patient's experience in the transference is not so much a noninteractive, wholesale displacement of the past onto the present (as in earlier Freudian theory) as it is a response to the patient's experience of interactions with the analyst in the here-and- now. But important, interesting differences remain regarding what that experience is and who knows about it.

In the recent analytic literature, some of the harshest rhetoric has surfaced in the clash between the Kleinian and the self-psychological sensibilities. The issue of the adjudication of meaning is at the heart of those clashes. The Kleinian analyst sees through the patient's conscious experience and concerns as surface, manifest material concealing unconscious meaning underneath. This "policy of suspicion" could not be further from what Kohut had in mind by the "empathic stance" he recommended for analysts. The patient requires, Kohut (1984) believed, a conscious experience of being accepted, validated, and understood, certainly not seen through. Meaning, for Kohut, the developmentally most significant meaning, lies in the way the analyst manages the surface. Both these approaches have made important contributions to our understanding of the analytic process and the complex interactions between analysand and analyst. The chapters that follow develop an approach to the analytic relationship and analytic interaction based on the principle that surface and depth, conscious and unconscious, meanings that are apparent and meanings that are elaborated, are dialectically enriching. What the analyst offers the patient is not suspicion about the patient's motives and the exposure of a truer meaning known only to the analyst, but a variety of complementary (and sometimes paradoxical) meanings that open up new experiential options.

CHAPTER 5

VARIETIES OF INTERACTION

E dgar Levenson (1983) depicted the two competing clinical paradigms in psychoanalysis, the more traditional intrapsychic and the maverick interpersonal models. He suggested that the former was concerned primarily with the question, what does it mean? The latter, the interpersonal model, was concerned primarily with the question, what is going on around here? At that time, the traditional, one-person model was clearly dominant, the interpersonal model an important, but distinctly minor countercurrent. In the past 14 years, the two-person model has come to dominate the concerns of clinicians and theoreticians alike. The question, what does it mean? has not become unimportant, but it has become subsumed by the question, what is going on around here? The question, what does it mean? no longer stands by itself in any meaningful way. Consistent with larger currents of postmodern thought, analysts now tend to address considerations of meaning only in context. What does it mean . . . with which analyst? at what point in the process? In what transference–countertransference configuration? In the traditional one-person framework, grounded in the myth of the generic analyst, the person of the analyst mattered little. The analyst was like the operator of a time machine, a technician who would provide the vehicle for the patient's encounter with her own past. If the technician was competent, he was invisible. Thus, Freud compared the personal impact of the analyst on the analytic process to the role of the sperm in gestation. The analyst gets things going, but, once started, the pregnancy proceeds on its own momentum.

If there is widespread consensus on the interactive nature of the analytic process, there is little agreement on how this interactive process actually works. There are many different ideas of interaction in psychoanalysis and little clarity about their relationship to each other. There has now been a whole generation of psychoanalytic writing in which authors contrast the interactive, two-person, intersubjective nature of their own work with the classical model. Occasionally there have been sidelong glances at others who are also contrasting themselves with the classical model, and then it has often seemed important for the author to claim to be more truly interactive, more fully two-person than the other guy (or gal). Both these projects are bearing diminishing returns: the one-person principles of the classical model have faded so much that one has to work hard to find anyone who will really defend them any more; and the claims to be more interactive "than thou" seem to imply that there is only one good way to view the analytic process in interactive terms.

Because interaction has generally been portrayed as a continuum, with the classical model on one end and a radical interactionism on the other, pressures have arisen for authors to demonstrate their interactive mettle. It sometimes seems as if embarrassing self-disclosure has become the implicit mark of good analytic work against which the timidity and self-concealment of others is to be measured. A contrived opaqueness was an unfortunate standard for traditional analytic work; simple self-exposure is an equally simplistic standard for our time. The finger-pointing, single continuum approach seems unnecessarily to deprive us of the rich variety of modes of clinical work and thinking about clinical process that have emerged in recent years. Current psychoanalytic candidates, struggling to develop their own ways of working, are faced with an array of charismatic models of distinctive analytic styles honed by master clinicians, but without a framework for determining what they have to do with each other or a methodology for developing their own personal clinical approaches.

In this chapter I would like to lay the groundwork for addressing several of the most important issues before us. First, I want to try to push beyond the customary binary framework by offering a comparative approach to analytic interaction. We need to recognize that the way interaction proceeds in the analytic process is profoundly personal and that there are many authentic modes of analytic participation. Second, the demise of the classical theory of technique has left us with profound doubts about how we know what we are supposed to be doing. Pay attention to the countertransference—fine. But what to do with it: interpret or not interpret? disclose or not disclose? be expressive or show restraint? I believe the next generation of analytic writing needs to concern itself with clinical choices and judgment: once the guiding principles of neutrality and abstinence have been abandoned, how do we decide what to do? Third, we are currently faced with the difficult problem of how to teach candidates how to do psychoanalysis in a way that is authentically personal but also responsible and rigorous. My hope is that an exploration and comparison of several of the important recent concepts of interaction will provide a basis for addressing these issues.

One way to explore differences both in conceptualizing interaction and also in using those concepts as clinical guides is to consider the methodology of those current analytic authors who have provided us with the richest and most extensive accounts of their work. Our communication with each other suffers greatly from the profound privacy of our work, so those who have found ways to make their clinical process available deserve our deepest gratitude. Theodore Jacobs, Darlene Ehrenberg, and Thomas Ogden are among those who have done so, and each has provided us with a strong, distinct interactional methodology. Of course, each of these authors works differently at different times and thinks about the process in many different ways. What I want to do here is to explore the hallmark, prototypical features of their clinical tales, the features from which, as far as I can tell, their readers draw guidance and inspiration. Each brings a different kind of interaction and a different kind of self-experience to the analytic process, making possible a use of self that is unique to them. And the ways they approach interaction reflect the psychoanalytic traditions from which they themselves have drawn inspiration: the Freudian tradition for Jacobs; the interpersonal tradition for Ehrenberg; and the object relations tradition for Ogden.

In the traditional one-person framework, transference was understood simply to emerge, of a piece, once the neutral medium of the analytic stage was set. From our current perspective, we view transference as much more contextual and more constructed—a response within a particular constellation of interpersonal circumstances for a particular purpose. Similarly, countertransference is often now written about as if it simply emerges. And this certainly is the way it feels most of the time. To borrow from Donnel Stern (1990), countertransference generally has an "unbidden" quality; it catches us by surprise. But this feature of its phenomenology can conceal the extent to which countertransference is also an action, within a particular context, with an implicit purpose. We might consider countertransference as the form through which the analyst attempts to reach the patient. Since we all have our own idiosyncratic styles of engaging the world, it is not surprising that we each participate in analytic interaction in a distinctive fashion.

Schafer (1992) has described the technique of transference interpretation as one in which we "try to establish disturbing manifestations of past relationships in the present analytic relationship" (p. 188). We are looking for a point of entry. In the recent exploration of a two-person, interactive framework, we might think of countertransference similarly, as the analyst's effort, largely unconsciously, to read himself into the patient's story. The term enactment is often used precisely for this purpose.

In Jacobs's approach to interaction, the analyst brings to the analytic process a kind of elaborate, looking-glass world in which important features of the patient's dynamics are mirrored in the analyst's dynamics. Jacobs's clinical descriptions are enormously rich in their detailing of the evocation in the analyst of memories, affects, and self-states, generally from the analyst's own distant past, that are mirror images of the patient's central relational configurations. All the more remarkable because of his training in classical theory of technique, with its traditional undervaluing of the constructive use of countertransference, Jacobs illustrates the ways in which the analyst comes to know and understand the patient's childhood conflicts through the evocation of parallel childhood conflicts in the analyst.

Thus, for example, Jacobs (1991) comes to understand the way in which Mr. V's intimidating rages covered over a wounded vulnerability through the revocation of his fear, in the countertransference, of his own father's tyrannical rages. As Jacobs puts it,

> Mr. V's attitude toward me in the transference, and historically toward his father and brother, resonated with feelings I had struggled with toward my own father - feelings that I found threatening and that I had tried to keep at bay. Working with Mr. V had, no doubt, stimulated affects and memories connected with these childhood experiences that were defended against, as they had been originally, largely through repression and isolation, but also by unconscious efforts to minimize their intensity. It was only when I could put myself in close touch with the strength of the emotions stimulated in me that I could grasp affectively, rather than intellectually, the power of Mr. V's rage and his destructive urges [pp. 40].

Similarly, crucial to Jacobs's effective analytic work with Mr. C's conflictual disillusionment with his father was the evocation in the transference–countertransference of Jacobs's conflictual disappointments in his own father. Such resonating parallels are a central element in Jacobs's (1993) most moving clinical tales.

> Mr. C's story resonated with my own history and for me threatened to awaken troublesome ghosts. Patient and analyst, then, each for his own reasons, formed a conspiracy that had as its purpose the avoidance not only of current conflicts but of memories rooted in parallel life experiences. . . . Correspondences between the lives of the two participants in the analytic situation occur with some frequency, and memories and fantasies of the therapist's that interlock and interweave with those of the patient can prove to be an important source of the analyst's resistances [p. 61].

An image that comes to Jacobs (1993) during another session with another patient seems paradigmatic of his approach to interaction: "I think of two swimmers engaged in the art of synchronized swimming, moving in perfect harmony, each mirroring the other" (p. 12).

What use does Jacob make of his countertransferential experiences? On the whole, he keeps them to himself and employs them to broaden and deepen his understanding of the patient's dynamics. Jacobs defines the analytic project in the traditional terms of the patient's development of insight into his own dynamics and own childhood conflicts. The richness and intensity that the patient's dynamics generate in the analyst's looking-glass countertransferencial world are, ultimately, a vehicle for understanding the patient better. Jacobs (1991) is careful to emphasize the secondary significance of "interpretive work at the interpersonal level." It does not, he stresses, constitute the core of the analytic process" (p. 222). In this sense, the silent use Jacobs makes of the countertransference is perfectly consistent with the ways he uses himself in the analytic process. Jacobs (1993) has a genius for making available past self-states and drawing on them to deepen his affective understanding of the patient's struggles:

> For reasons that I cannot easily explain, I have, as quite regular companions in my office, a band of revenants, friendly—and sometimes not so friendly—ghosts from the past. They are especially fond of listening to a patient's material and come alive, so to speak, when they hear it [p. 1144].

Darlene Ehrenberg's approach to interaction has a very different quality from Jacobs's. Whereas Jacobs seems most in touch with past selves, Ehrenberg seems very much grounded in the present. Jacobs's way of being in the analytic setting seems to require little from the patient. Ehrenberg, by contrast, is seeking an intense kind of engagement. When Jacobs is upset, he is upset because past relationships with his early significant others have been stirred up. When Ehrenberg is upset, she is upset because she wants something from or is threatened by something with this particular patient right now. If Jacobs is looking for the patient in echoes from his own past, Ehrenberg wants to contact the patient in the here-and-now. Where Jacobs writes of parallels and resonances, Ehrenberg writes of boundaries and edges. In reading Jacobs, we learn a great deal about his own childhood and family. In reading Ehrenberg, we learn nothing about her childhood and family, but a great deal about her personal reactions to her patients, what it feels like to be her in their presence. If Jacob's writing sometimes suggests a literary wistfulness, Ehrenberg's (1992) writing suggests heat and intensity:

> Making the immediate interactive experience the crucible of the work and the arena for working through often enables us to facilitate the awakening of desire even in individuals who seem to have long since given up wanting, feeling, and caring, as well as the willingness to risk the kind of vulnerability these imply [p. 6].

The interpersonal clinical tradition from which Ehrenberg's work emerges (in conjunction with other influences) was greatly influenced by Fromm (1960),whose emphasis was on the existential urgency of the analytic situation. For Fromm and Ehrenberg, the interpersonal dimension is not secondary but central to the patient's difficulties. We are what we do with others, and to withhold the analyst's reactions from the patient is to deprive the patient of precisely the insight she might find most helpful in understanding their experience.

Thus, the kind of data Ehrenberg discovers in the countertransference are not past relationships and past self-states but present affects and present self-states. Ehrenberg pays careful attention to what the patient seems to be asking of her, expecting from her, ignoring in her—where the patient is placing her. For example, with her patient Dani, who seems to have a commitment to feeling victimized, Ehrenberg (1992) experiences herself as burdened with the "major share of the responsibility for the treatment" (p. 7) and feels threatened and punished. With Paula, by contrast, Ehrenberg feels "more moved by her distress than frightened by her behavior" (p. 17). Because she feels a very fragile connectedness to Paula even in extended periods of silence, the affective intensity Ehrenberg seeks is established without words. With Edward, she felt deadened and humored; with Sara she felt an uncharacteristic distraction; with Jeff she felt hurt, and so on. In each clinical tale Ehrenberg uses her feelings about the patient and her sense of self in the presence of the patient to generate hypotheses about the patient.

But for Ehrenberg, countertransference is best used actively and verbally not silently. The analyst's self-disclosure to the patient is a central technical option for Ehrenberg. The presumption is that her affective experiences of connection and disconnection vis-à-vis the patient are likely to contain vital information that can be important to the patient.

The contrast with Jacobs here is instructive. For Jacobs, self-disclosure seems very rare, and so it should be. The content of his experience in the presence of the patient is largely tangential to the patient; it has often been precipitated by the patient and, in its parallels contain affects and ideas relevant to the patient. But, within Jacobs's frame of reference, disclosure to the patient would be distracting and unnecessary. By contrast, a greater degree of self-disclosure seems to be a natural extension of Ehrenberg's (1992) mode of participation in the process. Because she characteristically scans her experience for data about the patient's impact on her, about what it feels like to be in the presence of the other, a lack of self-disclosure would often seem a contrived withholding. Although she does not reveal her countertransferential experience impulsively or indiscriminately, the burden of proof for Ehrenberg seems the reverse of what it is for Jacobs. There would have to be exceptional reasons not to make such disclosures.

Further, for Jacobs, as for Racker (1968), the forerunner of so many modern developments, countertransference is carefully processed before it is acted on in any fashion. Ehrenberg (1992), on the other hand, sees great value precisely in the sharing of unprocessed reactions. The affective immediacy that accompanies such disclosure generates a sense of safety and connection for the patient in the analyst's presence:

> The "intimate edge" ideally becomes the point of maximum and acknowledged contact at any given moment in a relationship without fusion, without violation of the separateness and integrity of each participant. Attempting to relate at this point requires ceaseless sensitivity to inner changes in oneself and in the other, as well as to changes at the interface of the interaction as these occur in the context of the spiral of reciprocal impact. This kind of effort, in itself, tends to have reflexive

impact on both participants, and this in turn influences what then goes on between them in a dialectical way [pp. 33–34].

It is noteworthy that Ehrenberg goes out of her way to stress that her notion of analytic intimacy avoids "fusion" and preserves the "separateness and integrity of each participant" (p. 33) because the idea of interaction that Ogden (1994) has written about recently calls for precisely a carefully defined, constructive, distinctly analytic kind of dedifferentiation in which the boundaries around the self-experience of the two participants become permeable.

Ogden has introduced this development in his thinking about the analytic process, an extension of his earlier work on "projective identification," in connection with the term "the analytic third." We noted in the previous chapter that Bion interpersonalized Klein's original, purely intrapsychic concept of projective identification to begin to explore the way in which certain more disturbed patients get under one's skin. Grotstein (1981), Joseph (1989), Ogden (1982), and others have greatly extended this approach to processes of impact and influence in pathological, normal, and analytic relationships. Ogden has suggested that the distinguishing feature of the analytic relationship is precisely the analyst's offering himself as a container for the patient's projections of dissociated dimensions of experience. Following Harold Searles's (1979) earlier work on therapeutic symbiosis, Ogden depicts the cocreation, by analyst and analysand together, of a "third" subjectivity that belongs to neither of them individually but requires both of them, in their different roles, to emerge. Thus, Ogden (1995) is suggesting neither Jacobs's parallel, resonating worlds nor Ehrenberg's encounter between two separate subjects, but rather the generation of a uniquely constituted, combined subjectivity:

> I do not view transference and countertransference as separable entities that arise in response to one another; rather, I understand these terms to refer to aspects of a single intersubjective totality experienced separately (and individually) by analyst and analysand [p. 696n].

Ogden's (1994) idea of the interpenetrating quality of the analytic process was introduced in the dramatic and disquieting opening of his book, *Subjects of Analysis.* I am including it here in some length, because the state of mind Ogden creates in the reader through his carefully controlled use of language seems designed to generate the powerful sense of intersubjective permeability created by the psychoanalytic situation:

> It is too late to turn back. Having read the opening words of this book you have already begun to enter into the unsettling experience of finding yourself becoming a subject whom you have not yet met, but nonetheless recognize. The reader of this book must create a voice with which to speak (think) the words (thoughts) comprising it. Reading is not simply a matter of considering, weighing, or even of trying out the ideas and experiences that are presented by the writer. Reading involves a far more intimate form of encounter. You, the reader, must allow me to occupy you, your thoughts, your mind, since I have no voice with which to speak other than yours. If you are to read this book, you must allow yourself to think my thoughts while I must allow myself to become your thoughts and in that moment neither of us will be able to lay claim to the thought as our own exclusive creation [p. 1].

The patient, like Ogden's author, has (dissociated, presymbolic) thoughts but no voice with which to speak them; has experiences, but no subjectivity to know them in. The analyst, like Ogden's reader, surrenders his subjectivity to the process, emptying it to some extent, so that it can receive, process, and bring to life the voiceless experience of the other. Unlike early notions of projective identification in which the analyst was viewed as, or at least aspired to be, a squeaky-clean container for the patient's projections, Ogden's understanding is that this process is profoundly interactive. There are two active minds in operation. Each reader understands the author through the filter of his or her own subjectivity; each analyst would house and give expression to the patient's projected experiences in his or her own distinctly personal fashion, through the complex internal prism constituted by his or her own experiences, associations, and memories. Thus, the patient's dynamics, conflicts, even the patient's past, are uniquely created in each analytic dyad. Because it is partially through the analyst's subjectivity that the patient's dissociated present and past come alive, the analytic process is, ultimately, profoundly interactive and interpersonal.

Thus, in Ogden's way of working, the analyst is slowly, inexorably engulfed by the deepest levels of the patient's pathology. The analyst comes to feel rage, isolation, futility, stuporousness, desperation, despair, panic, and, most of all, deadness. Ogden (1995) has suggested that "every form of psychopathology represents a specific type of limitation of the individual's capacity to be fully alive as a human being" (p. 2). In each analysis, inevitably, the deadness that the patient's psychopathology houses, and is an expression of, seeps, unannounced, into the analyst's experience. Ogden (1989) wrestles in the analytic process neither with ghosts, as does Jacobs, nor with the patient in the interpersonal present, as does Ehrenberg, but with his own internal objects:

> For both analyst and patient, the danger posed by the first meeting arises to a large extent from the prospect of a fresh encounter with one's own inner world and the internal world of another person. It is always dangerous business to stir up the depths of the unconscious mind. This anxiety is regularly misrecognized by therapists early in practice. It is treated as if it were a fear that the patient will leave treatment; in fact the therapist is afraid that the patient will stay [p. 172].

Ogden has increasingly pointed to the importance of the analyst's peripheral thoughts, fleeting associations, somatic sensations, and personal ruminations as indications of dissociated affective states that the patient and analyst, in the creation of the analytic third, have come to share. Very slowly, over time, the analyst struggles to put into words the inchoate affective experiences they experience together in the analytic third they have created. Ideally, as the analyst is able to convey his understanding of the patient's experience, through the gradual articulation of his own countertransferencial experience, areas of primitive splitting and dissociation in the patient are overcome.

Ogden's clinical tales suggest a form of analytic participation entailing an exquisite emotional presence and reactivity that, for extended periods of time, is largely silent. Ogden (1995) makes a point of noting that in his approach to analytic interaction there is little self-disclosure of the countertransference in the spoken word:

My own technique rarely includes discussing the countertransference with the patient directly. Instead, the countertransference is implicitly presented in the way I conduct myself as an analyst, for example, in the management of the analytic frame, the tone, wording and content of interpretations and other interventions, in the premium that is placed on symbolisation as opposed to tension-dissipating action, and so on [p. 696].

With Ogden, as with Jacobs and Ehrenberg, the approach to self-disclosure of countertransference is consistent with the mode of participation and ideas about analytic interaction. For Ogden, the most important dimension of the analyst's participation is the evocation, containment, and gradual symbolization of the deepest, most primitive features of the analyst's own internal object world. The kind of analytic presence that is possible with each patient in any particular hour is an extension of the analyst's relationship to his or her own internal world. The talk of disclosure is likely to serve as a distraction and an escape from the silent and often lonely work of struggling with the demons that have been stirred up in the transference–countertransference matrix.

Ogden regards the formal asymmetry of the analytic roles as crucial to the distinctly analytic form of intimacy generated by the analytic process. For Ogden, the patient is primarily the initiator of projective identifications; the analyst is primarily the recipient and processor of projective identifications. They are both deeply, personally involved, but, because of the differences in their roles, they are involved in different ways. The analysand is called on to express his experience as openly as possible. The analyst is called on to be as responsive as possible to the patient's experience, while bearing the responsibility for keeping the situation psychoanalytic. Ferenczi's clinical experimentation has defined, for us, his analytic descendants, the dangers of allowing the intense mutuality of the analytic experience to blur the distinct contrast in the roles through which analyst and patient participate. In a clear reference to Ferenczi, Ogden (1994) stresses,

the unconscious experience of the analysand is privileged in a specific way, that is, it is the past and present experiences of the analysand that is taken by the analytic pair as the principal (although not exclusive) subject of the analytic discourse. The analyst's experience in and of the analytic third is (primarily) utilized as a vehicle for the understanding of the conscious and unconscious experience of the analysand. (Analyst and analysand are not engaged in a democratic process of mutual analysis.) [pp. 93–94].

Psychoanalysis and Prestidigitation

The following two pieces of clinical interaction are offered as examples of my way of working clinically. I want to demonstrate the utility of the three ideas of interaction we have drawn from Jacobs, Ehrenberg, and Ogden in illuminating a complex clinical situation, one in which the issues of value and meaning—and, therefore, also influence and autonomy—are central. Although there is considerable overlap, my own work seems to me to be quite different in style from that of Jacobs, Ehrenberg, or Ogden. Of course, it is much easier to characterize the style of other clinicians than one's own. But ironic and comic dimensions often strikes me as important and helpful, and they sometimes come together in my clinical style as a form of playful engagement. These pieces of clinical process demonstrate the deeply personal nature of the way in which any of us applies theoretical principle ideas in our own work.

Andrew

Andrew sought analytic treatment because he felt caught in a complex dilemma that threatened to paralyze him and destroy his life. During his adolescence and early adulthood he had been totally absorbed in composing music, serious contemporary concert music, with some degree of success. But his aspirations were grand, and he did not develop his career in a realistic, step-by-step fashion. In his mid-20s he began to suffer states of depersonalization and chronic anxiety attacks and nearly became dysfunctional. He was able to pull himself out of his tailspin, but only by abandoning music altogether. He transferred from a graduate program in music to a business school and, with consider-able anxiety, was able to graduate and function quite successfully in a very demanding, middle-level managerial position. He was happily married and took great pleasure in fathering his three children.

But recently Andrew had begun to feel that there was something important missing in his life, and that had to do with a sense of mean-ing, a sense that he was involved in something that had value and importance beyond his own private concerns. He had a sense of hav-ing pulled himself up by his own bootstraps, having survived against great odds. Yet, having made it, he now had time to look around, only to discover that he was engaged in activities that did not seem to mat-ter. It was not that he really wanted, or felt it would be possible, to go back to his life as a composer; that time had passed; those opportuni-ties were gone. But he missed the intensity of that life, the sense of higher artistic and cultural purpose.

Andrew came from a broken home and a childhood that was char-acterized by extreme, relentless chaos. His mother suffered from bouts of depression and outbursts of manic activity. His father was an economically marginal, extremely detached, self-absorbed man who had little time for Andrew or anyone else. Both subsequently remar-ried following their divorce when Andrew was eight. The father's sec-ond marriage, like everything else in his life, seemed marked by a joyless tedium; the mother was remarried and divorced a second time and thereafter entered and abandoned a series of what appeared to be shallow, unsatisfying relationships.

Andrew spent a good portion of the first year of his analysis talking about the contrast between his experiences with music and his cur-rent life of economic stability and domestic tranquillity. When he was composing music, he felt that he was expressing something pro-foundly personal in himself. It was if he operated expansively, bliss-fully happy, in a secret, magical bubble; nothing else existed. In an unself-conscious way, he felt at one with himself and at peace with the world. It was not so much that he missed the composing itself, but he missed the sense of deep connection with himself that accompanied composing. If he could not find analogous meaning in his current work, he feared, he would end up feeling as if he had betrayed some-thing central in himself.

When he was in this state of mind, speaking in this way, I felt quite swayed in the direction of thinking that Andrew should pull back from his investment in his daily activities and functions and pursue meaning in a more committed fashion. I found myself musing about his rekindling his love of music, perhaps taking up composing again or cultivating hobbies that inspired a comparable passion. If he did not, he became convinced and I seemed to agree, he would never escape the sense that he had compromised his own potential.

On other days, Andrew would speak of the importance to him of his vocational stability and relative tranquillity. He felt, justifiably, that it was an enormous accomplishment for him to have built the dependable, responsible life he had. He liked his job and enjoyed being valued by people for his competence. He worried about the impact of pulling back from it, even a little bit, and feared the return of his depressive breakdown, anxiety states, and depersonalization. He worried that a disruption of his functioning would have a disastrous impact on him and, ultimately, on his marriage and his children. He feared that he lacked the inner resources, that he was just not strong enough, to survive such an upheaval. In this state of mind, he felt that his doubts about the meaning and value of his job were the self-destructive rantings of a lunatic, the pursuit of a romantic version of the Holy Grail, which would leave him with nothing but emptiness. When he spoke along these lines, I found myself similarly swayed, but now in the opposite direction. He will try to deepen his commitment to his current life, I found myself musing; he needs to stop torturing himself and come to terms with the limits of a finite, mortal life and its inevitable choices and losses.

One thing that impressed me greatly as Andrew and I moved back and forth between these two starkly contrasting perspectives was how skilled he was at maintaining them in an exquisite balance with each other. I told him that I thought he was a genius at "reverse cognitive dissonance." Recall how Leon Festinger (1957) described the way in which people deal with intense conflicts and difficult choices by moving in one direction or another and then minimizing features that are dissonant with the choice they have made. If I choose A over B, the negative features of A and the positive features of B start to become less salient to me and the positive features of A and the negative features of

B begin to seem much more important. By recalibrating positive and negative considerations, we build a sense of conviction about the rightness of our choices.

Andrew operated in an opposite fashion. When he felt himself significantly drawn to the conclusion that the work of a business manager was just not sufficiently engaging to sustain him, that he needed to reconnect with deeper, more creative dimensions of himself, he found himself savoring those elements of his current job that were dear to him. The possibility that he could lose the satisfactions that accompanied his sense of stability and competence was deeply anguishing. It seemed unthinkable that he would do anything to put his current life at risk. On the other hand, as he moved toward concluding decisively that he would renounce satisfactions that accompanied the life of a composer, he began to focus on the pleasures of composing that he would never know again and became wrenchingly depressed and desolate. It seemed as if either emotional commitment involved an impossible, devastating loss. And it seemed as if his conscious process of trying to locate where meaning for his life might be found was designed not to arrive at a sense of conviction and commitment but to preserve this state of anguished indecision.

In this agitated paralysis, Andrew seemed to operate on the illusion that his ambivalence about value and meaning was not a choice, that as long as he did not feel himself firmly committed in one direction or the other he would escape one or the other of the devastating losses he envisioned. I noted that his cultivation of ambivalence could forestall loss only in the short run; in the long run, his waffling served to erode his capacity really to enjoy the satisfactions of either domain. He was able to discern the countertransferential impatience expressed in such remarks. I was reminded of Sullivan's (1956, pp. 28–33) understanding of obsessionalism as a "substitutive activity" that has to be sufficiently distracting to be effective. It was clear to both of us that part of what was happening was my struggle to stay with him in his anguished ambivalence.

Andrew was, of course, very interested in what I thought should matter to him, and I was, of course, very interested in what he thought I thought should matter to him. He went back and forth on the question, which tended to correspond roughly to my conscious attitudes.

One thing I thought a lot about was the extent to which analysts' responses to this kind of struggle for meaning and value in their patients' lives often have a lot to do with their own histories. In hearing case presentations and talking with colleagues about different clinical situations, it has become quite apparent how one's own choices form the basis of a sense of life and what it has to offer, a model of maturity, an attitude toward risk. Each one of us makes choices along these axes, and the way those choices turn out has a lot to do with how we define maturity and immaturity, realism and idealism, health and pathology, value and meaning. What is realism through one set of analytic eyes is masochistic surrender through another; what is daring, robust vitality to one analyst is flirting with omnipotence or oedipal triumph and disaster to another.

So, I wondered how my own history affected my responsiveness to Andrew's dilemma. There was something about his somewhat romantic sense of his own creativity and its peremptory importance that I could certainly identify with. There certainly have been choices I have made in my life that entailed taking risks to preserve a sense of freedom and personal expression. On the other hand, the kinds of satisfactions Andrew drew from his vocational stability and general good citizenship were also experiences not unknown in my life, although fraught with conflicts deriving from my own family and early relationships.

In one session when Andrew was in his romantic state of mind, he spoke of composing music, of artistic creation in general, as the "gold ring" of life. He had overcome many different hardships and won many prizes. Perhaps making it as a composer would have been the ultimate prize, and he had irreversibly passed it up. I found myself associating to a very formative moment in my early adulthood.

In my sophomore year of college, during the Vietnam War, I was part of a group of students trying to figure out what to about our draft status: should we apply for conscientious objector status? burn our draftcards? publicly announce our intention not to serve? privately make plans to leave the country? We spent a great deal of time talking among ourselves about these options and then decided to expand these discussions by inviting various members of the faculty to speak with us.

One of the first speakers was an internationally known cleric and political activist. He spoke a lot about "bearing moral witness." He considered experiences like being awakened in the middle of the night by the voice of one's conscience to be the defining moments of life. Not to heed that voice might be to feel that one's moral integrity has been compromised for the rest of one's life. He clearly thought that the best place to view the war was from a prison cell, and he was very persuasive.

One of the subsequent speakers was a member of the philosophy department. We asked him about voices in the middle of the night. He said that if he were awakened by the voice of his conscience in the middle of the night, he would go back to sleep and see who else was talking in the morning. In retrospect, I have come to understand that he was a pre-post-modernist who believed in multiple self-organizations. Since we are composed of more than one voice, he suggested, the one speaking in the middle of the night might very well not be the one to heed. I have remembered that advice often, particularly at gripping moments in the middle of the night. I thought of it when Andrew was going on about his gold ring. "Maybe there is more than one gold ring," I found myself saying.

Andrew began the next session by announcing that he'd had an interesting dream (a voice from the middle of the night?). Before he related the dream, he prefaced it by saying that he'd been thinking about what I had said about there being more than one gold ring. He had noticed since the last session that he found the kind of intensity and satisfaction he experienced in composing music in other settings as well. There were projects he was working on that involved composition of a different sort, some involving writing, some involving complex administrative tangles. Perhaps he did not require only the totally absorbing life of a composer to feel fulfilled. Perhaps he could survive the loss of that path without a crushing sense of loss and desolation. That night he had the following dream:

> You were a kind of prestidigitator. [One great benefit of my work with Andrew is that he is improving my vocabulary. For those of you who are not quite sure, a prestidigitator is a magician who uses sleight of hand—fast fingers.] You were a prestidigitator, doing

a trick. You were using your fingers very rapidly, manipulating brass coins, five or six of them. There were very rapid movements. I could see that there were nearly invisible strings between the different coins, so thin, like filaments. The filaments were part of how the trick was done, and there for all to see. The point was not magic really, but skill.

Andrew had many associations to this dream, but for our purposes here I want to focus on those pertaining to the problem of value and his relationship to me. Andrew was clear about the connection between the brass coins and the gold ring of the previous session. But what, exactly, was the relationship? He thought the image referred to his sense of me as knowing how to find value in life in many different ways rather than in a single, engulfing creative focus. I wondered about the devaluation from gold to brass, whether he sensed a danger of my robbing him of or seducing him away from something precious. And then, I suggested, there was the illusionist nature of my feat in the dream. Were there things about me that he felt I did not want him to see?

Andrew was determined to use the dream in a different way. The brass suggested to him "common coinage," not a devaluation but a hope that he could find meaning in ordinary life rather than in a transcendent, perhaps transitory, creative ideal. And he connected the multiple coins to the alternative satisfactions he'd been thinking about since the previous session. Further, he insisted that there was no illusionist element to the prestidigitator's feat. The filaments suggested a knitting together of meaning and value. They were there for everyone to see. The skill was in keeping them moving together. I made one last effort to interpret what I suggested was his effort to protect me from what might be his unconscious doubts about me and my influence on him. He shrugged off this suggestion, and we explored the importance to him of believing that, in my life, the anguished choices he was paralyzed by had been resolved in some form.

One question I am interested in is the use Andrew seemed to be making of me. Was the image in the dream a comment on the illusionist, shifty claims of psychoanalysis? Was he giving voice to perceptions about me? Did he feel I had sold him a bill of goods? Did he sense a need in me to present myself as powerful, magical? Were issues of his autonomy at stake? Did I need to find a way to interest him in addressing those?

Or, alternatively, was he using me to provide for him an important, growth-promoting kind of experience he had never had? Given the emptiness he sensed in his parents' lives, Andrew seemed to need to see me as someone who knew something about personal meaning and could guide him in this regard. We might think of this need as a missing developmental function, a very constructive way he was using my influence on him in the service of his own growth and autonomy. We might think of it as the overcoming of splitting and the knitting together of a depressive position. What was real and what was illusion? Perhaps he had trouble envisioning how anyone could sustain a life that is both stable and creative, responsible and intensely meaningful, so the connecting filaments were expressive of a vision he could scarcely imagine, a filmy hope.

There seemed to be an important parallel (of the sort that Jacobs writes about) in my association to my own search as a student for role models in a desperate time. The philosophy professor became an important intellectual mentor to me, the advisor of my senior thesis, which absorbed virtually my whole attention during my senior year. What was the process through which that association, that piece of my life, emerged?

An important part of the countertransference with Andrew, I had come to see, was sustaining, with him, his anguish about loss. I worked hard to overcome my episodic impatience, perhaps my own characteristically manic tendencies, my temptation to say something like, "Come on, get on with it already." In a fashion suggestive of Ogden's notion of the analytic third, it was as if I had entered with Andrew into a mode of experience in which I, too, could not imagine how one could accept the losses of the roads not taken. No life course seemed possible; every choice seemed to reek of loss and death. I had long since given up the expectation that he would emerge from his ambivalence and sense of defeat any time soon. There was something about my sustaining the anguish with him that seemed important. Eventually it helped me to learn about the early history of his sense that to choose his father was to lose his mother forever, and that to choose his mother was to lose his father forever, and that to choose to love them meant to lose any satisfactions in living, and that to choose to enjoy life meant losing them and his childhood forever. What bubbled up out of my internal world at that moment was a quasi-paternal object of my own, someone who had helped me find my way. Although not at all consciously, perhaps I was trying to lend him this paternal object of mine or evoking it so that by reliving that point in my life we might together find a way out of his impasse.

In mulling over this clinical moment, it seems useful to bring together the kinds of analyses Jacobs, Ehrenberg, and Ogden offer. Andrew's ruminations had a powerful interpersonal impact on me in the here-and-now. The paralysis I found myself sucked into, undermining any real connection with myself as potentially helpful or analytically therapeutic, precipitated the emergence in my own internal world of presences entailing self-doubt, loss and death, internal objects of a persecutory, abandoning nature. The internal objects, in turn, seemed to awaken ghosts from a troubled, indecisive time of my own. The ghosts, in their turn, seemed to provide an internal resource for me that I was able to draw on in my struggle to stay with Andrew, which in turn transformed my sense of myself with him and, probably, his experience of me. We could characterize the movement as one from present interpersonal action to internal world to past interpersonal events back to internal world to transformed interpersonal action; from edges to internal presences to ghosts to internal presences to renegotiated edges.

Would it have been useful for me to tell him about my ghostlike association, to bring my earlier experience into the discussion of gold and brass? I imagine someone else might have, but I decided not to. My simple statement about there being more than one gold ring seemed sufficient to give to him whatever it was I was providing him at that point. Would it have been better if I had not brought in the issue of illusion, since it was not in his associations? Or should I have pushed harder on the question of his protecting an image of me? I can well imagine other analysts making other choices here. It felt to me that to talk more about his use of me at that point was to undercut the use he wanted to make of me.

I noted in Chapter 3 that Merton Gill (1994) struggled repeatedly with this issue in his final years. Gill wanted to insist that all interactions in analysis must be talked about, if it is to be analysis and not therapy; yet, talking about relationships changes them, sometimes foreclosing possible dimensions that require silence to stay alive. Commentary on the analytic relationship does not arrive from outside the field; it emerges from within the field and thereby changes the relationship.

My sense of what might be best for Andrew here clearly also reflected my own degrees of comfort and discomfort in being used in different ways, as potential for different kinds of influence, in the analytic process. My choice to go on record (but without continuing to push it) with my sense that he was protecting me in some fashion undoubtedly had something to do with my own conflicts about being idealized and my own experiences of the advantages and dangers of idealizing. So my choice not to disclose my thoughts about my own participation derived from my sense, conscious and implicit, of where the process seemed to be going at that point, the ways Andrew was using me, and the advantages and dangers of that usage. My choice clearly reflects what Renik (1993) has described as the irreducible subjectivity of the analyst's participation.[1]

A Piece of Writing

Consider another sequence in Andrew's treatment that touches on similar issues in a very different way and exemplifies the kinds of microprocesses of interactional patterns that I believe constitute analytic change over time. It occurred a few months after the prestidigitator dream.

Andrew had been referred to me by someone in the field who was familiar with my writing. Andrew decided to read something of mine

---

1. In a commentary on a version of this chapter presented as a paper, Aron (1995a) offered an interesting alternative view, that Andrew's relative lack of interest in or readiness to address the question of his idealization at this point may have resulted not only from Andrew's need to use an idealized version of me, "but because Mitchell's discomfort with exerting his influence on Andrew kept him from addressing this more directly" (p. 13).

to get a sense of me. Apart from reactions to the content, he felt there was an artistry in my use of language that he admired, and that was a factor in his deciding to call me.

Andrew had done some writing himself in graduate school, short pieces of fiction thematically linked to some of the musical compositions he was working on. In the middle of a session in which we were talking about the devastating struggles he had had during graduate school with setting reasonable goals and judging what he could do and not do, he asked me, in a somewhat offhand manner, whether I would be interested in reading some of these pieces of fiction. I found myself saying yes without thinking too much about it. I thought later about why I had agreed so quickly. With other patients in other circumstances I have been much more careful about reading or viewing their extraanalytic productions. I am well aware that these are complex choice points. But with Andrew, at this point, I almost jumped at the offer. Reflecting on the issues, I felt that there was a playful, somewhat omnipotent part of Andrew that had been crushed in his near decompensation years ago. I had a strong sense, again without articulating it to myself, that this part of him was to be found in his writing and that I was being offered something quite precious. To turn it down, or to call for time for us to talk about it, would not have been a neutral reaction. I think it would have been experienced as a rejection. Further, as I thought about it, I knew I would like his writing. He had a wonderful, quasi-musical way with words that was often apparent in the sessions, and he often made me laugh. I was pretty sure, correctly as it turned out, that I would enjoy his pieces of fiction. Thinking about it afterward, I reasoned that, if I had felt intuitively less sure that I would respond positively, I would have wanted to talk more about the significance of what we were embarking on.

As it turned out, I thoroughly enjoyed these pieces. I did not work out a preplanned response. It was not clear to me that he expected one. When I returned them, however, thanking him for letting me read them, he looked expectantly at me and said, "Well, what did you think?" "I really enjoyed them," I said. "I think you are a great writer." Nothing else was said about the writing that session; I (and Andrew as well) felt it best to let things gel and settle in before I thought about whether and how to talk about it. But in the very next session Andrew said that he been thinking a lot about my reactions to his writing. "Great writer . . . Boy, great is a strong word. I mean how many really great writers are there? Or great anythings? Let's see: there was Alexander the. . . .—well, maybe Alexander wasn't so great." He continued for a while with this riff on "greatness," and I played along. He ended by saying, in a way that I believe was both very serious and very tongue-in-cheek at the same time, "It meant a lot to me that you said that, coming from you, a writer yourself. I mean I don't know if you are a *great* writer, but . . ." There was something exhilarating, I think for both of us, in this interaction. Eventually his thoughts drifted to related features of the issues connected with his writing, his ambitions in general, his difficulties in establishing and maintaining a workable sense of where he fit into the world.

We might think of this moment as an opening of the kind of intimate edge Ehrenberg (1992) writes about. To hold back, either in reading his writing or in sharing my spontaneous reactions, felt to me as if it would have created something artificial between us and foreclosed an avenue for working on important dynamic material. Andrew's intensely conflictual feelings about his own sense of omnipotence was a central issues in his presenting paralysis as well as in the prestidigitator dream. Retrospectively, there seemed to be something very important and healing about our being able to play with the issue of "greatness," both taking it seriously and having fun with it. I think there was something very valuable to him in my admiration of his writing. But there was also something dangerous in it. What if my admiration precipitated a manic explosion of his own grandiosity? In the joking, he was able to tell me that my taking such pleasure in his productions made him a bit uneasy, yet not so uneasy that he could not play with it. He could also enter a competitive banter with me. How seriously did I take myself? Could I bear the possibility that he was a greater writer than I?

What if I had not had the anticipatory sense that I would enjoy his writing? That would have been a different situation; it would have felt different; it would have had different meanings. I believe that each analytic clinician has a kind of technical compass and conscience in connection with clinical choice points like these that operates something like Socrates' oracle. In "The Apology," he says that he has an internal voice that never tells him what to do but warns him if he is about to make a disastrous mistake: "it always forbids but never commands" ("Apology," p. 414). In clinical situations like this one with Andrew, I have come to realize that it is very hard to know what to do and that generally we are making choices in situations where we will come to understand many of the relevant meanings only much later on. In the classical theory of technique, one could always decline or postpone deciding and believe that in so doing one was being neutral and therefore not participating. But I don't find that frame of reference useful. Not accepting Andrew's offer or sharing my reactions would not have been a nonreaction. As Hoffman (1996) has noted, in psychoanalysis, unlike basketball games, there are no time-outs. But there are times when I am invited to do something or I feel tempted to do something that I have a sense will get me and us into a mess that I don't understand enough about to proceed. If Andrew's request had felt coercive, or awkward, or distracting, or seductive, I would have felt forewarned and would have suggested we take more time to understand its meanings. It did not, and so I felt reasonably safe in proceeding.

What sort of interaction characterizes my version of psychoanalysis? Ghosts play a role, but my affinity for the interpersonal and object relations traditions probably has something to do with what is for me more vibrant and richer in the exploration of edges and boundaries and the stirring up of internal presences. Ultimately, all these general concepts come alive in the analyst's own experience and vision of life, which for me generally includes a playful tension between grandiosity and irony, passion, and an appreciation of the transitory quality of human experience.

Let me conclude by reiterating that the entire manner in which the analyst participates with each patient is distinctly personal to that analyst. That idiosyncratic form of participation includes the analyst's very ideas of interaction and of psychoanalysis itself. Within the heterogeneity of today's analytic community, the "frame" the analyst establishes, the very methodology through which he works, is itself a personal expression of the analyst (Aron, 1992). Although the roles of the analyst and patient are strikingly different, certainly because of the responsibility the analyst has for safeguarding the process and the well-being of the analysand, I don't regard the analyst's role as primarily one of respondent to the patient's projections. In a certain sense, psychoanalysis might be regarded as originating in Freud's projections. Whether we are looking for ghosts, intimate encounters, or internal presences, each of us devises his or her own way of using the analytic process to reach other people, find them, understand them, and be understood by them.

CHAPTER 6

THE ANALYST'S INTENTIONS

I have done much teaching over the years, and, like any teacher I have my favorite stories to illustrate different points. Whenever I teach clinical process, if I have more than about 20 minutes or so, I am likely to find a way to work in my all-time favorite story about psychoanalysis, which is not really about psychoanalysis at all. It is about music. But somehow it always seems to convey some of the central concepts I am trying to get across. I have recently realized that it has even broader significance for some of the issues with which I am struggling now. In fact, I have come to think of this story as an allegory of the recent history of psychoanalytic ideas.

As the story goes, the composer Stravinsky's recently written violin concerto was in rehearsal by a major orchestra. The solo violinist was having a very difficult time, and when the famous composer dropped by for a visit, the violinist stamped his foot, put down his violin, and announced his intention to quit. "I can't play this; nobody can play what you have written." Stravinsky replied, "Of course, of course. I know you can't play it. What I was after was the sound of somebody *trying* to play it."

The anguished cry of the violinist and Stravinsky's reply express a central feature of my experience of trying to do psychoanalysis. *What* is done in psychoanalysis is ultimately less important than the effort made and the intentions expressed in that effort. But recently I have come to realize that the fate of that poor violinist also captures something of the recent developments in thinking about the psychoanalytic process. Each psychoanalytic tradition has its own notion of what it is that the analyst should try to be: neutral, empathic, holding, containing, authentic. We have been witnessing the gradual dismantling, one by one, of any illusions about the possibility of all these projects. We have been discovering that, like Stravinsky's concerto, none of them can be accomplished as written. Of course, psychoanalysis is not alone in its self-deconstructive disillusionments. In a broader sense, every intellectual discipline in this era of postmodernism has been faced with a profound challenge to its claims to expert knowledge, authority, and technical competence.

The task of this chapter is to explore the question, given the impossibility of our traditional goals, of what we should be *trying* to do. What sort of efforts, what kind of goals, generate the best forms of specifically psychoanalytic influence? I shall begin by unpacking a moment I found particularly dense with meaning and choices as a way to set the stage for the kinds of questions I want to explore.

A Fork in the Road?

Rachel came for treatment because she felt profoundly lost. She'd been in a symbiotic relationship with her largely unemployed, extremely passive, artist boyfriend for five years. He spent virtually all of his waking hours high on marijuana, watching television and playing video-games, and she spent most of her time with him, stoned and numb. She made various efforts to do things, both out in the world and in the small house they shared, but he tended to mock or sabotage these efforts, for they had taken on the significance of acts of disloyalty to him. I believe she came for therapy at a point when she'd had enough, which she couldn't quite say directly, because being in treatment was the ultimate act of disloyalty to him.

Because of practical considerations with regard to commuting into the city and limited financial resources, we began twice-a-week therapy. Rachel was very thin, almost ethereal. There was a waiflike quality to her appearance and a gossamerlike quality to her voice and thoughts. I almost could picture the pot she smoked enveloping her with thick clouds of smoke, obscuring her presence and mind, and I occasionally found myself associating to the hookah-smoking caterpillar of "Alice and Wonderland."

Rachel's parents were wealthy and very troubled. The mother was a talented but profoundly frustrated woman who became alcoholic and emotionally abusive to her children. The father was a warm but extremely narcissistic man whose energies were occupied in business ventures and extramarital affairs. The mother felt trapped, deeply embittered, and self-pitying; the father was charming and fun to be around when he was available, but he was only episodically and randomly available. For example, in later years he might call Rachel on his car phone when he happened to be traveling in her vicinity to see if she was available for lunch, but he would never call ahead of time. It was as if she was never in his mind unless she was right in front of him. The parents maintained a very stormy marriage with a polished veneer. The children were required to appear at their dinner parties, where everything would seem wonderful and gay. But when she was not posing as her parents' "daughter," Rachel felt invisible to them.

Somewhat to my surprise, Rachel turned out to be the sort of patient that seems overripe for analytic work, and almost instantly she was able to use our work to great advantage. With some fits and starts, she quit the addictive pot-smoking, became more active in the world, and began to make her voice heard in the relationship with the boyfriend. She became increasingly vivid as a person for me, and, as the clouds cleared, I began to realize that she was quite brilliant. She decided to go to graduate school in philosophy, in which she had majored in college, as if she were reanimating her life again after an hiatus of seven years. She knew a little of my writing and dabblings in philosophy; I don't think that played a significant part in the reanimation of her involvement, although it did make possible an area of shared interest. At the last moment she applied to a handful of master's programs in the area. She was turned down by several universities, probably because of her spotty record since college, but got into a reasonably good program. Over the year and a half of the master's program, she did remarkably well, writing papers that she told me a little bit about, that were very well received and caught the attention of her teachers.

My experience of Rachel changed a great deal over the course of our work. My initial sense of her as spacy and ethereal persisted for a few months, even though she managed to make such good use of therapy. At times it seemed to me that the sessions had a shallowness to them, that I was finding myself drifting, spacy myself and fatigued, having trouble engaging her more deeply. I tried to develop useful ways of thinking about my countertransferential experiences. Perhaps there was something in them of the alcoholic haze that had saturated so much of her childhood family experience, of the schizoid absences of her parents' ways of being with her, of the depletion of vitality in her own way of using language and expressing herself. But my speaking to her about my experiences with her did not appear to alter them.

I tried to force myself to be more alert, pay more attention, but that didn't always work. The treatment hit a difficult but very important point when she started to become angry at me. The things I was saying to her sounded trite; my interpretations were merely parroting back to her things she herself had already said. She felt that she was an anonymous patient in a long and exchangeable series; I showed no evidence of really knowing *her*. I told her I thought she was partially right. There was sometimes a sense of our constructing the appearance of therapy sessions, like her parents' elaborate construction of the appearance of a family. We did not arrive at too much clarity about what had been going on, but something about our joint exploration of the problem seemed to engage us more fully in the sessions. She felt like an increasingly fuller presence to me, and she experienced me as increasingly related to her in a personal fashion. I have rarely had a sense of someone's becoming so visually transformed. I don't know if she actually gained weight or not, but she seemed to fill out, and a kind of radiance replaced her initial faded pallor.

The moment I want to describe took place several months later, when Rachel mentioned in an almost off-hand sort of way that she was thinking of applying for a transfer to one of the more prestigious philosophy departments for her doctorate. However, it was already late, she wasn't sure how to proceed, and she would probably wait until the last moment. I got very interested in the differences among the programs, which I didn't know much about. The more she told me, the clearer it became to me that she really belonged in one of the better programs and that there was no good reason why she would not be admitted.

In responding to my questions, she seemed to be somewhat phobic about the higher status universities, and as we tried to understand that fear she began to tell me about her experiences in applying to college. Her parents had had a considerable narcissistic investment in her getting into a good school, but, as with virtually everything else, they left it to her to deal with the application process on her own. Her father especially hoped she would go to the Ivy League school from which he had graduated (from which, coincidentally, I had also graduated). She messed up the application form and, again all on her own, tried to duplicate the form in a makeshift fashion. This botching may very well have contributed to her surprising rejection by the school.

I was listening to all of this with considerable concern about the extent to which she might really be sabotaging herself and the serious consequences of lost opportunities. One of the major things going on in my life at this time was my own daughter's applications to New York City high schools, which had turned out to be an extremely engrossing and anxiety-filled process. In the past several weeks I'd spent hours filling out applications and working with her on her test and interview preparations, with occasional thoughts about the longer trajectory of my daughter's applications to colleges four years hence. I found myself getting angry at Rachel's parents for what felt to me like their neglect of her, and I was concerned about what I thought might be Rachel's current repetition of that neglect in her failure to become active on her own behalf.

We explored her possible ambivalence about graduate school; there had been considerable prior exploration of her conflicts over her own growth and development as a powerful, competent woman. We both sensed that she really wanted to proceed but was inhibited about putting herself fully into it. I said a few things about her passivity and her hopes that somehow all that was necessary for the betterment of her situation might be taken care of by someone else. She agreed, but our discussion of these issues, although important, had a flat quality.

The session was drawing to a close, and I wanted to reach her with more impact. I wasn't sure whether my sense that this was a potentially fateful moment reflected my own anxiety and characterological action-orientation, or whether I was responding to a sense that she and I were both not engaging something important to her at this possibly crucial juncture in her life. I knew that I was also feeling a countertransferential competitiveness with her parents, a sense that I could be a much better parent than they, both with my own children and with her as well. I was worried about my mild sense of urgency, even though it might be justifiable in view of the deadlines in her real world options. Was I being seduced into being a rescuing father? Was I seducing her into being a neglected daughter in need of rescue? What could I make of the partisanship I felt inclined to take up on her behalf? It was certainly not neutral, nor did it seem particularly empathic. But it felt important.

Was there a danger of encouraging her into a regressive dependency on me? Was the greater than customary intensity in the countertransference a sign that I should remain silent to avoid an "enactment?" Or would remaining silent in an effort to avoid enacting something itself serve as an enactment in which, like the parents', my own concerns (in this case for appropriate analytic intervention) would lead me to fail to respond to Rachel and her needs? Would self-reflection on my own countertransference lead to a less impassioned intervention? Should I dispassionately describe to her some features of my understanding of her conflicts between her own growth and her masochistic allegiance to her neglectful parents as internal objects? Would a less impassioned response be better? Should I strive in my feelings and my tone toward a perfect Aristotelian balance between caring and respect for her autonomy? (See Mr. Palomar's efforts in an analogous project later in this chapter.) Is balance always the most analytically useful response? What to do? One important and comforting recurrent point made by some contemporary authors is that what the analyst does at any particular moment is probably much less important than the way the analyst and patient reflect on and process the choice and what happens subsequently. But still—we have to do something. We will return to this moment between Rachel and me later in this chapter. First, I want to consider the history of ideas about the analyst's intentions.

In most spheres of human endeavor, professional or otherwise, we have some sense of the goal we are trying to achieve and the way in which our efforts will move us in that direction. Psychoanalysts are surely professional practitioners of a complex and intricate craft. It takes many years to learn to do the work, and that process of learning is generally accompanied by an increasing sense of competence. Good analytic work tends to be easily recognizable, certainly within the community constituting any particular analytic school, and sometimes, despite our passionate disagreements, even cutting across different schools of analytic thought. Supervising beginners is often a startling and exhilarating experience for recent graduates, because it confronts them with just how much they *do* know, just how much they have absorbed, generally imperceptibly, over the course of their own training and practice.

But what is the activity, the set of skills, the technique that psychoanalysts become professional at? One of the major lessons in the literature on the analytic process and theory of technique over the past few decades is a lesson of profound humility—the specific activities previous generations of analysts thought they were expert at were, it turns out, actually much more complicated than they thought, and, in fact, not really possible to do, in their purest form, at all. Whatever it was we were trying to do, it turns out, actually cannot be done. We are probably most familiar with this deconstruction of the analyst's expertise with regard to the classical model.

Trying to be Neutral

The practitioner of traditional Freudian technique, as it was developed within mainstream Freudian psychoanalysis in this country, knew what the patient was supposed to do and what the analyst was supposed to do, or, more importantly, knew what both the patient and the analyst were not supposed to do. The patient was required to free associate and not to act, neither "acting-out" important unconscious conflicts outside the sessions nor "acting-in" important unconscious conflicts within the sessions. The patient was instructed to assume a passive, receptive stance toward his own mind, which allowed the entrance of all unbidden thoughts: the consequent free associations provided the raw material from which the analyst shaped his interpretations to generate insight. The locus of change for Freud is inside the patient's head, in the lifting of repression barriers and the overcoming of amnesias.

The analyst's task in the classical model was also fairly clear, although not always easy to accomplish. The analyst was supposed to be thinking about and responding silently to the patient's free associations and delivering occasional interpretations. In its purest form (although certainly not in practice, if Freud himself is taken as representative), no other speech on the part of the analyst was required or desirable, because talk other than interpretation was likely to affect and alter the flow of the patient's free associations. Noninterpretive interventions were therefore regarded as subjecting the patient to the analyst's personal influence; formal, technical neutrality protected the patient's autonomy.

Actions by the analyst, "acting out" (e.g., by forgetting a session) or "acting in" (by drifting off and letting his attention wander) were outcroppings of countertransference that operated as counterresistances, as obstacles to the analytic process. In the early decades of psychoanalysis, such countertransferences were assumed to stem from unanalyzed, unconscious conflict in the analyst. Something in the patient's material happened to trigger some unresolved experiences and conflicts from the analyst's past or current life. Thus, my associations to my own daughter and my involvement with her would be regarded as an intrusion into a more appropriate analytic state of mind of irrelevant and contaminating material. They would, by definition, suggest some neurotic, conflictual need of mine that was compromising my functioning as analyst.

In recent decades, such countertransferences have been generally assumed to include important information about the patient's material. The analyst's wandering off may very well parallel the patient's dynamically determined wandering off; where the analyst wanders *to* may provide important clues about the patient's unconscious inner conflicts. Within this framework, my thoughts and feelings about my own daughter might be regarded as relevant and useful in shaping an understanding of Rachel's own conflicts, perhaps even a projective identification of a more loving and constructive parental response toward herself that she longed for but could not herself give voice to (S.Stern, 1994). In the early decades of psychoanalytic history, the patient's resistances, including actions, came to be regarded not simply as obstacles to free association but rather as potentially useful detours. Similarly, the analyst's counterresistances, including actions, have more recently come to be regarded not simply as obstacles to the analyst's interpretive activity but as potentially useful adjuncts to it.

Nevertheless, in the traditional approach to these matters, actions on the part of both the patient and the analyst are regarded as, at best, preludes to thought and speech (e.g., Chused, 1991). To the extent that patient and analyst together continue to act rather than to think and speak, they are enacting the patient's crucial conflictual material or reenacting the patient's important historical configurations rather than thinking and speaking, remembering, and interpreting them. Greenberg (1996) has recently pointed out that Freud, in his effort to deal with the dangers of irresponsible activities on the part of the analyst, attempted "to do the impossible: he tried to ban the act" (p. 201).

Thus, the traditional analyst stayed out of sight, literally and figuratively, while the patient free associated and became active interpretively when resistances to free association emerged. The three fundamental pillars of the analyst's conduct became abstinence, anonymity, and neutrality. The classical practitioner of the craft knew she should remain scrupulously nongratifying (so the patient's drives would not find satisfaction and thereby elude the frustration that motivates thought), blankly anonymous (so the patient's transferences would emerge uncontaminated by the person of the analyst), and dispassionately evenhanded (so as not to exert any personal influence of the patient's autonomous working through of their own internal conflicts). The patient's autonomy was felt to be preserved by removing the analyst's personal impact. It was this strict emphasis on asceticism and restraint that was reflected in the once popular term "strict" Freudian.

I think it is accurate to say that there is now a widespread consensus that the analyst, despite his best intentions, actually cannot successfully operate in this way, that it simply cannot be done. There have been many contributing factors to this growing consensus, including 1) the way in which the very notion of "objectivity" itself has become problematic within the philosophy of science in general; 2) the proliferation of different schools of psychoanalytic theorizing, each with its own take on the meaning of the patient's productions; 3) the gradual admission (Silverman, 1985; Abend, 1986), even within the most conservative circles, that countertransference is not a rarity, an aberration, but, rather, is normative for analytic practice, that the analyst's own dynamics and conflicts are inevitably evoked and operative in interactions with patients; 4) the growing appreciation of the ways in which a great deal about the analyst, despite his best efforts to remain anonymous, becomes known to the patient (Hoffman, 1983; Aron, 1996); and 5) the appreciation, along with expanding theorizing about multiple levels of preoedipal as well as oedipal dynamics, that the analytic relationship, no matter how ascetically managed, is inevitably gratifying and not only frustrating to various of the patient's conflictual needs.

One of the most important and complex questions for contemporary clinicians is whether these changes within and around the field of psychoanalysis have resulted in a need for a fundamentally different model of the psychoanalytic process, which is my belief, or whether the traditional model can merely be amended and updated to meet the challenges (Spezzano, 1995). This is a very difficult issue to get a clear grasp of, because of the muddle of trying to distinguish among what clinicians actually do, what they think they are doing, and the way they talk and write about what they do with each other. Mayer (1996) has noted the very destructive impact on younger generation clinicians who, owing to the anachronistic features of the classical model, find themselves working in nontraditional ways and then struggling with a deep sense of inauthenticity, of being impostors as analysts:

> many analysts start to feel less and less like "real" analysts doing "real" analysis. As they honestly examine how they actually work,

those analysts develop an increasing and often uncomfortable sense that much of how they think they help their patients doesn't fit with the model of analytic technique to which they in principle adhere...
. A variety of consequences can follow—ranging from an insistent muddiness of thinking which is required to prevent contradictory ideas from encountering each other, to severe and disturbing lapses in conscience [p. 173].

And apologist authors defending the classical model often argue that "neutrality" was never meant to suggest detachment, as if the austere, ascetic demeanor of the traditional psychoanalyst was merely a fantasy of *New Yorker* cartoonists and tendentious critics.[1]

Because of this disingenuousness and general avoidance of an honest acknowledgment of real changes and breaks with tradition, Kernberg's (1996) recent essay "The Analyst's Authority in the Psychoanalytic Situation" stands out as a startling good-faith effort. Kernberg accepts a major portion of the critique of classical psychoanalysis of recent decades. His problem is to concede what is anachronistic about the classical model while at the same time preserving what he regards as most essential. Kernberg's central strategy for dealing with this problem is to distinguish between "anonymity" and "technical neutrality."

Kernberg links what is wrong with traditional analytic technique with the misguided concept of "anonymity" and jettisons this burdensome baggage by renouncing any aspirations to anonymity. Because the patient can easily perceive many features of the analyst as a person, the analyst's claims to be a perfect cipher are wrong, Kernberg suggests. Further, reiterating (although not citing) an argument recently made by Renik (1995), Kernberg argues that *trying* to

---

1. Defenders of the classical principle of "neutrality" as never suggesting detachment or austerity need to explain why works like Leo Stone's (1961) *The Psychoanalytic Situation* had such enormous impact. As Merton Gill (1994) put it, "An important landmark in the swing of the pendulum to counteract the overly rigid stance was Leo Stone's (1961) monograph *The Psychoanalytic Situation*.... Stone's monograph was an important step toward the revision of the concept of the analyst as an uninvolved bystander" (pp. 41–43).

be anonymous actually does great mischief because it pressures the analysand to agree that the analyst operates as an interpretive function, a faceless oracle. Ironically, the anonymity that was understood to protect the patient's autonomy by leaving the transference uncontaminated results in a demand for submission to the analyst as an idealized authority, thereby contaminating the transference.

> I believe that the concept of anonymity that strongly influenced the teaching and practice of psychoanalytic work from the 1940s through the 1960s, perhaps especially within the Kleinian and ego psychological schools, contributed to exaggerating the idealization processes in the transference to an extent that interfered with the full analysis of the transference. It fostered splitting and displacement of the negative transference and a nonanalyzed submission of the patient to the idealized analyst [Kernberg, 1996, p. 144].

This is an extraordinary admission regarding mainstream American Freudian practice, roughly equivalent to Merton Gill's (1983b) provocative statement, "Psychoanalysis as it is generally practiced is not of good quality technically" (p. 1).

Having rid himself of what is no longer defensible, Kernberg circles the wagons and rests the credibility of his method on a defense of another traditional conceptual pillar, "technical neutrality." The adjective "technical" is important here, because Kernberg seems to be reducing the kind of neutrality that he feels the analyst can credibly claim, from a more global attitude to a more narrowly defined position vis-à-vis the patient's conflicts at particular moments. In his early work on borderline conditions, Kernberg was one of the first traditional authors to suggest that countertransference is both normative and often useful. Listen carefully to the way in which Kernberg (1996) shifts back and forth between a definition of neutrality as something the analyst attains and the definition of neutrality as an ideal, as something the analyst strives for:

> Technical neutrality . . . is an objective, concerned stance regarding the patient's problems, an unwavering effort to help the patient clarify the nature of these problems, and a position equidistant between the contradictory forces operating in the patient's mind. Technical neutrality

implies an equidistance between the patient's id, superego, acting ego, and external reality, and a position of closeness to, or alliance with, the observing part of the patient's ego. Undoubtedly, such a position of technical neutrality may be considered an ideal position from which analysts tend to be torn away again and again by countertransference developments, a position that analysts must attempt to reinstate again and again by self-analytic working through of the countertransference [p. 143].

Thus, unlike earlier authors who regarded the analyst's neutrality as a steady state, Kernberg regards neutrality as a posture that is regularly lost and regained, a "perch," to use a term Modell (1991) has suggested, from which the analyst is regularly knocked off and which he just as regularly reestablishes. Similarly, Schafer (1983), another influential progressive traditionalist who has been struggling to grant increasing significance to countertransference, defines neutrality in terms of "a high degree of subordination of the analyst's personality to the analytic task at hand" (p. 6) and suggests that "the term neutrality specifies that the analyst should not take sides in the analysand's conflictual or paradoxical courses of action" (p. 167).

The claims that Kernberg and Schafer now make for the analyst's knowledge and authority are much diminished from the claims made even a couple of decades ago. Kernberg, who regards psychoanalysis as a science, thinks of the analyst as providing objective understanding of the patient's conflicts. Schafer, who regards psychoanalysis as a hermeneutic discipline, thinks of the analyst as providing master storylines, customized to the analyst's own personal dynamics and tastes, but sanctioned by the analytic community to which he belongs. But the linchpin of the analyst's credibility for both is the analyst's neutrality, the claim that, at the point of interpreting, the analyst is reflecting, not acting; dispassionate, not affectively embedded; considering the patient's conflicts, to use Thomas Nagel's (1986) phrase, from "the view from nowhere," speaking with a voice that is outside any countertransferential partisanship. By jettisoning the concept of anonymity, Kernberg is renouncing traditional claims to invisibility; but, by clinging to the concept of neutrality, Kernberg still claims that the analyst has no appreciable impact on the direction of the process, no personal impact on the patient.

It is difficult to escape the impression that defenders of analytic neutrality are fighting a losing battle, that more and more ingenuity is required to preserve less and less. What happens if one gives up this fight? What is the alternative to the insistence that the analyst has a diminishing, increasingly fragile, unstable, transitory, neutral perch on which to rest his authority? The alternative (Aron, Hoffman, Greenberg, Spezzano, Stolorow) is to view the analyst's participation as inevitably subjective, to regard the analyst's understanding of the patient as at least partially a product of the analyst's "irreducible subjectivity" (Renik, 1993). In this alternative view, countertransference is less like a storm from which one emerges periodically to regain one's perch and more like the weather itself.

Countertransference, like the weather, continually changes, but one is never without it. In this view, all actions have interpretive implications, and all interpretations are actions. Thought is not regarded, as Freud understood it, as generated through the inhibition of action; rather, thought and action are simultaneous, and continually interpenetrating facets of experience. Enactments and reenactments are not understood as detracting from interpretations, but rather as providing powerful, ongoing examples on which interpretations can be based. And sometimes, in the analytic relationship, action must precede thought and word, because the action expresses something unconscious for both patient and analyst. Because it is something unknown and unnamed, it can become known only by being inhabited and lived out in the treatment.

Thus, interpretations themselves are increasingly regarded not as alternatives to, or solutions for, enactments, but as forms of enactments themselves, or as relationship-transforming "performatives" (Gergen, 1994; Havens, 1997). As Greenberg (1996) has noted, interpretations are words, and "words are never neutral; they are our main way of acting upon others. Words plead, coerce, seduce, wound, embrace, draw in, push away. For each of us, what we say and how we say it is an extremely important part of our repertoire of actions" (p. 201).

Another way to understand the growing untenability of analytic neutrality as an attainable posture is that there has been (as noted in Chapter 4) a growing awareness of the difference between what the analyst intends and the meaning to the patient of the analyst's actions.

The largely silent analyst might well intend his silence as a neutral observational perch, while the patient may experience that silence as a sadistic withholding. In the old days, the analyst could declare the patient's experience a distortion and his own intent the reality. And Kernberg is clearly struggling hard to retain this right. But such claims seem increasingly arbitrary today. How can the analyst possibly be so motivationally unidimensional? How can the analyst, no matter how well analyzed, possibly assume that in her struggles in the counter-transference, at the moment she makes the interpretation, she is standing clear of the *"Sturm und Drang"*? How can she possibly claim to be so transparent to herself? Doesn't the analyst's "standing firm" in the face of the patient's experience of being abused often become sadistic? Isn't the posture of not "taking sides," as Schafer has put it, itself a partisan position, a side one is taking? (I am reminded here of recent rethinking of the implications of Switzerland's "neutrality" toward Nazi Germany during the Second World War.) Isn't the act of withdrawing or ascending to the analyst's perch rife with meanings to both parties? Is there only one accurate, objective meaning to the ana-lyst's actions or restraints from action, or is it plausibly interpretable in different (not all) ways (Gill, 1983b; Hoffman, 1983).

What would have been a neutral response to the clinical moment I have described in my work with Rachel? Would it have been neutral to say, "You want to be active on your own behalf but restrict your actions for fear of your own aggression and its consequences." Or "You want to be active on your own behalf but fear abandonment by your parents or the internal objects that represent them." Or "You long for a parental sort of person, like me perhaps, to take care of you in this matter, but fear the consequences of that dependence." The nice thing about these kinds of interpretations is that they reflect a cer-tain balance, as all interpretations of conflict tend to. "You want this, and also that" or "You want this and are also afraid of this." But there is something very deceptive about the internal balance in each of these interpretive sentences. They are merely balancing two things that the analyst himself has designated as important; they are hardly neutral or balanced with regard to the entire situation (Greenberg, 1997).

There is an elegance to Anna Freud's original definition of neu-trality in terms of the geometric metaphor of "equidistance" from the various constituents of mind, as a result of which we have been slow to realize the antiquated positivist assumptions upon which that definition rests. Any possible interpretation of this moment in Rachel's treatment, no matter how internally balanced, rests first on an interpretive construction of several different factors that are assigned central importance. Each interpretation leaves out, and is therefore nonneutral, with regard to the others; each one has implications for repeating qualities of the parents' involvements with her at various times, gratifying or abandoning. Equidistance depends completely on how one defines the points from which one is supposed to be equidistant. Exactly where shall we locate the id, the ego, the superego, external reality, at this moment?

Is Rachel's id manifesting itself in school as an aggressive break with her family, invested with oedipal and sexual significance? Or does school represent a dutiful playing out of superego expectations? Or does it represent the ego's healthy attempts at mastery in external reality? Perhaps it is seductive id energy that is defensively manifesting itself in Rachel's apparent longing to be guided and sheltered. Or is that her ego seeking developmentally missing ego provisions? Perhaps it is a strategy engineered by her superego to undercut her independent sexuality and aggression by channeling her newly found energy into a defensively intellectualized form of expression. Surely, before one could execute the exquisite balancing act suggested by the term "equidistance," one would have to make the various points of reference hold still. But these are not objectively determinable as if through some sort of sounding instrument; these are constructions of the analyst, who in his very aspirations to be neutral is imposing a landscape on the fluid, dynamic moment in question. To believe that one can actually be neutral in the classical sense is to believe that the psychical landscape of the patient comes predesigned, like a botanical garden, with little tags naming the specimens and arrows marking the pathways, making possible a geometrically determinable point of equidistance. The claim that equidistant neutrality protects the patient's autonomy from the analyst's influence actually masks and disclaims what is often the most powerful influence the analyst has— his impact on constructing the very terms in which the patient comes to think about and strauggle with her conflicts.

Analysts have always claimed to be neutral in relation to external reality. The analyst should not need anything particular to happen, and we have pointed to that unhurried, nondirective, nonpartisan timelessness to distinguish psychoanalysis from the more directive, behavioral, pragmatically oriented psychotherapies. But to be neutral vis-à-vis reality, one first has to decide where and what it is.

There is nothing more real than aging and the reproduction of the species, but what, exactly, are those realities? I recently heard the argument advanced by an older male analyst that young women in their 30s, feeling an urgency to marry and have babies because of their "biological clock," might do better working with male analysts, because women in this country, including female analysts, tend to be socialized to believe in the reality of that metaphorical clock. Male analysts, the argument goes, are free of that illusion and therefore are more able to attain the desirable neutral posture and discern the use of the urgency to bear a child as a resistance. But who can possibly determine the "reality" of the relationship between a woman's capacity to bear a child and her age? The biological clock itself is unquestionably real (although metaphorically expressed), but who could possibly decide where a neutral position with respect to this reality lies? (The tension between "reality" and its constructions with regard to gender is taken up in detail in the last chapter.) Surely male and female analysts construct different realities in regard to this question, as do older and younger analysts, analysts who are parents and analysts who are not parents, analysts who are relatively satisfied parents and analysts who are embittered parents, and so on.

Race is another reality all of us need to take into account. (See Altman, 1996.) But what exactly is the reality of race in our culture? The most stunning feature of the O. J. Simpson phenomenon is the dichotomous, race-linked perceptions of the relationship between the accused and the Los Angeles police. It became clear that whites and blacks in this country may live in the same geographic locale, but, psychologically speaking, their realities are, in some respects, strikingly different. I am very much a realist, and I believe that bodies, minds, and lives all come with many properties and constraints; but it is difficult to imagine how one might nonsubjectively determine what those properties and constraints are so as to position oneself equidistant from them.

The only realism that makes sense to me is a perspectival realism, in which the constituents of reality, minds as well as worlds, are necessarily viewed from some particular vantage point. Equidistance is possible only in an abstract realm of pure geometrical forms.

We noted earlier that Kernberg regards neutrality as an ideal that is episodically attainable, regularly lost and regained. Another fallback position would be to concede that, although neutrality is not attainable, it is important to preserve it as a useful goal nevertheless.[2] Of course, according to this line of argument you can't be neutral, but the analyst's job, like that of the struggling violinist, is to *try* to be neutral. Friedman (1996) seems to have taken just this position:

> If . . . the problem is merely that analysts do not know with certainty what the patient is experiencing, or what they have contributed to that experience, why wouldn't they try to standardize their behavior as far as possible so as to make the job easier? Even without pretending to obliterate one's influence or predict one's impact, it is not wholly senseless to try to keep the static down [p. 263].

Trying to be neutral certainly seems like one feasible way to define the analyst's activity. But the way Friedman uses neutrality as an unattainable ideal to strive toward illustrates how easy it is to slip back into assuming that the meaning the analyst assigns to his behavior ought to be the same to the patient. For example, the analyst might feel that he is trying to be neutral, but what does his trying to standardize his behavior mean to the patient? That depends greatly on the place in the patient's history that conventionality, standards, and efforts to conform to them hold. For a patient like Rachel, who comes from a family in which her real needs as a person were continually sacrificed to social appearances, an analyst trying to standardize his behavior might represent a nightmarish retraumatization and not be making his

---

2. W. W. Meissner (1983) notes that "it becomes for all practical purposes impossible for the analyst's values not to impinge on the analytic process, and this would include both technical and personal values. . . . value judgements seem to seep into the therapeutic process through every available pore" (pp. 581–582).

job easier at all. How does the analyst know what the "static" is without assuming that there is a clear, static-free tone somewhere? (Friedman's interest in eliminating static recalls the story of the squeaky chair of the analyst from Chapter 1.) We might consider, along with the composer John Cage, that the unintended noises sometimes make the most interesting music. Friedman is not saying, try to be neutral and learn from the ways you fall short; he seems to feel that the trying itself actually protects the analyst from getting into trouble.

There is a wonderful episode in Italo Calvino's (1983) Mr. Palomar (pp. 9–12) that may serve as an allegory on the perils of the analyst's trying to be neutral. The fact-seeking, scientific, objectivity-seeking Mr. Palomar encounters a topless sun bather on the beach and struggles to find just the right attitude toward her. At first he looks determinedly away, to prevent the woman from feeling that he is an intruder and a nuisance. But then, he reflects, by his refusal to see, he has created "a kind of mental brassiere suspended between my eyes and that bosom" (p. 10) that implicitly endorses the reactionary attitude that any sight of the breast is illicit. So, later, on returning from his stroll, he keeps his gaze rigidly straight ahead, in a studied interest in/indifference toward all features in his visual field, including the breast. He has, he hopes, "succeeded in having the bosom completely absorbed by the landscape. . . ." (p. 10). But, on further reflection, he worries that, by "flattening the human person to the level of things" he has objectified this woman and thereby expressed an expectable, offensive attribute of male superiority. So he turns to make another pass, this time allowing his gaze to pause ever so briefly in a darting glance, so as to grant that piece of the visual landscape the greater value its human significance calls for. But this is not quite right either. Mr. Palomar is an enlighted man, so wants to do his part in releasing the female bosom from "the semidarkness where centuries of sexomaniacal puritanism and of desire considered sin have kept it. . . ." (p. 11). He does an about face once again, this time expressing, through a lingering gaze accompanied by good will and gratitude, the perfect blend of "detached encouragement" (p. 11) that seems just right. However, as you've probably guessed, by this time the sunbather has had it, covers herself, and leaves with a huff. "The dead weight of an intolerant tradition prevents anyone's properly understanding the most enlightened intentions, Palomar bitterly concludes." (p.12) It is hard not to wonder how many analytic patients have similarly departed the scene in response to their analysts' striving so hard to get it just right.

One might disparage such tilting after windmills as ill advised, but all the most important of the postclassical models of therapeutic action seem similarly based on efforts to reach unattainable ideals.

Alternative Ideals

Consider the place of empathy in self psychology, which Kohut established as a precondition of psychoanalytic cure. Sometimes Kohut seems to have believed that the empathic stance is attainable as a more or less steady state, and critics of self psychology have routinely disparaged self psychology as canonizing the analyst as a creature of infinite empathy and kindness. But a more sophisticated reading of self-psychological texts suggests that what Kohut felt was important was not the attainment of an impossible steady state of empathic goodness, but *trying* to be empathic, especially trying to be empathic concerning the patient's disappointments in his subjective experience of the analyst's empathic failures. Because empathic failure is a subjective experience for the patient, there is no way for the analyst even to begin to know how to be perfectly empathic. Flawless empathy, Kohut came to believe, is not only impossible, but also undesirable. It is the trying itself, and failing, and trying again, that creates the new selfobject experience wherein lies the developmentally reparative impact.

Currently, all psychoanalytic schools claim that empathy was always part of their repertoire, but not everyone agrees that trying to be empathic should be the focal point of the analyst's efforts. Trying to do one thing allows other things to fade into the background, and one cannot try to do everything at once. Bromberg (1988), for example, suggests that, from his vantage point in interpersonal psychoanalysis, with its emphasis on the two parties in the analytic situation and their impact on each other, the self-psychological approach draws attention away from the analyst's experience and is therefore like "listening with one deaf ear." James Fosshage (1992) has responded to this sort of critique by attempting to stretch the self-psychological methodology into an oscillation between listening from what he calls the patient's vantage point to listening from within the analyst's. Of course, perfect stereophonic balance is unattainable, but this new ideal certainly shifts and broadens what the analyst is trying to do.

Interpersonal psychoanalysis developed in a dialectic between two very different ideals: Sullivan's image of the therapist as expert, micromanaging the patient's anxiety level the way a conductor plays an orchestra: and Erich Fromm's image of the analyst as truth-speaking and honest. Ultimately, (as noted in Chapter 3), Fromm's approach had the greater clinical impact, as contemporary interpersonal analysts strive for a mode of engaging the patient that emphasizes authentic responsivness. But authenticity has proved more complex and elusive than it seemed in Fromm's day, and the current interpersonal literature speaks much more of continual deconstruction, emergence from embeddedness, and enactments, than it does of a steady pulpit for speaking the truth. In a sense, deconstruction itself has emerged as a new ideal. As I noted in Chapter 3, contemporary interpersonal authors (e.g., Levenson, Gill) emphasize continual analysis of the transference–countertransference interaction as a device for factoring out the analyst's influence. But this methodology merely perpetuates the ideal of an influence-free analysis so central to the classical notion of neutrality. It has been recently noted (Mitchell, 1993; Hoffman, 1996) that there is, in fact, no way to factor out the analyst's participation. Continual deconstruction and analysis of countertransference does not simply remove impact—it is a powerful, very influential form of announcing the analyst's values and concerns.

Other ideals have emerged through the developmental concepts of British object relations theory. Bion (1967) offered analytic practitioners the rich notion of "containment" to describe the analyst's function of housing and registering the projected dimensions of the analysand's experience. Bion suggested that the analyst work with "neither memory nor desire" to fashion herself into the broadest, most uncontaminated vessel for containment. Taken as literally attainable, Bion's "containment" poses all the same problems as the classical ideal of neutrality but here a squeaky-clean container substitutes for the neutral, blank screen. But taken as an ideal, it certainly seems like an interesting thing to *try* to do.

Winnicott's concept of the "holding environment" has provided a similarly useful postclassical analytic intention. The analyst might usefully be seen as providing various maternal functions, some by trying to provide them, and others by just showing up and acting responsibly. It becomes a bit fuzzy sometimes to try to decide whether Winnicott-inspired authors believe that the analyst actually serves universal parental functions, or something close enough to universal parental functions to compensate for early maternal failure, or something the patient merely believes to replace missing experiences, sometimes getting it right, sometimes merely coming close, sometimes failing miserably.

Winnicott has been criticized by interpersonalists as proffering a model that infantalizes the patient, and Jessica Benjamin (1988) has developed a powerful, but sympathetic critique of Winnicott's notion of the "holding environment." She argues that it reproduces the destructive, ultimately sexist idealization of women in general and mothers in particular as lacking their own subjectivity. A mother or analyst as a perfect holding environment would be a disaster, this argument goes, because it obliterates the "other" and undermines the central struggle for intersubjective recognition.

Joyce Slochower (1996a, b) has built upon these interpersonal and feminist critiques of traditional psychoanalytic romantic developmentalism by presenting a much more sophisticated version of the "holding environment" as clinical technique. She argues that, although the analyst can never, in fact, obliterate her own subjectivity by attaining a perfect "holding" posture, and that although the patient is necessarily always in some sense aware of the analyst's imperfections and struggles in this regard, *trying* to hold the patient's experience at the expense of one's own is, for many disturbed patients, a necessary and constructive thing to do.[3]

One of the ironies that has accompanied the tumbling of one analytic ideal after the next has been the establishment of a state of nonin-

---

3. Anthony Bass (1996) has challenged the notion of a generic sort of "holding" in which the analyst's own subjectivity fades into the background, and Slochower (1996) and Bass have engaged in a fruitful and illuminating dialogue about the varieties of "holding," always in intersubjective terms.

tention and even nonknowledge as a counterideal. Bion and Lacan are important figures in this trend. Both were very sensitive to the delicate relationship between language and experience, the ways in which words, like the analyst's interpretations and analytic theories, become easily frozen into shallow, static reifications. This is why Bion (1967) warned us about the limitations of the analyst's remembering anything about and wanting anything for his patient and recommended that readers burn his books after reading them. Similarly, Lacan, emphasized the need for the analyst not to collude with the patient's idealization of him as "the one who is supposed to know."

Avoiding ideals is one thing; avoiding intentions is something else. How one can desire to have no desire, or intend to have no intentions, is the sort of conundrum practitioners of meditation spend a lifetime struggling with. Phillips (1994) has captured some of the paradoxical impossibility of Bion's injunction by pointing out that, when Bion "advocated that the analyst should engage in the psychoanalytic session 'without memory or desire' . . . he had both to remember to do that, and want to" (p. 30).

The fate of Bion and Lacan as figures within the analytic world is instructive concerning the impossibility of deidealization as an ideal. The cultlike followings they have attracted and the absorption with their writings as esoteric texts with hidden meanings, speak to the charismatic power of appealing, brilliant analytic authors who claim no knowledge. The avoidance of false knowledge claims and idealization through the eschewing of intentions is the latest in a series of ideals that have proven unattainable. The traditional analyst cannot really be neutral. The self-psychological analyst cannot really be empathic. The developmentalist, no matter how hard she tries, cannot really reparent. The Lacanian cannot help being one who knows things. And the interpersonalist who might actually *try* to be authentic involves himself in the same contradiction in terms as the poor consumer of popular psychology who is *trying* to be spontaneous.

Much of the namecalling and disparagement among current psychoanalytic schools derives from a confusion between intentions and claims of attainment. Critics of classical psychoanalysis accuse traditional Freudians of acting in a robotic fashion, while the most thoughtful defenders of traditional theory of technique, like Lawrence Friedman, argue the importance of *trying* to be neutral and objective, despite its impossibility. Critics of self psychology accuse the self psychologist of soppy sentimental reassurance, while thoughtful defenders of self psychology and intersubjectivity theory argue that change occurs not in the moments of empathy but in moments of empathic failure. Critics of interpersonal psychoanalysis accuse interpersonalist's of a sort of impulse-ridden, blurting-it-out approach, while thoughtful defenders of interpersonal psychoanalysis (Ehrenberg, 1992; Aron, 1996) argue that meaningful authenticity requires a selectivity of disclosure and that what might seem authentic at one moment is likely to appear in more complex terms later on (Mitchell, 1993; Hoffman, 1996). Thus, each group tends to regard itself as realistic in terms of its own ideals while regarding advocates of other models as blind believers in illusions. Probably the most accurate way to characterize contemporary models of psychoanalytic technique would be not as clinicians practicing neutrality, empathy, authentic engagement and holding, but as clinicians who feel that trying to be neutral, trying to be empathic, trying to be authentic, or trying to "hold" the patient's experience is likely to have the most desirable impact on the patient.

The Analytic Compass

Is trying to do something that is impossible the most useful framework for the analyst's intentions? I think not. I am in sympathy with Hoffman's (1996) argument (see also Renik, 1996) against the perservation of impossible ideals for the analyst's participation, no matter how modestly one acknowledges inevitably falling short of those ideals:

> I do not think it is good to set up intrinsically irrational ideals that do violence to human nature. Aspiring to walk on water and striving to be able to do that are bound to *interfere* with learning to swim. Such a standard of locomotion is no less wrongheaded if we humbly "admit" that, since nobody is "perfect," those attempting to walk will surely get wet. The ideals of accurate empathy and perfect affective attunement, like the ideal of perfect neutrality, encourage the development of inap-

propriate ego ideals which in turn promote defensive illusions about what we have been able to accomplish, along with misleading acknowledgments of our "imperfection." All of that distracts us from the more relevant issue which is to consider, not whether, but *how* we have been personally involved with our patients [p. 122].

What is it that I try to do? I would describe the intention that shapes my methodology as a self-reflective responsiveness of a particular (psychoanalytic) sort. In putting it this way, I am suggesting that my way of working entails not a striving for a particular state of mind, but an engagement in a process.

I find that aspiring to states of mind like "evenly hovering attention" (Freud), the "analytic attitude" (Schafer), and "reverie" (Bion) foreclose other possibilities, other kinds of responsiveness to my patients. There are times when it seems useful for my attention to be highly focused, not evenly hovering; there are times when I feel that my patients need a more genuine response from me, not an attitude; there are times when concerted, careful reasoning seems more fruitful than reverie. I find that I am using myself most productively when I struggle to understand the ways in which a patient is presenting himself to me in a particular session and then to try to reflect on the kinds of responses I find myself making. What version of myself is evoked by the patient's presence today? Who am I? What am I like when I am with them?

Because learning to do analytic work is such a harrowing business, because there is so much intensity, responsibility, confusion, and dread, we work hard to cultivate a version of self that we can recognize as professional, psychoanalytic, and competent. But the most interesting and productive moments and periods of analytic work are often precisely those spent outside that familiar, reassuring professional self—times when confusion, dread, excitement, exasperation, longing, or passion is the dominant affect. This does not involve a cultivation of not knowing or noncontrol, but an effort to free oneself from compulsive knowing and mandatory control. What I find most helpful is not aspiring to a state of nonintention, but remaining as open as possible to a flow of a variety of intentions, all of which then become the object of self-reflective scrutiny.

This kind of analytic participation is neither simple nor naive; self-reflective responsiveness to the patient is a highly cultivated skill. It assumes that the mind of the analyst, like that of the patient, is characterized by shifting, discontinuous self-states and self-organizations; it presumes that mind is generated in interpersonal fields of reciprocal influence; it presumes that self-reflection is itself always, necessarily, perspectival and highly selective. It takes a long time to learn to experience and use oneself in this fashion. Doing so involves hearing and following different levels of meaning at the same time, something like the way a simultaneous translator learns to hear one language and speak another or the conductor of an orchestra can hear separate lines that generate polyphony. The analyst, in this view of analytic process, learns to track and engage in, simultaneously, different lines of thought, affective response, self-organization.[4]

There are, therefore, in the same analyst, many kinds of analytic minds. I don't try to keep them in a state of suspended, even balance. I move back and forth among different states, different modes of participation; sometimes rapidly, sometimes continuing one particular mode of participation for an extended period; sometimes finding myself responding in a particular fashion, sometimes willing myself into a mode of participation that feels more useful. This is why I find different sorts of inspiration from reading very different analytic writers. I have learned a great deal about detailed, focused inquiry from Sullivan, richly imaginative reverie from Ogden, emotional connection from Searles, a respect for the patient's privacy from Winnicott, a playfulness in the work from Phillips, a psychoanalytic form of sacredness from Loewald. And there are many more. What has been most useful to me has been the freedom to respond variously at different times and to be able to draw on a wide variety of potential responses in my repertoire when it seems useful.

---

4. Renik (1993) has described a similar approach to the analyst's participation with a new set of guiding metaphors—the analyst as skier or surfer—to replace the traditional ones of the analyst as surgeon or reflecting mirror, "someone who allows himself or herself to be acted upon by powerful forces, knowing that they are to be managed and harnessed, rather than completely controlled" (p. 565).

Thus, one goal the analyst might usefully try for is a self-reflective responsiveness to the patient in each particular session.[5] I am suggesting that, within that global intention, we are always committing ourselves to one or another form of responsiveness and participation and foreclosing others. At any particular moment, we might choose to be even handed or explicitly partisan; sympathetic or self-expressive; dogged or yielding. I believe that we make these continual choices on the basis of an implicit sense of an ongoing analytic process that we are trying to enrich and deepen through our participation. There are times when it feels to me that keeping quiet is the best way I can help to deepen the process; other times an interpretation seems necessary, or the expression of a feeling, or a concern, or a fantasy. I believe that each clinician maintains an implicit model of rich, particularly analytic experience, and that implicit model serves, as I suggested in the previous chapter, as a kind of preconscious compass, guiding the perpetual choices that constitute analytic participation.

The compass used by each analyst is unique. There is in psychoanalysis, unlike in navigating the earth, no objective, singular electromagnetic field and generic compasses. Each analyst's clinical judgment is shaped by his or her personal integration of psychoanalytic models and concepts, seasoned with his or her personal dynamics, character, and life experience. Theoretical concepts are a crucial part of this personal guidance system. Psychoanalysts spend a great deal of time absorbing psychoanalytic ideas, adopting some, abandoning others, transforming many, to arrive at their own synthesis. (This is why I am opposed to atheoretical ecclecticism or model-mixing, which ignores the way each clinician molds his or her own, distinctly personal model.) That conceptual integration, saturated with our own life experience, provides each of us with an implicit sense of the richness and depth of experience, and that integration in the point of reference in relation to which we make clinical choices.

---

5. There have been several, recent, closely related conceptualizations of the analyst's responsiveness. See, for example, Sandler's (1976) notion of "role responsiveness," Bacal's (1985) notion of "optimal responsiveness," and Hirsch's (1987) reversal and extension of Sullivan's concept with his own notion of "observant-participation."

In actuality, these choices go by too fast to allow prior conscious reflection on all of them. But when I try, retrospectively, to articulate the implicit, preconscious nature of these choices, they go something like this: does the reverie I find myself in now seem related to the patient's material in some fashion, or does it seem to be taking me further away? Does focusing hard and closely on the details or confusion in what the patient is saying open up impacted areas of the patient's experience, or does it feel as if it is diverting me into an obsessional muddle and away from a fuller emotional response? Is what I am feeling now about the patient likely to be useful to her in the service of her own self-understanding, or will expressing it draw her into a diversionary preoccupation with me? Are the words we are using bringing light into unformulated areas of experience (Donnel Stern,) or narrowing and deadening them? Is the sense of affective attunement we are both feeling at the moment opening up a new kind of sharing, or is it perpetuating a collusive sheltering from the world? Is the privacy the patient is experiencing at the moment serving as a potential space for new experience or is it a chronic retreat from old fears? Is the playfulness of the moment establishing a ground for self-exploration (a la Winnicott and Loewald), or as if a playing around, to avoid grappling with serious and very real features of life? A good part of the time, the anwers to these questions are not clear, and yet the choices are continually made anyway. These microchoices, which constitute clinical judgment, can be made only with relative degrees of uncertainty and a commitment to later revisions. But the questions themselves are significant, and our dedication to this kind of questioning represents our greatest commitment to the integrity of the process.

In the classical theory of technique, the fundamental axis on which clinical choices were made consisted of the alternatives of gratification or frustration. Gratification was undesirable because it locked infantile instinctual derivatives into place; frustration was desirable because it set the state for remembering and insight. This classical frame of reference lent an intellectual, rationalistic cast to traditional clinical practice, which, I believe, has been broadly replaced by a concern for the deepening and broadening of the range of experience in postclassical practice. A more relevant axis for clinical choices in contemporary psychoanalysis is the distinction between opening and closing, or vitalizing and deadening. Thus, one of my fundamental concerns is to shape my participation in a fashion that minimizes my constraints on the patient's range of experience and to help her to minimize her own constraints.

The Boundaries of Psychoanalysis

Some forms of participation are outside the boundaries of what I would regard as psychoanalysis, such as, to use extreme examples, forming a business partnership or having sex with a patient. I believe that in the long run, the constraints that the patient would accrue through those kinds of participations would far outweigh the immediate potential enrichment of experience. But the debate about less obvious options is instructive because it forces each of us to consider our own process of clinical decision making.

For example, when does talking about the interaction between patient and analyst enhance the process, and when does it detract from the process? In the classical literature, dating back to Freud's (1910) important paper on "Wild Analysis," the major consideration with regard to this question was timing. The goal was to achieve as close to total insight as possible, and the analyst's job was to time interpretations so that they corresponded with unconscious material whose derivatives had just begun to spill out into the preconscious. That way the patient could recognize and use the analyst's interpretations. Today, when the interactive features of the analytic relationship are regarded as such a central element in both the process and the cure, there is another set of considerations. What impact is putting something into words likely to have on the affective experience of both participants and their relationship to each other? Talking about what is happening in any relationship (analytic or otherwise) tends to have a significant impact on that relationship—it creates self-consciousness. The double meaning of that word suggests its dual potential, constructive and destructive, in the analytic process: sometimes consciousness of self expands awareness, agency, and the potential for growth; sometimes self-consciousness scares away the tentative emergence of anxiety-filled, conflictual feelings. The factors governing the decision either to interpret various kinds of feelings in the patient or to disclose various kinds of feelings in the analyst are complex indeed.

Consider what has probably become the most controversial technical issue in recent years. Should the analyst ever disclose erotic feelings in the countertransference? Kernberg (1995) says no, never, because the very prohibition against disclosure makes it safe for him to experience his sexual fantasies about his patients. This is an interesting point, but it avoids the equally important question of the impact, and potential constraints, on the patient's experience of being in the presence of an analyst who gives himself over to his sexual fantasies in the context of an absolute prohibition against the patient's ever knowing anything about what is going on. I am sure that for some patients this might be a condition of safety, but I imagine that others would experience it as perverse and dangerous. Glen Gabbard (1994) has insisted that the disclosure of sexual interest in the countertransference is simply too arousing to be safe, and I am sure there are analytic dyads for whom this is true. But Davies (1994) has described a case in which not disclosing sexual interest in the countertransference locked patient and analyst in a retraumatizing reenactment, in which collusive disavowal of what seemed to be an essential aspect of the transference–countertransference process posed a more dangerous risk than the disclosure itself.

Gabbard and Lester (1995) provide a very helpful exploration of the complex problems of trying to balance a more open, contemporary model of the analyst's participation with a responsible approach to protecting the patient's boundaries. But their concerns often seem one sided to me. The metaphor that recurs throughout the book is the "slippery slope" from a more expressive use of countertransference experience to disastrous sexual transgressions with patients. What Gabbard and Lester don't appreciate is that the transference–countertransference mountain has two sides: there is also a slippery slope from excessive analytic restraint and avoidance of countertransference to a frozen, disastrous detachment from the patient. Excessive emotional detachment is just as fertile ground for sexual violations as excessive intimacy. The failure to recognize the dangers of denied involvement as well as of confessed involvement threatens to become a kind of "reefer madness"-approach to countertransference disclosure. In my clinical experience, I continually find myself on one or the other slope of that mountain, readjusting my participation accordingly. There are all kinds of dangers, not just one, and restraint, while often desirable, is not a universal safeguard. It is in the very nature of the analytic experience that the analyst's intentions are disrupted and fail (Slavin and Kriegman in press), just as it is inevitable that the patient's intentions, derived from old object relations, are disrupted and fail. A crucial piece of the work is the creative, mutually vitalizing, and satisfying negotiation of that situation (Pizer, 1992).

The relationship between feelings and talking is very complex. As Greenberg (1996) suggests, talk is a form of action. Some talk intensifies feelings; some talk creates a self-consciousness that squashes feelings; some talk creates a constructive kind of self-consciousness that enriches and transforms feelings. Talking about sexual feelings can be a form of seduction or foreplay; alternatively, talking about sexual feelings in a context in which those feelings have silently come to dominate an interaction can open up the possibility for something else to happen. Again, the relevant concern is not whether talk will be gratifying or frustrating, but whether talk will help open up and vitalize the patient's experience or contribute to shutting it down and deadening it.

It is essential to avoid the illusion that these choices are made simply objectively. A sense of the depth and richness of experience can be arrived at only by a particular person, a particular analyst, with her own life experience. But it is also essential to avoid a false and postured humility that fails to differentiate between analysts and everyone else. Analytic clinicians make informed choices; we learn a great deal about the depth and richness of experience from our cumulative clinical practice, the analytic literature, and our own analysis.

Returning to Rachel

I want to return to the moment between Rachel and me I have used as a take-off point for these reflections. What I said was something like this:

You know, it is my impression from talking to you and listening to what you say about other people's responses to you, that you are an extremely talented woman. Because you so expect a lack of positive response, you play it safe by setting things up to make it unlikely that you will get where you want to go. I think your parents really neglected you by not helping you with the college applications and that you are in danger of repeating that neglect yourself by not being more active now. I am aware of having the impulse to ask you to bring in the applications so that I can go over them with you. I am not sure whether actually doing that would be a good thing or a bad thing, helpful or not, but I wanted to tell you what I was thinking.

Rachel had an immediate and powerful response to this. She smiled broadly, sort of lighting up, and said she thought I was right. She made a few other comments, but the session soon came to a close. The following session she came in with a bad cold and spoke about depressive feelings, past and present, in relation to being sick. I decided not to ask her about her reactions to the previous session. A Kleinian would probably feel my departing from the strict function of an analytic object had made her sick. In retrospect, I wonder whether she was testing to see whether our connecting around a view of her as strong and competent precluded my allowing her to be sick and in need of care. I decided not to ask her either about her applications or about her reactions to the previous session; I tried merely to stay with her in her sick, depressive state.

Rachel opened the following session by reporting that there were various tasks she had set for herself in relation to her applications but that she had not been able to accomplish them. She reported this in a sort of sing-song, little-girl voice, as if she were explaining to a third-grade teacher why she had not done her homework. I asked her about that tone and her feelings about what I had said in the previous session. I wondered whether she had taken on these tasks ambivalently in connection with some conflictual concerns about pleasing me. She acknowledged some such feelings but said that she was sort of playing with them by starting the session the way she did. The major reaction, she felt, was that I had been right about her losing touch with who she was and what she could do, and that insight seemed very important to her. She felt that the applications were the right thing for her and that she was frightened to take that seriously. She remembered my reporting only that I had the impulse actually to help her with them, not that I thought that we actually should. She realized that she was certainly capable of doing them, but there was something frightening about taking herself so seriously in that way. In later sessions, we tracked her movements historically in and out of a sense that she and her life were important and her powerful longings for someone to care enough about her so that it was possible for her really to please that person by fulfilling his or her hopes for her. There were some very poignant moments when she and I realized how much she felt that to take herself seriously meant giving up her deep longing to be taken in hand and nurtured in that loving way by someone else.

Rachel and I came to regard this part of our work as very important. In retrospect, I think its importance lay not in my trying to be neutral, empathic, authentic, or holding, but in my becoming aware of an intense reaction to what felt like her self-denegration and my strong inclination to become actively partisan on her behalf. There seemed to be something important about sharing this caring feeling toward her and expressing it in a way that she could feel as real.

I offer this vignette not as an example of the "right" thing to do, but as an example of a clinical choice at an intense moment, in an effort to unpack the implicit intentions that form the context for such choices.

This is both the worst of times and the best of times for psychoanalysis. In this age of delegitimsted authorities and cynical management of care, we have been challenged to shed anachronistic claims to authority and knowledge and, at the same time, to refind what is best and most imporant about psychoanalysis to anchor a renewed sense of pride and relevance in the impact we have on people's lives when we do what we try to do.

CHAPTER 7

THE ANALYST'S KNOWLEDGE
AND AUTHORITY

T here is no issue on the contemporary psychoanalytic scene, either in our literature or in our clinical conferences and discussions, more important than our ongoing, wide-ranging efforts to understand and redefine the nature of the analyst's knowledge and authority. In some sense, this problem subsumes all other current issues and developments, for it raises questions both about the very claims psychoanalysis makes for itself as a discipline and about what we, as clinicians, think we are offering our patients. It is also a key ingredient of any position on both the history of psychoanalysis and the important question of the relationship between contemporary psychoanalysis and the classical tradition.

What sort of expertise do psychoanalysts have? Is the kind of knowledge and authority we claim for ourselves today the same kind of knowledge and authority claimed by Freud and his generation of clinicians? There are many different facets to the problem of knowledge and authority in psychoanalysis, and it would take a hefty volume even to begin to do them justice.

What I intend to do in this chapter is to outline the kind of knowledge and authority that I believe today's analytic clinician can justifiably claim, an expertise in meaning making, self-reflection, and the organization and reorganization of experience. The kind of authority and knowledge that I highlight in this chapter, however, has often been difficult to see clearly and hold on to because it becomes obscured by other, closely related problems concerning psychoanalytic politics and transformations in philosophy of science. Our task here is to get to the heart of the problem for today's clinicians, but to do that, we first have to peel back other dimensions of the problem, to traverse some sweeping historical and philosophical terrain.

The Nature of Knowledge: Psychoanalytic and Otherwise

Let us begin by peering out from the seemingly self-contained community of matters psychoanalytic onto the world around us. There we find pervasive changes in ideas about ideas, in understandings of what it means to know anything. For almost 350 years, from the beginnings of the scientific revolution in the 17th century to the mid-20th century, Western culture moved more and more pervasively toward a world view and self-understanding dominated by rationalism, objectivism, and scientism. Of course, there were counterpoints and countercurrents, but in many respects, Freud's era, the last decades of the 19th century and the first decades of the 20th century, was the apogee of this extraordinary movement. Freud took great pains to argue the scientific status of psychoanalysis as a discipline. Psychoanalysis was a part of science, the part involving the exploration, understanding, and control of that domain of the natural world constituted by the human mind. Psychoanalysis was part of the general scientific *Weltanschauüng* of the time and claimed for itself what any other science claimed for itself, no more and no less (Freud, 1933).[1]

---

1. Although the major thrust of Freud's positioning of psychoanalysis as a discipline is as a science, there are many complex subplots within the richness of Freud's writings. Many commentators have argued that Freud also viewed psychoanalysis, at least in potential, as a very different sort of discipline, of a

It is important to distinguish science from scientism, the former referring to the accumulation of certain kinds of knowledge by way of certain methods, the latter referring to the belief that such knowledge will tell us all we need to know about human experience, meaning, and values. It is not insignificant that Freud considered religion to be the greatest adversary of psychoanalysis, because he believed that psychoanalysis, and science in general, were in the process of generating knowledge that would serve as a much firmer basis for answering all the questions that religion had previously addressed. As Loewald (1977) has put it:

> Freud's insistence on the centrality of sexuality vis-à-vis Jung was in good part a fight against the religiously and theologically tinged, moralistic separation of and opposition between the sacred and the profane, between earthly body and sexual lust versus heavenly spirit and divine love or, in more secularized terms, between instinctual life and spiritual life. It was a fight against what Freud saw as a religious or philosophical escapism in the face of the human condition [pp. 413–414].

Psychoanalysis in Freud's day was both scientific and scientistic; the analyst's knowledge and authority were one and the same. His knowledge, scientific knowledge, gave him the authority, authorizing him to pronounce the definitive understandings about the realm of nature he was in the best position to understand—the patient's mind.

Since Freud's time, the pendulum has swung back in the other direction. Science itself has continued to advance, to generate knowledge, in often astounding fashion. But scientism, the faith that science would toss off, as a byproduct, the ultimate answers to the questions that are most important to us in human terms—scientism—has faded. There are many signs in contemporary culture of an often desperate groping around for some other footing to serve as a basis for self-understanding, the establishment of personal values and meaning, even to provide an ethical framework to help us best use science itself.

---

spiritual, hermeneutic, or intersubjective nature (see Bettelheim, 1982; Habermas, 1968; Lear, 1990).

Both religion and spirituality more generally have made comebacks, and one sees the search for a framework for value and meaning in a wide array of contemporary phenomena, from the most abstract discourse about postmodernism to cynical political manipulation and rhetoric about "family values." There are many ways in which this swing of the pendulum has been too extreme, overcorrecting for previous skewing; pendulums have a way of doing that. In its more extreme versions, objectivism is replaced by a total subjectivism and facile relativism, rationalism by a celebration of irrationalsm, and science is reduced to cult status. The more useful approach emerges when we grasp that the problem has not been science itself, but scientism, our inflated expectations of science, the mistaken faith that science will provide answers to our most personal questions of meaning and value.

These broad, culturewide upheavals and developments have enormous significance for psychoanalysis. If psychoanalysis is to remain vital as a discipline and a treatment, it has to be responsive to the shifting cultural and historical contexts of the lives of both analysands and analysts. It can hardly survive in the monkish isolation traditionally generated by psychoanalytic pretensions of existing on a higher or deeper plane from the rest of humanity. Some of the recent attacks on psychoanalysis in the public forum are aspects of this broad reaction to the scientism of earlier analytic generations. Clay feet are being rapidly exposed beneath the robes of virtually every traditional institution and authority, and psychoanalysis is no exception.

Because of the swing of the pendulum away from the scientism most of us were brought up on, we are particularly vulnerable to a clinical state I have observed in psychoanalysts that I have come to think of as the "Grünbaum Syndrome." This may afflict psychologist-analysts more than others: I don't know. I have come down with it several times myself. It begins with some exposure to the contemporary philosopher Adolph Grünbaum's (1984) attack on psychoanalysis. Grünbaum wants to indict psychoanalysis for not meeting the criteria he designates as necessary for an empirical, scientific discipline. Since the analyst's interpretations operate at least partially through suggestion, he argues, there is no way of testing their validity in any independent fashion. What follows is several days of guilty anguish for not having involved oneself in analytic research. There may be outbreaks of efforts to remember how analysis of variance works, perhaps even pulling a 30-year-old statistics text off the shelf and quickly putting it back. There may be a sleep disturbance and distractions from work. However, it invariably passes in a day or so, and the patient is able to return to a fully productive life.

The most striking thing about Grünbaum's impact on psychoanalysis is the extraordinary play his critique has attracted despite its almost total irrelevance to contemporary clinicians.[2] The reason virtually all clinicians suffering from the Grünbaum syndrome put the statistics text back on the shelf within a day or two is that clinicians tend to be satisfied (if not complacent) with kinds of confirmation different from the singular empirical one Grünbaum insists on. Nevertheless, there are several important features of psychoanalysis as a discipline that have contributed to our vulnerability, as a field, to Grünbaum's kind of critique.

Knowledge Claims: Excessive and Legitimate

First, there are the cultist features of traditional psychoanalytic institutions and literature. Analysts have often claimed for themselves an esoteric knowledge of mysterious realms and expressed that knowledge in thickly jargonized accounts, inaccessible to the uninitiated. Because they felt they had singular, proprietary rights of access to the unconscious, traditional psychoanalytic authors claimed a unique, foundational knowledge of the underpinnings of all human experience. Every now and again someone like Grünbaum comes along to burst that bubble by arguing that the psychoanalytic situation is not methodologically pure enough to justify such claims; they have not

---

2. This is not to say that the issue of empirical validation itself is irrelevant to contemporary clinicians (especially outcome studies), but, rather, that Grünbaum's (1984) narrowly defined basis of validation misses so much of the very intersubjective nature of the analytic process. For an in-depth exploration of Grünbaum's work in this context, see Curtis, 1996; Fourcher, 1996; Jacobson, 1996; Protter, 1996; and Schwartz, 1996.

been convincingly substantiated by nonclinical (methodologically controlled) experimentation. Those advancing this sort of critique are right, but psychoanalysts had no business making those claims in the first place.

Second, there *has* been a strong authoritarian current in the political management of psychoanalysis (Benjamin, 1997), at times almost Stalinist in proportion. From Freud's secret Committee, to the banishment of dissidents, to the kind of control Melanie Klein maintained over the minds and publications of her followers (see Grosskurth, 1986), to the medicalization of psychoanalysis in the United States and the occasionally medieval practices of both the American Psychoanalytic Association and the International Psycho-Analytical Association—the reigning political powers within psychoanalysis have hardly allowed psychoanalytic theorizing to flourish in an atmosphere of freedom and open exchange. It is true that from Freud's day to ours psychoanalysis has often been under siege, in one way or another. But like the Bolsheviks, the guardians of psychoanalysis often seemed not to grasp that the greater danger is not the wrong ideas but rigidly held ideas. This has become much clearer to us today, and part of the vitality of postclassical psychoanalysis comes from its emancipation from the constraints of Freudian orthodoxy.

For many, there is a clear analogue between the illegitimate wielding of power in classical psychoanalytic politics and the orthodox analyst's illegitimate claim to a singular scientific knowledge and authority vis-à-vis the patient's mind. In recent years, there has been a broad-scale democratization of psychoanalytic institutes that has been constructive and liberating. And there have been attempts to democratize the analytic relationship. Some lines of contemporary psychoanalytic thought, in critiquing classical theory, seem to offer a kind of relativism or epistemological democracy as the major alternative to what is taken to be classical authoritarianism. It has seemed as if the alternative to the analyst's traditional, arbitrary claims to exclusive, objective knowledge is the renunciation of objectivity and the avoidance of truth claims altogether. This sort of relativism amounts to a kind of unconditional surrender to the kind of critique Grünbaum presents, and a confusion of political issues with problems of knowledge.

Often missed in these battles between anachronistic positivism and total relativism is that the convictions developed both by analytic clinicians and by their patients rest on an intuitive, pragmatic credibility, a kind of enriched common sense. Ironically, by claiming a special, esoteric knowledge and privileged expertise, and by trying to protect the Truth through institutional control, psychoanalysts have traditionally deprived themselves of the strongest, most compelling basis for the most important thing they have to offer—a method of self-reflection and participation that is, generally, extraordinarily useful, immediately graspable, and enriching.

The philosopher Thomas Nagel (1995) has offered, in response to Grünbaum and similar critics, a very persuasive account of psychoanalytic knowledge. Nagel views psychoanalysis as an extension of what he calls "commonsense psychology," the fundamental human activities through which we make meaning out of our experiences with other people. We are constantly making assumptions about what is going on in other people's minds without the benefit of methodologically controlled, empirical verification. This assumption of meaning is a precondition to functioning in a world of other people. He writes, "When we interpret other people . . . we are trying to understand, within the limits of a nonscientific psychology, what really makes people tick, and we often hope to be confirmed by the person's own self-understanding" (p. 28).

There is battle being waged in philosophical circles over whether science provides objective knowledge or merely interesting and useful narratives about things like rocks and stars. Radical constructionists like Richard Rorty (1991) and Kenneth Gergen (1994) regard science as no closer to objectivity in any absolute sense than any other belief system, only more useful for certain purposes. Neorealists like Nagel regard science as producing empirically verifiable knowledge; social sciences, like history and psychoanalysis, as producing knowledge (e.g., the concept of unconscious processes) verifiable through plausibility and the enrichment of common sense.[3] Of course, "common

---

3. Isaiah Berlin (1996) defines good judgment in politics, that elusive quality political scientists continually strive to grasp, in similar terms: "Their merit is that they grasp the unique combination of characteristics that constitute this paricular situation—this and no other . . . we mean nothing occult or metaphysical;

sense" in any realm is always, to some extent, bound by culture or paradigm. But the question is whether common sense in disciplines like history and psychoanalysis is common only within a small, esoteric cult speaking a highly technical language, or whether knowledge and judgment in these realms is an extension of ordinary life within the larger culture. Nagel stresses that different types of knowledge require different forms of confirmation to establish their credibility:

> Much of human mental life consists of complex events with multiple causes and background conditions that will never precisely recur. If we wish to understand real life, it is useless to demand repeatable experiments with strict controls . . . (in any particular case) we simply have to decide whether this is an intuitively credible extension of a general structure of explanation that we find well supported elsewhere, and whether it is more plausible than the alternatives—including the alternative that there is no psychological explanation (p. 31).

Whether the kinds of knowledge generated by historians and psychoanalysts are best termed science, social science, or hermeneutics is much less important than an appreciation of the nature of this knowledge and its legitimacy. The mystique in which psychoanalysis has traditionally wrapped itself has deprived us of our strongest claim to validity—its often stunning obviousness and utility in understanding human difficulties in living. This is why Rorty (1996) refers to "our common-sense Freudianism" (p. 42) and Nagel stresses the ways in which psychoanalytic understandings are an extension of those everyday assumptions that enable us to live with other people who, we assume, have minds like ours:

> The general Freudian method of extending the familiar interpretive scheme of psychological explanation to the unconscious in particular cases, the method on which all such theories depend for evidence, is

---

we do not mean a magic eye able to penetrate into something that ordinary minds cannot apprehend; we mean something perfectly ordinary, empirical and quasi-aesthetic in the way that it works" (p. 27).

something that all of us should be able to confirm from our own experience: it is simply a matter of making sense of irrational or unintentional or involuntary conduct, when it fits into the same type of pattern so familiar from ordinary psychology, with some of the blanks filled in by thoughts or wishes of which the subject is not aware [p. 42].

Freud's most important contribution was not the specific content he ascribed to the unconscious at any particular time (sexual, aggressive, oedipal, preoedipal), but the discovery of an enriched mode or method of explanation and meaning making itself. Thus, even though the relevance of many specific features of Freud's theories have faded, the principle of unconscious intentions linking present and past, rational and fantastic, interaction and interiority has become a constitutive feature of contemporary Western culture. And the broad shift from classical oedipal explanations concerning sexual and aggressive conflicts to contemporary relational explanations concerning conflictual attachments and discordant self–other organizations reflects a lawfulness grounded in the utility of such explanations in current lived experience.

It is crucial that psychoanalysis expand its newly established beachhead in the territory between anachronistic objectivism and irresponsible relativism. Believing that there is no single correct canonical version of the patient's mind does not suggest that all versions are equally valid or compelling. Many facts make up a life, and we are justified in having varying degrees of conviction about our beliefs concerning them. There is a great deal of work to be done here in establishing distinctions between *factual events* such as your mother died when you were five; your father lost his job, became depressed, and was treated with ECT; and *interpretations of complex interpersonal relationships*, such as your mother withdrew from you when your younger sister was born; your father gave up hope and became demoralized; or your father tended to act seductively with you. Different features of past and present allow for different degrees of interpretive conviction. The leveling that equates all ideas generated in the analytic situation with stories claiming equal degrees of validity confuses clinical with political realms of power and tends to destabilize the analyst's expertise, making us more vulnerable to the kind of critique Grünbaum proffers.[4]

We do not have to choose between facts and acknowledging the analyst's expert participation in generating meaning about those facts. As Michael Wood has put in a review of Italo Calvino's *Mr. Palomar*,

> A fact is what won't go away, what we cannot *not* know, as Henry James remarked of the real. Yet when we bring one closer, stare at it, test our loyalty to it, it begins to shimmer with complication. Without becoming less factual, it floats off into myth. Mr. Palomar looks at the sky, the lawn, the sea, a girl, giraffes, and much more. He wants only to observe, to learn a modest lesson from creatures and things. But he can't. There is too much to see in them, for a start....And there is too much of himself and his culture in the world he watches anyway: the world is littered with signs of our needs, with mythologies [quoted in Goodman, 1989, p. 85].

Human beings require systems of meaning, including a sense of personal history and motivation, to knit their world together. Psychoanalysts are experts at the way those systems of meaning become constructed and change. Compelling and generative meaning systems do not work well if they are contradicted by known facts; the patient who claims no responsibility for his actions, or no connections with or feelings about his parents, or extraterrestrial ancestry is likely to have those beliefs questioned over the course of an analysis. But personal meaning systems are not derived directly from facts, nor can the analysand wait for the facts to become clear and indisputable before he or she tries to make sense of their existence. Each individual, like each nation, requires a narrative of origin to locate himself on

---

4. The *International Journal of Psycho-Analysis* has explored the nature of psychoanalytic knowledge with its Special 75th Anniversary Edition (1994, Vol. 75, parts 5 and 6) on the theme of "What is a clinical fact?" These essays provide an illuminating array of different points of view. There seems to be a general consensus on both the impossibility of clinical facts outside of theoretical perspectives and the utility of a systematic, disciplined explication of the formulations and reasoning that leads analysts of various persuasions to arrive at their conclusions. For insightful discussions of the original essays, see Schlesinger (1995) and S. Cooper (1996).

the planet. And each analysand requires a narrative of the history of the analysis itself. Analysts are experts at coconstructing and helping to transform those histories in useful, illuminating ways. Contemporary philosophers like Richard Rorty have argued the need for philosophy to move from unanswerable questions like "What is the truth?" to pragmatic questions like "What are we justified in believing?" Psychoanalysts need not be hesitant to claim, and can demonstrate, that psychoanalysis, over many decades, has generated many ideas worth believing. What we are struggling toward in contemporary revisions of psychoanalytic epistemology is a framework that allows us to take what we might think of as the analyst's culture (and subjectivity) into account in the process through which he and the patient hold on to the facts and coconstruct a new mythology about them, "shimmering" as Michael Wood put it, "with complication" (quoted in Goodman, 1989).

On Whose Authority?

Consider the actual, clinical process of psychoanalysis in the simplest terms. The analysand enters treatment suffering in some fashion, whether symptomatically or characterologically. She leaves treatment, undoubtedly still suffering, but there is more *to* her now. In ironic contrast to the popular term "shrink," those of us who love the work feel that we help people expand and enrich themselves. There is an enlargement of their memories of their own past, of their awareness of the complexities of their present functioning, and of their sense of options in the future. There are many ways of describing this enrichment, but one of the best is as the development of a broader sense of personal agency.

Schafer (1976) has pointed out that action and agency have always been the "native tongue" of clinical psychoanalysis. The analysand entering treatment feels victimized by forces external to himself—an outside world with intractable features and an inner world of irresistible forces and damaged parts. The analysand leaving treatment experiences himself, to a greater or lesser extent, as the agent of much more of his experience, perpetually generating and reshaping both his outer and inner worlds, as the author of his own story. The heart of the clinical process, as Schafer has suggested, is the assumption of agency for previously disclaimed actions, a kind of self-authorization.

Consider the close relationships among a group of words central to the analytic project. These words continually reappear in any effort to describe it: authority, author, authorize, and, with increasing frequency in the analytic literature, authenticity. They derive from the Latin roots, *aug* and *augere*, meaning to increase or expand. Over time this word group took on an idiomatic sense of "origination." Each of these words refers, in one way or another, to the generation or increasing of something and, especially, to the question of claims to have the right to create or expand. Thus, they all deal in some respect with power.

On whose authority does the analysand come to assume greater self-authorization? Here's where things get tricky. The analysand generally grants great authority or, to use Sullivan's (1954) term, "expertise" to the analyst. Whether or not we want to consider such positive transference "unobjectionable," as did Freud (1912), it is certainly there most of the time. And well the analysand should grant such authority to the analyst. After all, that is why she is there, and that authority or expertise is delegated by social institutions like analytic training institutes, state licensing agencies, and so on. The analyst's authority is built into the very asymmetrical structure of the analytic relationship. Yet the whole process, as I have noted, is one in which the analysand gradually is to assume authentic, functionally autonomous, *self*-authorization. (As Phillips, 1995, has put it, "Freud, after all, had done a very paradoxical thing: he had invented a form of authority, the science of psychoanalysis, as a treatment that depended on demolishing forms of authority" p. 30.) What is the relationship between the institutional authorization of the analyst and the emergent authenticity of the patient?

Freud was spared having to think too deeply about this problem. For Freud, the patient's mind is part of nature, a particular part of nature that the analyst comes to know more about than anyone else. The patient appropriately grants the analyst the authority that does and should accompany this knowledge. The analyst's interpretations, in effect, teach the patient about the underlying structures and contents of her mind. The more the patient learns, the more she too can use this knowledge to assume an authority of her own. The analysand is in the same position as a student learning biology from a teacher. The latter makes available to the student objective information about a piece of nature and that increase in knowledge expands the student's understanding. What made it all easy for Freud was the nature of the knowledge the analyst could persuasively feel he was offering the patient. Consider a recent paper by Charles Brenner (1996), in which he reaffirms Freud's approach, arguing that it still works quite simply and clearly in our day.

Brenner declares that *his* understanding of psychopathology, in terms of the conflicts and compromises concerning childhood sexual and aggressive wishes, is empirically derived, objective fact. He validates this claim by appealing to the authority of Freud and the observations of "the majority" of subsequent analysts. Later in the paper he significantly qualifies what he means by the truth of the analyst's understanding of the patient. Psychoanalytic truth, like all scientific truth, is the best guess one can make on the basis of the available evidence. But the use of words like "guess" and "conjecture" toward the end of the paper do not change the claims Brenner makes for his position at the beginning of the paper. It is clear that Brenner feels that, just as with other scientific procedures, there is an objectively best guess to be made in any particular analytic context and that the analyst, armed with Brenner's particular model of pathogenesis, is in the best position to make that best guess.

Once Brenner has laid claim to his consensus, everything else follows. The analyst has a perfect right to claim expertise in the conduct of analysis. Any patient in his right mind would cede that authority and knowledge to the analyst. And if the patient is not in his right mind in this regard, the analyst should hold his ground until the patient comes to see it his way. Because psychoanalytic theory gives the analyst a blueprint of the inner structures of the patient's mind, the analyst, Brenner suggests, often, perhaps always, knows better than the patient what is going on in the patient's mind. Of course, the analyst must decide how much of that understanding is to be communicated at any given time, at what pace, and in what form.

Brenner represents the extreme end of the continuum of views on the nature of the analyst's knowledge and authority, in that he seems completely oblivious of the intellectual revolutions swirling around outside of psychoanalysis and still feels, as did Freud and his contemporaries, that the analyst can claim, with complete conviction, to know what is in the patient's mind. (It doesn't seem to bother Brenner that the consensus of analysts on which he rests his claim to objectivity has disappeared in the sweeping shifts of analytic clinicians toward postclassical points of view like object relations theories and self psychology.) In contrast, Kernberg is very mindful of the current philosophical context and seriously tries to address it.

I noted in the previous chapter that, by distinguishing "analytic anonymity" from "technical neutrality," Kernberg (1996) disassociates himself from the artificiality of the traditional image of the analyst's demeanor, which he links to the pursuit of a false and stilted anonymity. Kernberg suggests that the posture of anonymity, which was designed to remove the analyst from the analytic situation and protect his role as objective interpreter, had the opposite and ironic effect of establishing the analyst as a powerful, idealized, grandiose presence. On the other hand, Kernberg regards the concept of "technical neutrality" and its classical ideal of equidistance as generating and guaranteeing a true sort of objectivity.

> The concept of technical neutrality assures the functional authority of the psychoanalyst and protects the patient from an authoritarian imposition of the analyst's views or desires. . . . [p. 143].
>
> [The analyst's interpretations], if carried out within a broad observational basis while tolerating necessary periods of nonunderstanding, should eventually reflect what is actually dominant in patients' experience [p. 149].

Kernberg is committed to preserving the traditional claims to objective analytic authority, which is under siege from so many sides. By distinguishing anonymity from neutrality and acknowledging that the former is illusory, he is attempting to cut his loses: trying to be anonymous does not generate objectivity, but trying to be neutral does. What is striking about Kernberg's formulation is his belief that *trying* to be neutral actually makes it possible to *be neutral*, to arrive at a perspectiveless vantage point. Kernberg has been at the vanguard of exploring the constructive use of countertransference, and that concern, along with his genuine effort to take into account current trends in contemporary philosophy of science, leads him to qualify his claims to analytic objectivity. In the end, however, he wants to believe, like Brenner, that the analyst knows what is really in the patient's mind. While Brenner bases his claims on a historical psychoanalytic "consensus," Kernberg bases his on the state of mind "neutrality" creates. Perhaps the most chilling description of the kind of objectivity analytic neutrality is presumed to generate was provided by Theodore Shapiro (1984), who points to "the need for neutrality as a means of achieving the aim of understanding the unconscious." Shapiro suggests that physician-psychoanalysts will grasp the process through which subjectivity is transcended and objectivity is achieved by recalling their experience of dissecting cadavers in medical school: "The distressing feeling as we see its skin, its face, its fingers, is a common experience, but once we are at work on the organ systems below, we put aside the feelings about the surface. The task becomes more technical, more universal" (p. 277).

Minds: Uncovered or Constructed?

In my view, the traditional approach, claiming knowledge about what is going on "in the mind," as if there were something to be found there that is inert and simply discoverable, starts us off on the wrong foot. There are no clearly discernible processes corresponding to the phrase "in the patient's mind" (in contrast to neurophysiological events in the brain) for either the patient or the analyst to be right or wrong about. The kinds of mental processes, both conscious and unconscious, that analysts are most interested in are generally enormously complex and lend themselves to many interpretations. There is no uniquely correct interpretation or best guess. As with good history, there are many possible good interpretations of important events occurring in the analytic situation.

In this way of thinking, mind is understood only through a process of interpretive construction. This is equally true for the first person, who *is* the mind in question, and for someone in the third-person position who is trying to understand the mind of another. Further, this is true for both conscious and unconscious mental processes. In a complex interpersonal situation, one can present to another in many different ways what is or was in one's mind. In an important sense, consciousness comes into being through acts of construction either by others or, through self-reflection, by oneself. Daniel Dennett (1991), one of the most influential contemporary philosophers, proposes a "multiple drafts" model of consciousness:

> Just what we are conscious of within any particular time duration is not defined independently of the probes we use to precipitate a narrative about that period. Since these narratives are under continual revision, there is no single narrative that counts as the canonical version, the 'first edition' in which are laid down, for all time, the events that happened in the stream of consciousness of the subject, all deviations from which must be corruptions of the text [p. 136].

The phrase first edition is interesting to compare with Freud's (1912) phrase "stereotype plate" p. 100. Where Freud believed, consistent with the science of his time, that there is a discernible, objective prototype that the analyst comes to be able to identify, Dennet does not, because the edition, or draft arrived at is, for Dennet, partly a product of the process through which it is produced.

In this view, mind is an enormously complex set of processes of which anyone, including the person whose mind it is, can grasp only a small, highly selective segment. Thus, there can be no singular, authoritative version "in the patient's mind" about which either the analyst or the analysand can be right or wrong. Of course, this does not mean that anything goes, that all constructions of conscious experience are equally plausible or accurate. The actual experience, despite its malleability and ambiguity, provides constraints (in a way that is similar to form level in Rorschach cards [Hoffman, personal communication]) against which interpretations are measured. But it does mean that events in the patient's mind are knowable both to the analyst and to the patient only through an active process of composing and arranging them. Many arrangements are possible; although some are better and some are worse, there are no *best* guesses.

Unconscious processes, by definition, are even more ambiguous. As Ogden (1994) suggests, they are experienced as absences in presences and presences in absences. To understand unconscious processes in one's own mind or that of another is not simply to expose something that has a tangible existence, as one does in lifting a rock and exposing insects beneath. To understand unconscious processes in one's own mind or that of another is to use language in a fashion that actually discovers and creates new experience, something that was not there before. And there is an additional, crucial factor in the psychoanalytic situation: through interaction with the patient, the analyst is also cocreating new conscious and unconscious experiences, including our very efforts to interpret what took place previously.

This is really the crux of the matter. Traditional claims to analytic knowledge and authority presupposed that the central dynamics relevant to the analytic process are preorganized *in the patient's mind* and that the analyst is in a detached and privileged position to access them. As Friedman (1996) suggests, this is not a question of humility, but of epistemology and perhaps ontology:

> What carries us beyond the question of the analyst's modesty is the more radical question of whether a hidden meaning is known even to the Eye of God. If it is, then perhaps some piece of it might also be known to the eye of the analyst. If it is not—if there is no already given predisposition from which momentary developments are lawfully elicited—then the analyst's "co-creation" of meaning is, indeed, an adventure of a vastly different sort than we have imagined [p. 260].

When it comes to the question of what is *in* the unconscious, determining the best interpretation, the heterogeneous state of contemporary psychoanalytic schools is probably the most persuasive evidence against a singular standard of objectivity. Each school, each theory, each clinician organizes interpretations of unconscious dynamics in a particular fashion, and there are many, many plausible interpretations, or, in Nagel's (1995) terms, many ways to enrich commonsense.

Most interesting about Friedman's position is that, although he grasps the ways in which the "co-creation of meaning" makes psycho-analysis "an adventure of a vastly different sort," he wants to retain the trappings of classical authority as a hedge against what he fears will turn out to be an abyss.

> It is hard to picture how an analyst would work who no longer believes in hunting for something that is already there to be discovered. For instance, Hanly observes that the strongest pillar of analysts' authority has always been their dedication to objective truth; it is that dedication that prevents analysts from pulling rank on patients, or engaging in other personal manipulations. If there is no objective truth to be known, what self-discipline will take its place? [p. 261].

Friedman (1988) often comes to the conclusion (this is true in many places in *The Anatomy of Psychotherapy*) that the psychoanalytic process cannot possibly work in the way that traditional psychoanalytic theory told us it did, but that there is something valuable, indeed absolutely essential, in analysts' acting as if they still believe it works in just that way. Belief in a fictional objectivity is retained as a barricade against unretrained feeling and activity on the analyst's part. This seems a weak rationale for retaining a dubious, increasingly anachronistic doctrine.[5]

Yet, it is possible to anchor self-discipline, clinical responsibility and a respect for the patient's autonomy in an acknowledgment of the intersubjective nature of the analytic enterprise rather than a denial of

---

5. The link between the epistemological claim of neutrality and the emotional and behavioral restraint of the analyst has a long history. Thus, Warren Poland (1994) argues that "neutrality is . . . a principle used to circumscribe the interpersonal aspect of the transference process from eccentric intrusions by the analyst's intrapsychic forces" (p. 285). Robert J. Leider (1983) notes that a key element in subscribing to Freud's basic principle of neutrality has always been "keeping the countertransference in check and avoiding imposing values upon the patient" (p. 673). And Michael Basch (1983) similarly notes approvingly "the desirability of . . . controlling his (the analyst's) affective needs and emotional predilections so as to maintain an even-handed attitude towards his analysand's productions" (p. 697).

it. Indeed, in my experience, "rank pulling" tends to be found more often in clinical work where the analyst believes he represents objective Truth (often under the banner of "standing firm") rather than in clinical work where truth and meaning are regarded as coconstructed. The patient's autonomy is more honestly and meaningfully protected through the acknowledgment of the analyst's influence than through claims to illusory objectivity.

A fundamental difference between the traditional approach to the analyst's knowledge and authority and more contemporary approaches is that many of us believe that each analyst provides a model or theoretical framework that does not reveal what is *in* the patient's mind, but that makes it possible to organize the patient's conscious and unconscious experience in one among many possible ways, a way that is, one hopes, conducive to a richer and less self-sabotaging existence. Thus, I would make very different claims for my model of psychopathology, based on conflictual relational configurations, than Brenner makes for his model, based on conflictual childhood sexual and aggressive impulses. I do not regard my model as empirically derived and objective, although it has certainly been influenced by empirical data and would likely be changed in response to disconfirming empirical data and any growing consensus of clinicians regarding some other viewpoint. I regard my model as one among many possible and valid ways of viewing psychopathology, one that reflects both the interpretive community that I was drawn to and trained in, and also my own distinctly subjective experience. Thus, my approach to the problem of the analyst's authority and knowledge is different from the traditional one, because it presupposes a different phenomenon (a different kind of mind, ambiguous and amenable to multiple interpretations rather than prefigured and distinct) about which the analyst hopes to have authoritative knowledge.

The analyst, if he or she is meaningfully engaged in the process, inevitably becomes touched and moved by the patient, and happily so. The understandings that emerge within the analyst's mind about the patient are embedded in the fluid, interpenetrating mix of their encounter, with their perpetual impact on each other. The analyst's guesses about the patient are not simply derived from the application of his or her theory but are saturated with the analyst's countertransferential responses to the patient. The traditional notions that the analyst is essentially invisible to the patient and that the properly functioning analyst understands the patient largely in dispassionate terms are essentially illusions, serving to disclaim the analyst's personal impact.[6]

This is not at all to deny that most, if not all, patients begin by attributing vast authority of various kinds to the analyst. That initial authority, which Freud (1912) approvingly called "the unobjectionable positive transference," is not the authority that the patient will ultimately come to respect as a meaningful feature of analytic change. The latter authority is not brought *to* the treatment but is a product of the analyst's participation *in* the treatment.

One important implication of the approach I am suggesting is that any understanding of a mind, one's own or another's, is personal; it is one's own understanding, based on one's own assumptions about human life, one's own dynamics, and so on. So, unlike Freud and Brenner, I do not regard any analyst's understanding of his or her patient's mind as a best guess in any sort of objective, generic sense, but rather as that particular analyst's best guess, embedded in the analyst's experience and in the context of the predominant transference–countertransference configurations. The analyst always participates in and, inevitably, cocreates precisely what she is also collaborating with the patient to try to understand. As Donnel Stern (1997) has put it, "psychoanalysis is not a search for the hidden truth about the patient's life, but the emergence, through curiosity and the acceptance of uncertainty, of constructs that may never have been thought before" (p. 7).

The analyst's expertise lies, most fundamentally, in her understanding of a process—what happens when one begins to express and

---

6. Renik (1993) has mounted a strong critique of the traditional presumption that a striving for neutrality generates anything approaching objectivity: "Instead of saying that it is *difficult* for an analyst to *maintain* a position in which his or her analytic activity objectively focuses on a patient's inner reality, I would say that it is *impossible* for an anlayst to be in that position *even for an instant*: since we are constantly acting in the analytic situation on the basis of personal motivations of which we cannot be aware until after the fact, our technique, listening included, is *inescapably* subjective" (p. 560).

reflect on one's experience in the presence of a trained listener, in the highly structured context provided by the analytic situation.

Perhaps these differences will be sharpened if we consider a brief clinical example of a patient beginning analytic treatment.

Robert and His Inner World

Robert, a 40-year-old corporate executive, seeks psychoanalytic treatment because he is tortured by bad dreams in which he is swamped with tasks and demands on his time and discovers that he has overlooked or forgotten about some crucial detail, leading to disastrous consequences. Robert has a simple, unidimensional view of his own mind. His parents were devoted to their children and made enormous personal sacrifices to fund their education; they were poor but happy. Robert understands his nightmares as due to the pressures of his job, but he does not understand why he cannot handle those pressures with greater ease.

Within the first several weeks of sessions it becomes clear that the affect in the dreams vis-à-vis work-related pressures corresponds to a more general worry about his wife and children that he has suffered from for many years. Robert fears that he will become absorbed in some project or distraction and will not be available to them when they are endangered. He has particular concerns about his son, David (he also has two older daughters). He sees David as caught up in the greedy, television-inspired materialism of American culture and worries about how he will be able to instill in him the self-sacrificing devotion he learned from his own parents. He then reports his first dream in analysis:

> I am climbing down a stone wall in my backyard; David is with me. I am lowering him down to the ground by holding on to his arm. He was about a foot from the ground when I let him go. It should have been safe, but he punched a hole in the ground and sank into some kind of chamber. He disappeared into the hole. There was some sort of light, as if there were a floor five or six feet below the ground. He bounced and rolled off to the side. I

couldn't see him. I started screaming for my wife to call the police, an ambulance, something. I began digging frantically. I wasn't getting anywhere. There were sliding rocks. Then there were rescue workers, lots of people. There was an horrific feeling that David was dying. Then I noticed a piece of wood poking out of the dirt some distance away. It was moving. I dug down and uncovered a box like one of my filing boxes in which I keep all sorts of things I think I might need someday. I pulled the box up, and inside was David. He was alive and well.

Several features of the interaction between Robert and myself around this dream are of particular interest. After exploring and developing many of his rich associations to the dream, which included his chronic fears that his world and his mind might suddenly give way, I told Robert I thought the dream might be understood to suggest that there were places in his mind that he was not aware of, places where pieces of his own experience had been placed for safekeeping for future reference. I also suggested that his struggles with his son were in some measure reflective of struggles with a part of himself that had been long buried.

Robert began the next session by complimenting me on my "creative" understanding of the dream, by which it soon became clear he meant far fetched. But he then told me another dream in which now his wife (who has an interest in psychoanalysis and had encouraged him to enter treatment) disappeared into an elaborate system of underground pipes. In his associations to this image, he recalled that the house in which his family had lived when he was a child had a septic system underneath the backyard. The tank in this system would need to be drained periodically by a visiting truck, at considerable expense. To save money for the education of the children, his father undertook the massive project of digging trenches for lateral pipes to the tank, which would increase the available drainage underground. The children would be enlisted in these massive digging projects. Robert remembered his mother's concern for his safety, since the trenches were at times deeper than he was tall. There was one memory in which he struck at some rocks with his shovel and water from an underground spring began to fill the trench. But he was pulled to safety before the trench filled with water.

Through the lens of relational psychoanalytic theory, Robert's conscious, isolated sense of himself is embedded within a complex network of relationships within his own mind of which he is largely unaware. His father, whom he remembers only lovingly, was internalized by him in a complex fashion. There is a part of him—a greedy, aggressive part of him, perhaps a phallic, sexual part of him (as suggested by the waving stick)—that had been buried in his father's world of devotion and hard work. The sector of his experience that was buried and remains dissociated seems to correspond to, and resonate with, his son and his typical childish egotism and greediness. Robert becomes involved in desperate efforts to control his son, partly because the son stands also for the version of himself that he has long entombed and that he deeply fears. Yet his dreams of something important that has been forgotten suggest to me that he is struggling with a sense that he has tragically mutilated his own inner resources and potentials.

This is just one way of understanding this dream; there are no doubt many others. But to be occupied primarily with figuring out what the dream "really means" is to miss the point. Dream interpretation must facilitate the analytic process. If one thinks about the analytic process as generating insight by correctly identifying the patient's dynamics, then the "best guess" decoding of the dream is essential. But for me the analytic process is about expanding and enriching the patient's experience of his own mind and facilitating his capacity to generate experience that he finds vitalizing and personally meaningful. From this perspective, arriving at a "best guess" decoding of the dream is neither possible nor desirable; what is important is engaging him about the dream in a way that sparks and quickens his own analytic interest in himself (Bollas, 1987; Phillips, 1993).

What does psychoanalysis offer this man? The dream suggests some possibilities, because we might regard the dream as a reference not just to his childhood and the world of his father, but also to his feelings about the psychoanalytic project on which he has just embarked.

Psychoanalysis seems to provide Robert entry into a complex, labyrinthine world in which he might very well get lost, as he did in some sense in the world of his father. (The anal metaphor of the septic system suggests fecal passageways, a fantasy of paternal bowels in which he was hiding and trapped.) Partly because it becomes a self-fulfilling prophesy, we can certainly make the guess that his relationship with his father will reemerge in the same basic forms in the transferential relationship with the analyst. My analytic concepts and vision will become an analogue of his father's septic vision. In fact, at a later point in the analysis, this feature of the transference announced itself in what he experienced as a shameful admission of concerns that I might disapprove of his analytic efforts, at his not "digging deep enough."

What sort of claims can I, should I, make for my analytic understanding? I believe that if I present my ideas about his mind as if I knew what is there and that he would come to see it my way, I will likely be experienced by him as reenacting his relationship with his father, and he will be faced with the choice of either passive surrender or defiance. Freud and his contemporaries might have been able to proceed in just this way, because they were practicing at a time when everyone ceded enormous authority to professional, religious, and intellectual leaders of all sorts. In our day, virtually all authorities have come under attack and are questioned, and the same deference to authority that in Freud's day was normative and adaptive is in our day, a form of masochistic pathology.

I believe that what I can offer Robert instead is possible ways to view his mind and experience (including thinking about it in terms of metaphors of interiority) that I hope to show him will be both enriching and liberating. (As Phillips, 1995, has put it, "So instead of asking, Is there an unconscious?, we might ask, In what sense are our lives better if we live as though there is one?" p. 56.) I believe my expertise lies not in knowing what is there in him, but in devising ways of construing his experience that are potentially helpful, and also in inquiring into what happens between us when he is confronted by my ideas about him. Thus, with the emergence of his concerns about my feeling that he is not "digging deep enough," his ambivalent hopes and dread about my system, his sense of what my system means to me, become at least as important as his efforts. I don't believe that it is useful to insist on his recognition of my authority and knowledge as a contractual basis for our work. He has his ideas about what I can possibly provide for him, and I have mine. The proof is in the proverbial pudding. My authority and knowledge can become meaningful to him only *through* the process; it is not a precondition of the process.

My job, the way I conceive of it, is to find ways to show Robert that my conceptual diggings are likely to be safer than he imagines, perhaps even exhilarating; that, despite what might be a wish to surrender to my efforts, he does not have to participate in a way that is over his head and threatens to drown him; that he and I might collaborate in a new system of understanding that neither he nor I can envision at the start; that he and I will be able to find a way for him to use me without becoming buried in me. Robert's struggle with his father and his trenches will be fought in the analytic trenches with me.

So I am offering a view of the analyst's knowledge and authority that portrays the analyst as an expert in collaborative, self-authorizing self-reflection, in developing useful constructions for understanding the analysand's experience.[7]

Analytic constructions are neither uniquely objective nor idiosyncratically subjective. They are among many possible organizations of the analysand's experience that have proved helpful in generating a sense of personal meaning and value.

Mutuality/Asymmetry

Irwin Z. Hoffman, Lewis Aron, Thomas Ogden and other authors who have emphasized the "mutuality," the continual reciprocal influencing that characterizes the analytic relationship, also note that the forms through which analyst and analysand participate are asymmetrical. The effort to define this asymmetry precisely has been one of the trickiest features of the current reconceptualization of the nature of the analytic relationship. Ferenczi's (1932) experiment in "mutual analysis" foundered when he lost sight of the difference in the roles of analysand and analyst.

---

7. This is a claim for analytic knowledge that is perspectivist without being relativist (Elliott and Spezzano, 1996, p. 61).

One of the implications of the argument I have been developing is that it is crucial both that the analyst not pull rank and that he also hold his ground when necessary. In the self-authorizing empowerment of the analytic process, the analyst's traditional rank-pulling can only be counterproductive. Yet it is important that the analyst be able to hold on to a sense of the value of his input as offering potential utility for meaning making, self-expansion, and self-reflection. Sustaining desire for something important from someone important is the central challenge of emotional life. (The Kleinians call this depressive anxiety.) Can the patient learn to take in something important from the analyst without risking impossible self-betrayal in a myriad of forms? It is precisely in their collaborative struggle to find a way to make that possible that the most important analytic work is done.

One of the major features of the analyst's role is his or her function in preserving the relationship *as analytic* and conducting and protecting the inquiry. While the analysand's role entails giving oneself over to the experience of the analytic process, the analyst, in addition to that experiential self-monitoring, must also pay attention to holding and protecting the process. The asymmetry of the analytic relationship derives greatly from the necessity for the analyst to bear this responsibility. In some respects, the analyst's role is analogous to that of the "designated driver" at a party, or the designated negotiator of reality in a group drug trip. Someone has to be mindful of the bigger picture, and it is precisely that mindfulness that allows a surrender to the experience for the other participants. The person in the role assigned such responsibilities is, of course, expected to join the party, but she must also maintain a state of mind in which she can guarantee the safety of all involved, and that difference in roles makes possible a different range of experiences.

Does the enormous responsibility the analyst bears in safeguarding the analytic process suggest that his role is largely parental? From its inception, parental metaphors have been an important avenue for thinking about the analyst's participation. Freud conceptualized the analyst largely in paternal terms; postclassical theorizing, especially that derived from Winnicott and Kohut, has often cast the analyst in terms of maternal metaphors. Hoffman (1996) has argued that the analyst is inevitably experienced as reflecting a certain aura, a power that is an accompaniment of the developmental significance the analyst inevitably comes to play.

Yet, Phillips (1993) has pointed to the dangers of developmental metaphors, "playing mothers." When we presume that the analyst will serve specific developmental functions, whether defined as paternal, maternal, or in terms of an array of self-object functions, Phillips suggests, we foreclose the valuable possibility of being taken by surprise. But to argue against a universally assumed developmental significance or parental aura does not preclude an appreciation of the unique configuration of the analytic relationship, which for each analyst–analysand dyad, in its paricular way, makes possible an extraordinary intimacy.

The context-specific intimacy of the analytic relationship contributes to its oddness. So much cannot happen. The preset formal structure of time and place, the almost exclusive conversational focus on the experience of one participant and not the other, the prohibitions against touching—all this makes for an odd relationship indeed, one that does not translate easily into chance encounters on the street. Yet it is this very constellation of constraints that opens up the possibility of a kind of intimacy, self-expression, and self-reflection that is simply not available in any other way.

The setting of a patient's dream for me captured this creative tension at the heart of the analytic relationship. In the dream, she and I were in session in my office. Two of the walls were intact, parallel to each other, as they actually are. They seemed clear and close together. But the two ends of the narrowed room were open; there were no walls, only open spaces. For this patient, who struggles with boundaries and transgressions, imprisonments, and liberations, the analytic relationship provides both agonizing limits and dizzying possibilities. And for all patients there is something in the limits themselves, guarded by the analyst in his authoritative role, that opens up the uniquely analytic possibilities.

Over the course of an analysis, the analysand's experience becomes increasingly self-authorized. What sort of enduring presence remains of the analyst in the patient's mind? What, then, is the fate of the analytic object? In the early decades of analytic theorizing, when the analyst was thought to be solely a transference object, the analytic relationship was understood to leave no residue. If the transference were "completely resolved," the analytic relationship would vanish like a figment of the patient's imagination, which, in fact, it was understood to be. In recent decades, there has been increasingly greater emphasis on the ways in which the analyst is internalized in lasting identifications. We are generally most comfortable speaking of these identifications as generic functions, like the analyst's "observing ego," analyzing function, and so on. But more and more we are able to acknowledge to ourselves and to each other that the specific person of the analyst, in his or her unique subjectivity, becomes a lasting presence in the postanalytic world of the analysand.

For many patients, the most difficult thing about the analytic relationship is precisely the differential importance analyst and analysand have in each other's lives. For the analysand, the analyst is at or near the center of his or her emotional life. For the analyst, each patient necessarily occupies a more peripheral spot. Many of us began doing analytic work with one or two patients and quickly learned something of the dangers of depending on too few for too much. No matter how reciprocal the analytic relationship, the patient starts in need, while the analyst starts by offering a service. The patient has one analyst; the analyst has many patients. The patient will go on to a life without analysis; the analyst will continue to practice with other patients.

Part of what the analyst has authoritative knowledge about is the shimmering complications of these facts, these givens of the context-specific intimacy of the analytic situation. But there is a great deal about what this will be like for any particular analysand that neither analyst nor patient know beforehand. One function of the analyst's self-reflective interpretations, especially during the final phases of an analysis, is to try to help facilitate a tolerance of and a sense of excitement about precisely those unknowns.

CHAPTER 8

GENDER AND SEXUAL ORIENTATION IN THE AGE OF POSTMODERNISM

The Plight of the Perplexed Clinician

number of years ago I had occasion to drive around the sub-
urban neighborhood in which I grew up. Although things
had changed enormously, true enough to Proust, some vivid
memories were stirred up. There was a park just a block away from
my apartment building, and I remembered the many times my father
and I would go there to play baseball during the years in which I
played in Little League, when I was between 8 and 13. These were
very nice memories of precious time with my father, and one feature of
them stood out particularly vividly—his teaching me how to field
ground balls. This had been one of those preconscious fragments that
I had been aware of from time to time, but my visit stimulated me to
dwell on the implications of that particular lesson.

Now, the tricky thing about fielding grounders is this. Anyone in
his right mind crouching down to try to grab a rapidly approaching,
very hard ball traveling toward him across an uncertain terrain would
turn his head away to keep from getting smashed in the face. But if
you do that with most grounders, you are finished, because you can't
see the ball well enough. My father taught me that I had to keep my

face down, directly in front of the ball, so that I could move my glove quickly if it took a bad hop. I had to squelch the impulse to turn away. What would help me control that reflexive impulse was the belief that, ironically, turning away actually made it more likely that I would get hurt by cutting down my vision and, consequently, the mobility of my glove. Looking straight into the path of the approaching ball, which seemed somewhat lunatic, was actually my best protection. After many Saturday mornings with my father hitting grounders to me, I was able to absorb this principle well enough to become a reasonably good third baseman.

The memory of this baseball lesson had floated through my mind from time to time over the years, but I had never really thought about its broader implications before. What a wonderful device for teaching a kid something about life, I thought. ~~Keep your eye on the ball; don't flinch. The best protection against the bad hops of life is not avoidance but directly confronting the problem.~~ Surely the baseball lesson had served me well as a prototype for confronting challenges. The more I thought about it, the more gratitude I felt toward my father, and the next time I saw him I reminded him of our time together and told him what I had come to realize were its larger contributions to my development.

It was something of a shock when he told me that we had, in fact, played ball at that park, or any other, only once or twice. My memory of many, many mornings spent learning to field grounders was, apparently, wildly exaggerated. Now, of course, it was possible that it was my father's memory that was faulty, but that seemed unlikely to me. He has an excellent memory for the distant past and always likes to recall things we did together, like, for example, the many hours we spent playing tennis. No, the more I thought about it, the more likely it seemed to me that I had elaborated the frequency of the baseball instruction with my father to correspond, somehow, with its psychological significance. What had been important was not the grounders themselves, but learning from my father to approach life's difficulties by looking at them head on.

As I reflected further, it suddenly occurred to me that my father was actually the last person in the world from whom I could have learned that larger lesson. My father was generally a very anxious person, and during my childhood he was under a great deal of stress, which he talked about frequently, often with great panic. To return to the baseball metaphor, he presented himself as if the next grounder would surely knock him over and out of the game for good. As I thought about it, I realized that the person from whom I had learned whatever I know about facing problems squarely and believing in my own resources and instincts was my mother, a much steadier, quietly steadfast, extremely resourceful person.

As we know, retrospective reconstruction of historical events and developmental processes alike is a hazardous business, but these reflections led me to the following current understanding:

I admired and identified intensely with the strength of my mother's approach to challenges and adversity. That identification was both precious and threatening. My mother, like many women of her generation, seemed to me to have a somewhat degraded status within my family. I wanted to be like the men, not the women. I must have taken the content of my identification with my mother and reworked it into something stereotypically masculine, drawing on my father's analytic ability to conceptualize important principles, so that the whole package could appear to me as coming from my father. Undoubtedly, constitutional features were also important. I was finding a way to use aspects of my own temperament, together with contributions from both my parents, by shaping and protecting an identity for myself. Certain fragments of experience were included in my self-concept; others were excluded, creating polarities and longings that contributed to my developing sense of both gender and sexual orientation and its accompanying desires.

This self-analytic account of a piece of my own development approaches gender as a construction within a relational context. It bears the stamp of my own preferred ways of thinking and also reflects qualities found in most contemporary discussions of gender, with its emphasis on early object relations and active, narrative construction. But, as we all well know, there is much controversy about the best way to understand many of the key features of such a psychodynamic vignette. Certainly, one of the most divisive points would be in understanding why it had been important for me to detach my identification with qualities of my mother from my mother per se and displace them onto my relationship with my father.

Discussions of gender in our time, in comparison with earlier periods of psychoanalytic history, are characterized by a much greater variety of intense convictions. Consider some of the most far-reaching questions about which there is broad and heated controversy: Is it necessary or desirable for a boy or a girl to consolidate a firm sense of gendered identity? Are masculinity and femininity, traditionally defined, still serviceable ideals? Or is it more desirable and healthier to strive to transcend traditional gender roles, to strive for newly emerging ideals of androgyny and bisexuality?

The problem I explore in this chapter is the plight of the psychoanalytic clinician in our contemporary world, in which issues of gender and sexuality are of great concern but about which we have an enormous diversity of theories and beliefs. Because these issues are so central in patients' lives, and because there is so little consensus either in the society at large or within the psychoanalytic community about the most useful way to think about them, a consideration of gender and sexual orientation brings into sharp relief many of the most important implications of approaching the analytic process within an interactive framework. The gender and sexual orientation of both analyst and patient, and the biases and preconceptions in each concerning these issues, bear directly on the problems of influence and autonomy we have been considering from various angles throughout this volume.

I have used the term postmodernism in the title of this chapter in a very general, slightly ironic sense, to characterize our contemporary cultural and intellectual milieu. There is, of course, great controversy surrounding this term and its meanings: historical, aesthetic, literary, political, and philosophical. For my purposes here, and for psychoanalysis in general, probably the most significant feature of postmodernism has been its antifoundationalism, the undercutting of any claims to certain knowledge or values.

> Not only has knowledge become uncertain, but more importantly the whole question of how to legitimize certain forms of knowledge and certain contents of knowledge is firmly on the agenda: no single satisfactory mode of epistemological legitimation is available. . . . In the

postmodern, it has become difficult to make the proposition "I know the meaning of postmodernism"—not only because the postmodern is a fraught topic, but also because the "I" who supposedly knows is itself the site of a postmodern problematic [Docherty, 1993, pp.4–5].

As we have noted repeatedly in previous chapters, the most common guide to the problems of influence in the analytic literature has been "neutrality"—stay out of it and let the patient find his or her own way. That guide is no longer helpful. As virtually all contemporary analytic schools of thought have moved in the direction of understanding psychoanalysis in interactive terms, the analyst is now regarded as having a considerable impact on the process, both conscious and unconscious, both intended and unintended. Given the current array of possibilities, even the analyst's choice of theories with regard to gender and sexual orientation must be seen to reflect the analyst's own dynamics and personality in some fashion. In working with gender and sexuality, the analyst's own preferences and values must be taken into account, reflected upon, and weighed.

In this chapter I consider some of the theoretical models that have been most important and interesting to me, the way in which they inform my own clinical work with respect to these problems, and the ways in which they apply to the dynamic issues in the autobiographical vignette with which I began. The literature in this area is vast, and I will not attempt a comprehensive review. My aim, rather, is to discuss some of the major conceptual options the literature makes available to clinicians struggling with these problems. To highlight the complexity of thinking about gender and sexual orientation in our time, let us take Freud as a point of comparison.

Theorizing Gender

One of Freud's (1937) most interesting discussions of gender-related issues is found in the late clinical reflections of "Analysis Terminable and Interminable." Anticipating the tremendous importance of gender in subsequent decades, Freud identified the most intractable resistances to analysis he had encountered over the years: "in the female, *an envy for the penis*—a positive striving to possess a male genital—and, in the male, a struggle against his passive or feminine attitude to another male" (p. 250). These apparently two different themes, Freud suggests, are related: "Something which both sexes have in common has been forced, by the difference between the sexes, into different forms of expression" (p. 250). And the something all people have in common, Freud went on to suggest, is what he termed the "repudiation of femininity."

The asymmetry in Freud's understanding of this problem for men and women clearly reflects the differential valuing of masculinity and femininity in his day. Both men and women are missing something; both long for what is missed. It is, Freud argued, "the attitude proper to the opposite sex which has succumbed to repression" (p. 251). But there is a critical difference. Women are missing the male organ, so their longing is fantastic and must be renounced. Men are missing passive feelings vis-à-vis other men, which they dread because these feelings are associated with femininity and castration. Men have all the organs they could possibly want; they need to overcome childlike, illusory fears. Women lack the most valued organ; they need to renounce their impossible striving for it.

> At no other point in one's analytic work [Freud laments] does one suffer more from an oppressive feeling that all one's repeated efforts have been in vain, and from a suspicion that one has been "preaching to the winds," than when one is trying to persuade a woman to abandon her wish for a penis on the ground of its being unrealizable or when one is seeking to convince a man that a passive attitude to men does not always signify castration and that it is indispensable in many relationships in life [p. 252].

Freud ended his pessimistic clinical retrospective by suggesting that these problems may constitute a biological, underlying "bedrock" (p. 252) and may be intractable to treatment.

I want to focus on two major distinctions between thinking about gender in our time in contrast to Freud's. First, many writers now would not presume Freud's differential valuing of masculinity and femininity. There are many examples of a contemporary emphasis on the desirability and power of femininity that makes it an object of envy as well as dread. Three of the most important contributions include

the stress on the omnipotent figure of the preoedipal mother among
the French Freudians (Oliner, 1988); the stress by Carol Gilligan
(1982) and her collaborators as well as the Stone Center authors on
the greater emotional connectedness and relational moral values made
possible in female development; and Irene Fast's work (1984) on a
common early developmental bisexuality and subsequent envy in
men of women's capacity to give birth.

A second major difference between thinking about gender in our
time and thinking about gender in Freud's time is that, for Freud, gender was simple and unproblematic as such. Although Freud introduced us to the complexities of psychosexual conflicts, cross-gender
identifications, and so on, gender itself was fundamentally grounded
in anatomy and the inevitable psychological consequences of psychosexual development. Because gender itself was regarded as fundamental and given, it is not even listed as a subject entry in *The Language of
Psychoanalysis* by Laplanche and Pontalis (1973). As Chodorow
(1989) has put it, in the classical model, "the creation of sexual orientation, the desire for parenthood, masculine and feminine identifications with the same-sex parent, all result from what the child does
with her or his sense of genital difference" (p. 180). Thus, gender
problems for Freud are biological bedrock, because men have
penises, which will always be experienced as vulnerable to castration,
and women never will have penises and will always want them.
Considering the baseball vignette from this model, all boys would
dread being like their mother in any important respect because such a
similarity would arouse fears about sexual differentiation and castration anxiety.

In our day, there are strikingly different accounts of how gender
develops and what gender is. I'd like to explore briefly some features
of the rich array of approaches to understanding gender by grouping
them according to conceptual strategies.

The counterpart to Freud's classical biologizing was the classical
culturalism of Clara Thompson, Karen Horney, and other interpersonal authors. There, gender is most fundamentally a cultural creation—roles are established by the assignment of social meanings to
biological differences. Thus, for Thompson (1942) a woman's wish
for a penis "is but demanding in this symbolic way some form of
equality with men" (p. 208). In a fashion that prefigures some of

Gilligan's (Brown and Gilligan, 1992) recent empirical work, Thompson saw the most problematic phase for girls not at the oedipal period, in the perception of anatomical differences, ~~but in adolescence, in the perception of differences in social power and constraints~~. Gender characteristics reflect cultural conditions. In this model, my attribution of the baseball lesson to my father was fueled by the sexist degradation of women in our society and in my family in particular. Thus, Thompson (1942) suggests, because of economic disparities and the use of seductiveness as a commodity, "woman's alleged narcissism and greater need to be loved may be entirely the result of economic necessity" (p. 214).

A very different but popular approach to gender has surfaced in recent years based on what might be considered a neobiological model: Freud was right that anatomy is destiny, but he simply misread the way in which anatomy destines us.

Chassequet-Smirgel (1988) and other French Freudians, for example, argue that the phallocentrism and phallic monism of Freud and Lacan were not just wrong but were defense-motivated errors against a deeper universal truth—~~the dread and denial of the preoedipal mother and her cloacal, devouring vagina~~. In this view, it is not the penis that is central and primary, but the vagina. Penises are valuable because they enable us to escape from the dedifferentiating threat of the preoedipal mother. Boys are lucky to have them and fear losing them; girls obtain them through intercourse and in a fantasized theft from the father.

But the game of reading destiny from anatomy can be played in many different ways. Whereas Lacan orients everything important, including language and culture, around the paternal phallus, Kristeva (1981) (in a fashion very reminiscent of Loewald, 1976) separates the paternal, symbolic function of language from its semiotic dimension, which she derives from the infant's presymbolic, "instinctual" relations with the mother's body. And, for another variation, consider Irigaray's (1977) imaginative view of the superiority of female genitalia:

[A man] needs an instrument in order to touch himself: his hand, woman's genitals, language—and this self-stimulation requires a minimum of activity. But a woman touches herself by and within herself directly, without mediation, and before any distinction between activity and passivity is possible. A woman "touches herself" constantly without anyone being able to forbid her to do so, for her sex is composed of two lips which embrace continually. Thus, within herself she is already two—but not divisible into ones—who stimulate each other [p. 345].

Mayer (1985) has proposed yet another biologically based view of gender that is somewhat reminiscent of Erikson, but with a contemporary twist. She suggests that "primary femininity" for the girl entails the development of certain mental representations of genital femaleness:

The young girl begins by assuming that everyone has a vulva like hers, with the possibility of an opening and the possibility of an inside space. Among the consequences of such an assumption may, in certain girls, be the development of a castration fantasy in which males represent the frightening possibility that such an opening in a female could be endangered, lost, or closed up as that opening is imagined to be in males [p. 345].

Of course, male experience can also be biologized in many different ways, and Freud's often discredited account certainly did not exhaust the possibilities. In my own clinical experience, for example, I have seldom found evidence of fears of castration as such. It seems to me that the distinction between flaccid and erect is much more important to many men than is the distinction between having a penis and not having a penis. I suspect a dimension of the psychological experience of masculinity for many men draws on the physical experience of the penis in its different states—the sense of episodic, expansive power, always with a shadowy sense of vulnerability and transience. I also suspect that these anatomical properties have something to do with the ambivalent power many women feel in relation to men—a deeply conflictual power both to generate and to deflate the potency of men.

That so many different destinies have, in recent years, been generated out of anatomy suggests that nature can be read in many different ways. I will return to this point momentarily, but we need first to complete our survey by noting two other important strategies of theorizing gender.

An approach I would call developmental essentialism has been developed by writers like Gilligan, Miller, and Jordan. Here the origins of gender differences are stressed less than the fundamentally different sensibilities that are felt to correspond to them. Thus, Gilligan's (1982) ground-breaking work rescued what she argues is a distinctively female set of values from being regarded as an insufficiently developed healthy, (i.e., male) consciousness. And Miller (1976) and Jordan (1992) suggest that women, owing to temperamental and developmental factors, are more attuned and related to other people: "Women typically demonstrate more emotional/physical resonance with others' affective arousal than do men" (Jordan, 1992, p. 63). Conversely, from this perspective we might wonder whether there was something about the physicality of baseball and the challenge of grounders that was expressive of the temperamental features of being a boy and hence linked in some essential way with masculinity.

A closely related, but also quite different strategy results from what might be termed a developmental/constructivist model. Here, gender differences are regarded, pointedly, not as essential, but as an artifact of social structures, most particularly inequalities in male–female participation in child caregiving. Thus, Chodorow (1980) suggests, "gender difference is not absolute, abstract or irreducible; it does not involve an essence of gender. Gender differences, and the experience of difference, like differences among women, are socially and psychologically created and situated" (p. 421). Chodorow, drawing heavily on Stoller, argues that in many ways, the primacy of female caregivers has made things easier for girls, because they do not have to disidentify, as do boys, with their primary female identification with the mother in developing a gendered identity. In this view, the essential feature of the baseball vignette revolves around the way in which a boy would have to dread being like his mother because of the developmental requirement to separate from early preoedipal mergers. Yet Chodorow stresses that these differences are artifacts of cultural inequalities, not essential male–female differences.

Similarly, Benjamin (1988) argues that essentialists like Jordan have simply reversed the values in the culturally created polarization of gender by elevating femininity and deprecating masculinity. Benjamin argues, as have Harris (1991) and Dimen (1991), for the value of a creative and continually oscillating tension between traditionally masculine and feminine identifications and themes, between assertion (which comes more easily to boys in our society, with its female caregivers) and connection (which comes more easily to girls):

> I am not suggesting that gender can or should be eliminated, but that along with a conviction of gender identity, individuals ideally should integrate and express both male and female aspects of selfhood (as culturally defined) [Benjamin, 1988, p. 113].

One of the constant features of theorizing about gender is the perpetual dialectic between biological/essentialist accounts and constructivist accounts. The former roots gender in some notion of nature or the natural. Constructivist accounts, often associated with postmodernism, argue that gender cannot be rooted in nature, because nature, as such, is purely a socially constructed category (see Gagnon, 1991, p. 274).

In my view, this dialectic is very stimulating—the two sides bounce off each other in a mutually enriching fashion. Either side, on its own, seems very problematic. In discussing biology-based theorizing, I noted that the very fact that biology can be viewed in so many different ways suggests that, in theorizing in this way, we are not so much reading a prewritten destiny as imaginatively creating one.

On the other hand, to regard gender as purely constructed, as unhinged from any presuppositions about nature, as a "free-floating artifice" (Butler, 1990, p. 6), seems to leave it hovering in thin air. One can certainly raise questions about our compulsory binary gender system, but, to be fully consistent, one cannot then argue that there is any other gender system or even the absence of a gender system that would be more natural. If all gender is constructed, then one would have great difficulty making a claim for the preferability of a system that is polygendered, or monogendered or nongendered. For example, Butler (1990), in her incisive, carefully reasoned fashioned, appreciates the limited choices her radical constructivism leads her to: "If sexuality is culturally constructed within existing power relations, then the postulation of a normative sexuality that is 'before,' 'outside,' or 'beyond' power is a cultural impossibility and a politically impracticable dream" (p. 30).

Foucault, on whom Butler draws heavily, suggests that the greatest subversive freedom lies in the desirability of forbidden sexuality—to do what has been declared bad and illegal. Butler (1990, pp. 93–106) demonstrates that Foucault's hope for an unregulated, freer, multiplicitous form of sexuality is contradicted by his own radical analysis of society's establishment and regulation of the very categories of sexuality and bodily experience. He overlooks "the law's uncanny capacity to produce only those rebellions that it can guarantee will—out of fidelity—defeat themselves and those subjects who, utterly subjected, have no choice but to reiterate the law of their genesis" (p. 106). Thus, Butler arrives at the conclusion, known well by clinicians, that negative identities are just as enslaving as conformity.

Butler locates greater freedom and subversiveness in both gender and sexuality not in any particular form of sexuality but in the attitude one takes toward those forms, establishing the ideal of a fluid, destabilizing multiplicity, complexity, and parodic irony. While it is a compelling political position, the values inherent in this deconstructive ideal may not always serve the perplexed clinician well. Fluidity is a kind of negative identity itself. One form may not fit all, when it comes to patients who are struggling to establish workable, consistent organizations of their experience, including their gender and sexual orientation.

I find it most useful to think of gender and sexuality in the way Chomsky understands language. Is language biologically destined or culturally constructed? All humans, across cultures, generate language, so language is biologically wired. Yet the content of any particular human speech is wholly determined by social context. What is biological is the capacity to generate language, but the language that is generated is a cultural construction. Similarly, until technology alters us in some unforeseen way, being human necessarily entails having the bodies we have, being part of a species that reproduces itself through conception generated by sperm and eggs, producing young that are dependent for many years, and so on. Our bodies and our reproductive nature serve as powerful organizers and constraints on what culture can make of us, yet they cannot speak to us directly, unmediated by culture. Thus, both gender and sexuality are entirely constructed, yet all human cultures necessarily construct ideas of the body, gender, and sexuality. Along similar lines, Benjamin (1988) urges feminists "not to ignore the importance of the body in shaping our mental representations" (p. 127) and values the continual reworking of bodily metaphors as sources of self-organization.

The variety of constructionism on gender and other related issues that makes the most sense to me struggles hard to take the constraints of that which is constructed into account. Consider an analogy:[1]

What is it like to drive a car? Is there a difference between driving a VW bug, a Saab turbo, and a Cadillac? Cars are interesting to think about in relation to bodies, because in our culture, for many of us, cars are almost a prosthetic device. They offer us greatly extended locomotion, vastly expanded power, a second skin, a range of visual embellishments—lots of things that bodies were designed to do over the course of evolution.

But what of the differences in the experience of driving the three cars in question? Of course, it depends on who is driving. The quality of the experience depends enormously on the meanings the driver assigns to the VW, the Saab, and the Cadillac, and the possible comparisons and constrasts are infinite. But are those meanings unrelated to the actual structures and capabilities of the cars? I think not. Or, at least, I would argue that anyone who could make a Saab out of a VW or vice versa is curiously out of touch with the physicality of the experience of driving, living too much in his head, in a way that deprives him of a dimension of richness of experience that the senses provide. Saabs have advantages for passing: VWs are great for parking in small spaces; and there is nothing like a Cadillac for displaying prosperity. These differences can be woven into an infinite variety of constructions, but the differences are real, and they do not even approach the differences between cars and roller skates or helicopters. Again, the

---

1. The following analogy and argument was developed in response to a very incisive and challenging critique of an earlier version of this chapter by David Schwartz (1996).

kind of car does not determine the experience, but the enormous range of experiences that are constructed are constructed *about* specific cars as physical entities in the world, with specific properties. In that sense, the materiality of the cars both differentially constrains and inspires the kinds of constructions generated.

But, it could be argued, are the differences between and among male and female bodies equivalent to the differences among the cars I chose? Or are they more like the differences between roller skates and helicopters? Or more like the differences among models of any one of the makes of cars? No one knows! Clearly, what one makes of the differences themselves is a construction, heavily saturated with cultural meanings. Nevertheless, the differences are real and, if they were different differences (like the difference between giraffe and elephant bodies), the range and types of meanings that could be made of them would be different.

Should we assume that there are necessarily common elements in the experience of living in male and female bodies or reliable differences? Is there a universal grammar of gender and sexuality? This is a question for which there can never be a definitive answer; yet it is vital that we keep asking the question. Any answer is bound to be temporary—any bit of biologizing (the construction of meaning, not the biology itself) will always be deconstructible, eventually found to express the culture in which it is generated; any bit of constructivism will always have to be reanchored to the body and human biology to keep it grounded and emotionally relevant.

In his final discussion of symbolism, Loewald (1988) argued that the symbol and the symbolized mutually enrich and reciprocally transform each other. The snake cannot be reduced simply to mean the penis. Once so symbolized, the snake is transformed by the penis and the penis is transformed by the snake. Neither the snake nor the penis is ever the same again. Both have become constructions. Similarly, when it comes to gender and sexuality, the construction and the constructed both constrain and transform each other. We construct our own gendered and sexual identities, yet that which is constructed cannot be our destiny unless it makes possible the expression and development of what we experience as our bodies and our nature. Biological and constructivist models of gender do not so much demand a choice as create a helpful tension that perpetually generates new forms of organizing experience, a kind of potential space that is particularly well suited to the analytic process, in its continual reworking of past and present, fantasy and actuality, internal and external, to generate new meanings.

Gender Mixes

Consider a woman somewhere between the middle and termination phase of her analysis who dreamed of having a penis. She was an artist who, when she began treatment, felt blocked in her ability to realize fully her own creative potentials.

This dream occurred during an extended period in which the dreamer had had a breakthrough in her painting, about which she was feeling particularly exhilarated and potent.

I am with my parents in a town I don't recognize. We are going to my studio, which is very lovely and is on Main Street. Then later we are at your office, which is on a lesser street. I have had a session with you, and now you are in the yard watering your flowers with a hose. I feel that I am dressed too warmly for the weather and would like to leave some article of apparel for safekeeping in your office. You have a large bureau, and there seems to be room in one of the drawers for me to leave my sweater. My mother tells me to quickly fold it and place it in the drawer before you see what I am doing. That seems too sneaky to me, and I feel I need to ask you if that is OK. I think I do that, and it is fine with you.

Later I am back in my studio, lying on my back, like I lie on the couch here, but with no clothes on. I have this enormous penis, and it feels wonderful. It is big and very thick, much bigger than any real penis, and it feels simply wonderful that I have it. Pretty grandiose, huh? I can't really remember how the dream ends. There is this vague feeling that my father is in a coma somewhere. I will have to give up the penis, and when I do, he will die.

The dreamer had a markedly distant relationship with her father, by whom she had always felt rejected in favor of her three brothers.

Her mother was a stereotypical woman of the 1940s and 1950s, who had given up her nursing career early in marriage and cultivated a brand of pseudo-stupidity in which her husband was seen as godlike.

One of my first responses to the dream, after she had supplied her associations, was to ask why she had to give up the penis. She laughed nervously and wasn't sure how to respond. She said it seemed like a very good question; as she thought about it, she wasn't sure whether the sense that she would surely have to give it up was in the dream itself or in her waking memory of the dream.

This dream is rich in detail and became greatly elaborated through associations. I would merely like to comment here on a few relevant features. The dream struck both of us as reflecting the emergence of a sense of potency and vitality that had been previously dissociated or, perhaps, was absent. The potency seemed organized within a male identification, as if the emergent sense of power could not quite be contained, not quite imaginable, within a female version of the dreamer. For this dreamer, her sense of being degraded, damaged, and embedded in the constraints of her family very much centered on her being female. Having a penis, being male, seemed to carry the hope of a more powerful, vital, expressive self-experience.

The dream turns around the complex interpersonal and intrapsychic relationships among the dreamer in relation to her father, the dreamer in relation to her male analyst, different versions of the dreamer in relation to each other. There is the suggestion of a connection between the dreamer's phallic power and a dissociated, dormant identification with her father. To feel stronger is connected to feeling a link to him that was too dangerous or painful in waking life. There had been a dream early in the analysis, several years before, in which the patient found herself in possession of a large house. There was a basement, into which she had never gone, and in the basement were snakes, taken care of by a boy. One of the snakes was ugly, and one was quite beautiful. They lived, along with the boy, in cramped compartments in the basement. She felt bad that they lived in such uncomfortable conditions, but the boy assured her they had everything they needed. That dream might be thought of as a precursor of the current dream. Earlier on, the phallic identification was completely dissociated and compartmentalized; now the phallic power had become part of her, at least temporarily.

The dreamer used her ideas about the maleness of the analyst as a kind of resource for creating a different sense of herself. She is involved in a curious exchange with the analyst. She deposits something in his drawers; she ends up with the powerful penis. Her mother recommends sneakiness, the kind of anal sadism Chasseguet-Smirgel (1988) regards as an essential ingredient of the development of female sexuality. But it is very important to the dreamer that she be forthright with the analyst, who holds on to his hose and seems content to water his garden. (It should be noted that in earlier phases of the analysis I was experienced, rather than as an alternative to the pathological father, more as a recreation of him in that she feared the potentially deadening impact of the analysis I offered.)

As is often the case with dreams, I came to regard the activity of our talking about the dream as an enactment of the content of the dream and as, perhaps, the locus of the greatest therapeutic traction. She was struck by my curiosity about why she would have to give up the penis, which to her suggested that I could envision her as powerful, even more powerful than I (the penis was a lot thicker than my hose, her studio grander than my office). It meant a great deal to her that I could enjoy her that way.

The analyst's thinking and speaking about gender, as in all other features of the analytic situation, has a crucial impact on the process. I would divide that participation into three components. First, the analyst is always likely to have some programmatic intent when it comes to gender. Listening to this dream, for example, one cannot avoid the question of attitudes about the anatomical differentiation between the sexes. The French Freudians emphasize repeatedly that the elimination of gender differences underlies all forms of perversions and that confusion in this regard generates psychosis: You go crazy if you aren't clear about who has a penis and who doesn't. As Chasseguet-Schmirgel puts it, "The man who does not respect the law of differentiation challenges God, [by] creat[ing] new combinations of new shapes and new kinds" (quoted in Goldner, 1991, p. 257). Listening to this dream from such a framework is likely to produce a different kind of response from mine, which tends to give more weight to the creative and healing power of imaginative identifications. It depends on where you stand. In my view, an interpretation of this dream informed by traditional notions of penis envy, the narcissistic denial of the differentiation between the sexes, and so on would have been very unfortunate.

This dreamer, by reflecting on her own dream as "grandiose," was testing me, I think, to see if I would concur that she had no business aspiring to own a penis. What the more traditional approach would miss is the extent to which the penis reflects not a grandiosity needing to be renounced but a longing for self-healing and wholeness and, perhaps, for retaliation (in relation to the immobilized father) in metaphors that are extremely compelling for some female analysands, perhaps particularly for those working with male analysts (see also Aron, 1995b).

A second dimension of the analyst's participation, often not clearly separable from programmatic intent, concerns the analyst's unconscious and preconscious biases, preferences, implicit judgments. My reaction to this dream, for example, might be understood to reflect a general tendency in me to refuse to accept limitations. Is this an omnipotent, Utopian longing, a counterphobic denial? Is this an adaptive trait (like fielding grounders)? It is probably both. This is not, of course, an objectively answerable question, since it depends on where one stands. It also should be noted that I might have responded quite differently to the same dream if it had been dreamed by a different patient. The work of Susan Coates and her colleagues (1991) with gender-disordered children gives powerful testimony to the anguish that gender confusion can produce for children in our society. It is possible that my response to this dream was based on an implicit sense it that was grounded in a stable gender identity, which she was trying to stretch through the dream; a patient who lacked such a stable gender identity and suffered from that lack might generate a different sort of response. The Zen master Sazuki was once asked whether schizophrenics were close to Enlightenment because they already lacked the stable ego that meditators are trying to transcend: "You have to have an ego before you can give up your ego," was his response (David Schechter, personal communication). The same might be true of expansion beyond the constraints of gendered identity (see Goldner, 1991).

A third dimension of the analyst's participation concerns his or her sense of the analytic process, its tone, its ambiance, the claims made for various kinds of analytic authority, the personal aesthetics of what Schafer (1976) has called the psychoanalytic "vision of reality." Both the dream and our discussion of it might be regarded as a form of play, in the Loewaldian or Winnicottian sense, as trying on different kinds of self-organizations and using her perceptions of the male analyst as material for self-creation. The dream seemed to herald and also to consolidate important changes that were taking place, intrapsychically, in terms of stretching and shifting self-organizations and, interpersonally, in a discovery of new versions of self that might work between her and others, in this case, particularly, a man.

The complementary situation, as Freud (1937) noted, is the struggle of male patients with conflicts concerning passivity. To take in something from another man, as Freud understood it, is equated with passive homoerotic longings, femininity, and castration and therefore arouses deep dread. What we can see from our contemporary vantage point (and what was inaccessible for Freud) is that many men—perhaps all men in one way or another—long to be free of the burdens of socially constructed, male-gendered identity.

Take, for example, an artist who sought a second analysis following an extremely frustrating seven years in a first analysis that had become stalemated. He had come from a family in which gender lines were tightly drawn. His father was an extraordinarily self-absorbed artist, with considerable skill but overreaching ambitions. He considered his work revolutionary and earth-shattering and cultivated an isolation that protected him from any feedback or other kind of engagement with the outside world. His wife had become increasingly embittered, and the parents eventually separated when my patient was 10 years old. His only sibling, a sister, was closely aligned with the mother; he, partly because of his mother's embitterment toward all men, became closely aligned with his father. But his father seemed largely unaware of his existence, and the boy's tie to him consisted mostly of a fantasized union based on how similar and superior they both were as suffering, unrecognized geniuses.

The son became a promising artist in his own right, much more successful in the real world than his father, yet with a talent at sabotaging himself at crucial junctures. There seemed to be something about really succeeding that was terrifying. There were also other ways in which he cultivated passivity. Although enormously bright and innovative himself, he sought leads from others regarding what he might do, what movies he might see, how he might spend his time. The very same idea, coming from another, seemed much more valuable than one he could generate himself. The most precious thing in life, he had come to feel, was someone bringing something, almost anything, to him. In sexual intercourse, he reported sometimes feeling, at moments of arousal, a confusion about who had the penis, the woman or he. There was something intriguing and exciting about the idea that the woman possessed the penis and was penetrating him, and he enjoyed thinking about what penetration by a penis might feel like. (Perhaps there was an implicit vagina envy there, I don't know.)

Not surprisingly, the transference in both analyses was organized largely around an intensely ambivalent longing for, and dread of getting, something from the analyst, in both cases, men. He saw the analyst as possessing precious analytic knowledge, but denying it to him. His first analyst was classical and quite laconic, and the patient felt that the analyst was deliberately and sadistically withholding his priceless knowledge from him. He sought me out after reading some things I had written and partly because he felt I would be more interactive. He was very pleased, at first, by my somewhat more forthcoming style, but soon, the same dynamic found new material, as it generally does, and he became impressed with the contrast between how insightful I seemed in my writings and how trite and dull I seemed in my communications to him. Once again, the good stuff, the really valuable stuff, was being withheld.

Hearing about earlier analyses always gives the current analyst a wonderful advantage. There seemed to have been two basic problems contributing to the earlier stalemate. First, the patient's idea of passivity and femininity was regarded as a regressive retreat from his anxieties (ultimately castration anxieties) about his own masculinity. The analyst, according to the patient's report, made interpretations about his wanting to be a little girl, as if this were a childish, ultimately cowardly withdrawal from manhood. What doesn't seem to have been considered is how desolate an image of masculinity this man had inherited from his father and to what extent his identification with his father condemned him to live in heroic solitude. Rather than being a regressive retreat, the longing to be penetrated—by ideas, by a penis, by scintillating analytic interpretations—seemed to represent both a desperate hope finally to get something from his father and an escape from the masculine confinement that constituted being a man.

A second problem concerned the extent to which the central dynamic was continually enacted in the transference–countertransference. The patient provisionally granted the analyst superior knowledge; then everything depended on getting him to deliver that knowledge or else suffering dramatically to protest his condition of deprivation. The patient knew all along that the analyst's claims to greater knowledge, like his father's claims to genius, rested on shaky ground. He derived a great, secret pleasure from demonstrating the ineffectuality of the analyst's efforts. Yet there was also a deeply embittered anguish in the face of the analyst's inability to help him.

As I noted in Chapter 2, one important difference between practicing analysis in Freud's time and in ours is the difference in people's attitude toward authority. In Freud's day it might have been possible to "convince" this patient, as Freud (1937) put it, that to accept authoritative interpretations is not to be castrated. In our day, any analyst who claims authority for his interpretations just because he is an analyst is asking for trouble. We have all come by our distrust of authority quite honestly, from experiences with politicians, religious leaders, journalists, doctors, lawyers. Why should one trust a psychoanalyst? Any real credibility the patient grants the analyst has to be earned, not presumed. So, in a situation like this, for the patient to accept the analyst's interpretations about his passive longings as authoritative is, in itself, necessarily experienced as a kind of sexual submission. The analyst's claims border on the crackpot, like the father's; the patient both very much wants to buy them and be swept up by them, but also knows he cannot do so without betraying himself profoundly.

In the early months of our work together, this patient had a great deal of trouble remembering anything I said, but one particular question had really struck him. He had been recounting his story of the previous analysis and his own doubts about his analyzability. For him to change, he lamented, he would have to give up a sense of himself as special, and he wasn't sure he would ever be prepared to do that. I asked where he had gotten the sense that the major factor in constructive change would entail his giving up something very precious to him. My question was quite striking to him because it defined our relationship in terms very different from the primary integration in the transference with the first analyst, which he experienced, quite conflictually, as a demand for submission. The first analyst seemed to be saying something like, "Your problems with assertiveness are due to your remaining your very special father's very special little girl. Cut it out; give all that up." Yet the patient experienced that injunction as implicitly claiming, "My penis/authority is bigger and better than your father's. I want you as my little girl. To make it with me, you have to give up him."

Over the months I came to experience features in the countertransference that could, and sometimes did, lead me to make similar claims: an envy of his relationship with his father, from whom he at least believed he had gotten more than I felt I had gotten from mine (remember my concocted baseball memory); seductive hints that he could certainly be a most loyal and rewarding devotee, if only I could convince him I had the right stuff; an intellectual toughness and competitiveness in him that made it clear that, if I was not man enough to make him want to be my little girl, he would certainly make me his; an admiration for his intellectual prowess and vast knowledge of things I was interested in that made a passive surrender to him both tempting and dangerous; and so on.

Thus, for contemporary male analysts, working with male as well as female analysands, the decisive arena for working on gender issues is in the complex interpersonal negotiations of the analytic relationship. This man needed to realize that he had cocreated the impasse in his first analysis (along with his analyst's help) with his horror of a surrender, which he also deeply longed for. Our joint task was to find a way for us to engage each other by which we could alternately give and receive, alternately exert power and be vitalized by the prowess of the other, and simultaneously lessen the threat of self-betrayal and humiliation.

I noted earlier Freud's speculation that wishes and fears pertaining to the opposite gender may be intractable. Schafer (1992) has written insightfully about Freud's evolutionary reductionism, in which basic features of psychic life, like reproductively defined gender identities, are biologically mandated and immutable. But if Freud's clinical observations are recontextualized into a more contemporary framework, they might be understood differently. Penis envy in women and passive longings and fears in men can now be regarded as secondary to a prior fractionation and splitting of experience into socially constructed, dichotomized gender categories. Looked at in this way, these longings and fears are not illusions to be renounced, but the anguished expression of thwarted potentials—for women, to be able to explore their power in their use of others without worrying about damaging them, and, for men, to be able to suspend a relentless pressure for self-sufficiency and control, to give themselves over to the activity and care of another. Seen in this light, these dynamics are intractable because they represent fundamental features of a fuller experience of being human in a culture that, until recently, provided for only two equally truncated deformations of a fuller human experience. Only a naive Utopianism could hope that everyone could be everything; Fast's (1984) work on gender suggests that the renunciation of an infantile bisexual omnipotence is a key developmental right of passage. One of the most perplexing questions of our time, at this point unanswerable, is how much the loss of opposite-gender development is inevitable, universal, and a tragic consequence of self-development, of becoming something; and how much such loss is an artifact of traditional overly polarized gender roles. But whether inevitable or ameliorable, penis envy in women and passive longings in men might now be regarded, like the bifurcated creatures in Aristophanes' story in Plato's "Symposium" who keep searching for their other half, as expressions of missing and very precious versions of self.

Sexual Orientation

The issues we have been exploring in regard to gender have implications for sexual orientation as well.

Freud regarded sexual orientation as largely constitutional; in many cases, homosexuality was not primarily defensive or psychodynamically derived, and, therefore, Freud thought, changing sexual orientation was not a proper goal of analytic treatment. One of the few of Freud's ideas to which the American psychoanalytic Establishment paid virtually no attention (in addition to his support of "lay" analysis) was his attitude toward sexual orientation. As psychoanalysis was accepted by American society, with its prominent homophobic currents, a different kind of biological determinism was established. In the 1950s and 1960s, the position that dominated the American psychoanalytic literature was that everyone is constitutionally heterosexual and that homosexuality is a pathological, defensive, phobic retreat from castration fears. In this directive/suggestive approach, analytic clinicians were urged to insist that homosexual patients renounce their sexual orientation and actively direct the process of conversion into what the analyst considered the "good," that is heterosexual life. It is a reflection of the passion and fear of those who shaped this position that how far it took us from Freud's own views on sexual orientation and the central analytic ideal of nondirectiveness seems to have gone unnoticed.

A brief consideration of the approach recommended by Lionel Ovesy (1969) is representative and particularly striking precisely because of Ovesy's important contributions to other areas of the analytic literature. Homosexual activity, Ovesy insisted, must be interpreted as a prima facie manifestation of resistance and disadvantageous to the progress of treatment. When the patient does establish a relationship with a woman, if neither he nor the woman initiates sexual behavior, the therapist should suggest it. With patients who have difficulties responding to this steady but relentless pressure, "the therapist should commit the magic omnipotence with which he is unconsciously endowed in the transference, and guarantee ultimate success . . ." (p. 123). The therapeutic goal cannot simply be full potency with women, since, Ovesey argued, the temptations for backsliding will be too great. The ultimate goal must be a "successful marriage," although the criteria for success in this context are not elaborated.

Over the past 10 years or so, the directive/suggestive approach to sexual orientation has been discredited in many quarters of the analytic world. To many of us that approach embodied a dark episode in American psychoanalysis. It subjected many patients to considerable pain and contributed to a massive interference in their pursuit of their own personal meaning and satisfaction. But what has replaced the directive/suggestive approach? What should replace it?

The array of conceptual approaches to gender we have explored is mirrored by a similar variety of models for understanding sexual orientation. Freud regarded sexuality as the most "natural" imaginable phenomenon, and authors of the directive suggestive approach regarded heterosexuality as "natural" and homosexuality as a phobic deviation. In contrast, many contemporary authors regard sexual orientation, as well as gender, as a complex construction, not at all a simple extension of our anatomically based reproductive capacities. Thus, Schafer (1992) comments on "his [Freud's] being preoccupied with the organs of reproduction, in consequence of his commitment to an evolutionary model and value system and a patriarchal bias. . . . Far more than it should have, anatomy had become Freud's destiny" (pp. 74–75). Once sexuality is unhinged from concrete, reproductive function, the pathologizing of homosexuality is no longer feasible. Conversely, heterosexuality can no longer be regarded as a natural blossoming of human biology, but, rather, as something to be explored and explained as well (Mitchell, 1981). As Chodorow (1992) has put it,

> biology cannot explain the content either of cultural fantasy or private erotism. We need a story to account for the development of any particular person's particular heterosexuality, and it is very hard to know where to draw the line on what needs accounting for in anyone's sexual development or object choice [p. 273].

As with gender, neobiological accounts of sexual orientation have also surfaced. Richard Isay (1990) has argued that sexual orientation is fundamentally constitutional and not subject to change, and some radical feminists argue that all women would be naturally lesbian if not for compulsory heterosexuality. But, as with gender, claims for the purely "natural" with regard to sexual orientation ought to be regarded as suspect. Thus, regarding heterosexuality as constructed and even genitality as a socially imposed hegemony (Marcuse, 1955) does not imply that there is some other form of sexuality that is unconstructed and therefore more natural and desirable. Bisexuality, polymorphously perverse sexuality—these are all equally constructions, and it is not at all clear on what grounds one might assign greater virtue or value to bisexuality, polysexuality, monosexuality, or, for that matter, asexuality.

Given the diverse range of thinking about what sexuality is and should be, how is the analyst to find a position from which to be helpful to patients struggling to establish their sexuality? I once thought that the answer to this question was fairly simple. In 1981 I argued that sexual orientation was not different from any other material that emerges in analysis (Mitchell, 1981). It was isolated as a special problem requiring a particular technical approach only by those with a homophobic ax to grind. I argued for a return to analytic neutrality, with no preconceived assumptions about the desirability of one or another sexual orientation.

The growing sophistication about countertransference and interaction in our literature over the past 13 years has, however, made insufficient any notion of the analyst's neutrality as the guardian of the integrity of the patient's autonomy. Neutrality with respect to sexual orientation is still crucial in terms of the analyst's programmatic intent, but, as Blechner (1993) points out, the analyst's biases and preferences are bound to be at work in more subtle fashion in the countertransference. David Schwartz (1993) argues that serious questions must be raised about whether it is possible for any analyst to be neutral about something as deeply personal as sexual orientation; he suggests that the problem often is not specifically homophobia, but what he terms "heterophilia." This suggests that the avoidance of programmatic intent be coupled with a continual reflection on one's countertransferential participation and, at times perhaps, a judicious disclosure of that participation to the patient.

My current thinking about these issues has been shaped by recent clinical work with several patients for whom the problem of sexual orientation was a central concern. The following is a composite of some of that work.

James began treatment with me in his early 20s when he moved to

New York City in connection with obtaining a very desirable job. He had been in treatment for several years in a different city with an analyst whom I know and whose work I admire. James had struggled for years with great confusion about his sexual identity and sexual dysfunction. He had had sexual relationships with a few women in which his performance was inconsistent and his satisfaction minimal. He had a few sexual encounters with men he did not particularly care for but by whom he had been courted.

James had always been terrified that his lifelong interest in boys and his phobic dread of sexual play with girls meant that there was something terribly wrong with him. He had many good male friends and very much liked being "one of the guys." He felt humiliated by his heterosexual failings, and the prospect of life as a gay man seemed a horrifying sentence. He wanted what he regarded as a "normal" life with a wife and children. He wanted desperately to be able to form and sustain a relationship with a women, and he wanted analytic treatment to help him.

James had been very much attached to his prior analyst, whom he found warm and supportive during a time in his life that was chaotic and very frightening. According to James's account, the analyst responded to James's fears that he might be gay by reassuring him that he probably was not, and it was clear that, on one level, James wanted a similar reassurance from me. A continued analytic exploration of his psychodynamics would surely lessen his phobic dread of sex with women and make possible a "normal" life. I felt torn.

On one hand, James did have some erotic responsiveness toward women, and there were some dynamic issues that related to fears of women, which, if they were worked through, might make sex with women possible. On the other hand, throughout his whole life James clearly had had a stronger erotic responsiveness to men. Would helping him fashion a heterosexual adjustment be collaborating in condemning him to self-betrayal? Is maximal sexual gratification the key to personal fulfillment, as so much of our contemporary culture seems to suggest? Or is his longing for a heterosexual life a legitimate wish to have things easier for himself, perhaps with fewer obstacles to fulfillment in other areas, like his career?

In Chapter 6 I explored the complex problems inherent in aspirations to neutrality with regard to these kind of issues. Sexual satisfaction is certainly important to me, but would assuming sexual satisfaction to be a central, universal need represent my own erotophilia? Is it really central for everyone? Should it be? Would helping James come to terms with a gay life represent a helpful avoidance of vestiges of homophobia in me or a righteous conformity with what is now politically correct? Would helping him adjust to heterosexuality represent my own heterophilia and a collusion with his homophobia or respect for what he wanted for himself? But patients sometimes want things for themselves that are terribly self-destructive.

As you can see, I wasn't getting very far with these considerations and was at risk of becoming as obsessively mired as he was. The following line of thought began to emerge, which, along with some of the questions I was struggling with, I shared with him. Neither he nor I knew with any certainty what his sexual identity was nor, in fact, whether he, or anyone else, had a preformed, irreversible sexual identity. I reframed the issue, therefore, from the question of which way he wanted to move to the question of whether he wanted to move at all. I suggested that his life, in many respects, had been organized around his lack of clarity about something that, because of his paucity of experience, he could not possibly be clear about. Perhaps his belief that psychoanalysis would help make him heterosexual was a device for preserving the status quo, and perhaps preserving the status quo was really his major interest. I suggested that his inaction was itself a choice and that while he was ruminating about heterosexuality and homosexuality, he was, in fact, choosing asexuality, which was itself a possible, viable life course.

The position I took (hardly neutral because of the differences in my own ability to identify with James's various options) was at first very disturbing to James, who felt I was less caring and supportive than the previous analyst had been. But he slowly began to think about what I had said and decided that an asexual life did seem the direction he was passively, implicitly choosing; and, when he thought about it, he began to feel he wanted to explore his other options. So he began to seek out sexual experiences of different kinds, and we worked on his anxieties from a number of different angles: his fears of unconventionality, his anxieties about performance, and, perhaps most important, his terror of actively seeking anything and the vulnerabilities inherent in desire itself. He eventually had extended relationships with two women in which he was able to perform quite adequately and with considerable satisfaction. Although these women fell in love with him, he felt that he could not quite give himself over to them. He still felt a stronger response to men and needed to discover what a romantic relationship with a man would feel like. So he sought that out and fell deeply in love for the first time. He began to make various kinds of contacts with other gay men, as well as with his straight friends, and felt at one with himself in a way he never had previously.

Some years later, looking back, James noted several times that he had felt particularly happy about the relationships he had with women before he moved in a homosexual direction. That he had been able to make it sexually with women—that he had been able to have a girlfriend for some time, that he knew he could have had a reasonably satisfying conventional, heterosexual life—all this made him feel that he was making choices based not on fears or incapacity but on his own preferences.

What was important about this experience for me was that we seemed to avoid, more or less, letting abstractions and beliefs get in the way of experience. Beliefs about either the pathology or the constitutional irreversibility of homosexuality, beliefs about either the desirability or the dangers of conformity—all these could have interfered with James's fuller exploration of his own experience and what was important to him. What seemed most helpful to James was exploring his conflicts without assuming that we knew things we were in no position to know. In this sense, I do not agree with Isay (1990) that assuming homosexuality to be constitutional provides the most open clinical position.

The work with James did not leave me with the conclusion that his particular solution is right for everyone. All patients do not feel compelled, nor should they feel compelled, to try everything. And not every inclination needs to be acted on if one is to feel that one has explored and knows one's sexuality. Different analysands need different experiences at different points in their lives. In fact, my hunch is that James's experience with his first analyst had less to do with that analyst's stance about James's sexual orientation and more to do with

James's need, at that very stormy and chaotic point in his development, for an analysis that allowed him to postpone dealing with the issue of his orientation. It is not clear to me that he could have used his experience with me earlier. What seemed most important was that I was able to work on my own various biases and values enough to arrive at a way of working with him that we both came to feel was relatively free of a programmatic intent, except for the value placed on action and responsibility embedded in my way of working analytically.

The current psychoanalytic literature is bursting at the seams with different ideas about gender and sexual orientation, about masculinity and femininity. Within this dense mix of beliefs and theories, new orthodoxies and ideals have emerged. There is a tremendous richness in all this that makes it possible, in fact necessary, for each analytic clinician to pick and choose among the conceptual wealth and ferment in shaping his or her own sense of gender and how it develops.

Some patients (perhaps all patients at some point) will look toward the analyst for authentication of their gender organization and sexual orientation. Analysts can never be free of their biases and ought to be constantly searching for them in their own experience and in their patients' reactions. The pursuit of a bias-free ideal seems futile and disingenuous; analysts serve their patients better by an openness to discovering and rediscovering their own prejudices, affinities, and fears as an inevitable and interesting feature of analytic inquiry.

How much gender interchangeability and object exchangeability is desirable? At what point does a fluidity of identifications undermine an acceptance of the anatomical differentiation between the sexes? How constrained are we by anatomy? By constitutionally based preferences? How gender- and sexually oriented should our identities be? The answers to these questions may be different for each analysand. In my view, the best position for the clinician in the land of postmodernism includes, in addition to claiming considerable knowledge about many things, not claiming to know things we don't know and probably never will know. And I think this also serves as a model for the most helpful approach for analysands in sorting out their own choices and shaping their own experience.

In many respects, the contemporary analysand is in a position similar to the contemporary analyst. It is up to him to develop a truly personal sense of his own life, its development and its future. What constraints do *his* biology, *his* anatomy, *his* temperament, *his* developmental history pose? How are the *analysand's* models, identifications, and choices molded together to create a gendered self-experience? There are many ways of thinking about these issues that need to be explored, tried out, and chosen from. One of the most important features of the analyst's role is to encourage the cocreating, with the analyst's participation, of each analysand's personal mythic imagination and metaphors, rather than borrowing Freud's or those of a currently fashionable ideology. Contemporary analysands, whether female or male, are faced with the same dizzying choices that confront analytic theorists, and it is the task of analysts to help patients confront those choices not with vertigo, but with a sense of extraordinary opportunity.

EPILOGUE
Toward A Personal Synthesis

W e have explored ideas of interaction across an array of different psychoanalytic traditions. The emphasis has been on interpersonal theory and, among various object relations approaches, the Kleinian tradition in particular. Because of its very nature, the interpersonal school has stressed interaction from its inception in the 1930s. The Kleinian school, through the concept of projective identification, has been in the forefront of the recent importance attributed to the analyst's interactive experience as a receptive repository of the patient's unconscious dynamics.

At the heart of the contemporary interpersonal approach to interaction, forged from many of Sullivan's concepts and brought to life in the clinical sensibilities of Erich Fromm and Clara Thompson (and through her of Ferenczi), is an emphasis on the importance of authenticity in the analyst's participation with the patient. Whatever traumas, wounds, longings, and predispositions the patient brings to the analytic situation, the patient is also engaged with the analyst as a person, here and now. The patient struggles to find, to know, to make contact with the analyst as a person (as well as a professional), and the analyst is inevitably affected by the patient's efforts, moved, touched, frightened, unavoidably engaged in many ways.

Because interpersonal psychoanalysis developed, to a great extent, in dialectical reaction to mainstream Freudian psychoanalysis, the dominant sensibility in interpersonal technique is toward open, collaborative discussion of transference–countertransference interactions. No interpersonal authors recommend an open, running commentary on the analyst's countertransference, and authenticity is not generally confused with blurting-it-out. Yet, the "grist for the mill" argument has powerful currency within the interpersonal school. If the analyst feels something intensely, and if that experience is not recognized as a feature of the analyst's own neurotic residue, that experience is likely to be regarded as having important meaning in terms of the patient's issues and is likely to benefit from a collaborative inquiry into its significance.

Contemporary Kleinian theorizing about interaction has evolved many concepts that provide a rich complementarity with interpersonal approaches. What I like about the Kleinian concept of the patient's "relationship to the interpretation" is that it provides a useful frame of reference for a kind of microanalysis and microinquiry into transference–countertransference processes. The analyst's communications are experienced by the patient as some sort of substance or body part or both. Is it good or bad? Does the patient take it in? spit it out? chew it up? rearrange his interior around it?

Similarly, when the concept of projective identification is used with a light touch, it can provide a very rich way of looking at the complex relationship between internal and external, the intrapsychic and the interpersonal. Although the language is quite different, the concepts are really very similar to the extension of Sullivan's ideas by family systems theorists. Consider the way in which conflicts tend to be distributed among family members: one is the "identified patient," representing everyone's madness and neediness; one expresses reckless, ruthless power, which the others enjoy and identify with but cannot own and feel dutifully horrified by. The Kleinian notion of projective identification is one way to think about the unconscious processes through which the conflictual richness of experience, too varied to be containable in one mind at any one time, becomes distributed in dyads and groups.

Kleinian and various other object relations theories provide tools for talking about these complementary self–other fragments that are evoked and played out in the analytic relationship. They suggest that, when the analyst becomes aware of some intense experience with the patient, that experience may be a clue to dissociated fragments of the patient's experience as well, roles in relationships and pieces of self that the patient has difficulty owning.

In contrast to the interpersonal approach, Kleinian authors, in continuity with traditional Freudian principles, advocate a taboo against self-disclosure on the analyst's part. In Chapter 4, we explored some of the presuppositions underlying that taboo and its problematic presumption of a shared, universal meaning to the analyst's function that corresponds to the ways analysts like to think about themselves.

The developmental-arrest approaches of Winnicott and Kohut also suggest a restraint in relation to countertransference disclosure, but for different reasons. Here the analytic process is not understood in interactional terms per se, because the analyst is viewed as participating largely in terms of the provision of functions (ego functions for Winnicott; selfobject functions for Kohut). Although the removal of the analyst as a subject in her own right is questionable, the contributions to technique provided by developmental theorists provide a useful corrective for the pressure toward disclosure in the interpersonal model. Developmental approaches tend to teach a humble attitude toward countertransference. The analyst is not supposed to be there as a person, with his own subjectivity; the analyst is there to offer himself for the patient's developmentally necessary "use." This calls for a noninterpretive, generally unspoken, malleability on the analyst's part, a willingness to allow himself to be shaped by the patient's subjectivity, to be created by the patient's need for new, developmentally necessary objects. Developmental approaches also call for a genuine appreciation of the patient's painful disillusionment in the face of the analyst's inevitable failure to completely provide those experiences.

The major limitation of approaches to interaction that have emerged within developmental traditions results from the overestimation of the extent to which the analyst *can* remove herself *as a subject*

from the interactional field.[1] The vision of the analyst as merely holding or containing the patient's experience in order to facilitate new
growth lends itself to a revised version of the myth of the generic analyst and casts a cloud over the idiosyncratic features of the analyst's
participation in the process. It is along these lines that Gilligan (1986,
p. 492) has suggested that mirroring, a favorite metaphor for both
Winnicott and Kohut, is not as suited to represent the development of
the self in a relational context as the metaphor of "dialogue."

As with most analytic concepts, if a humble approach to countertransference is taken too seriously, it becomes a false humility in
which the analyst's participation and influence is masked by making it
appear that the analyst's experience of the patient was *in* the patient
all along, just waiting for the right conditions to emerge. But the
developmental-arrest model has been of great value to me in that it
encourages us to allow the analyst to offer himself up to the patient's
"usage" in a Winnicottian sense. This often allows me to find other
ways to engage the patient more authentically than I would have imagined if I had staked out my own ground immediately. The developmental model mandates caution and restraint in the active expression
of the analyst's countertransference. Together with Kleinian notions
of projective identification, theorizing about the analyst's experience
in terms of the patient's developmental needs suggests ways of reflecting on, and playing with, countertransferential experience to generate
a richer interpretive vision.

Contemporary Freudians who have moved in a more interactive
direction add another useful sensibility to the mix of options and
ideas serving as the matrix for clinical judgment. We noted in Chapter
5 the way in which Jacobs has adapted the traditional intrapsychic
focus on the patient's past to a creative exploration of ways in which
the analyst's own past is evoked in interactions with patients and can
provide useful clues to instructive parallels to the patient's issues.
Jacobs's work has been instructive in the development of a distinctive
kind of countertransference reverie and exploration.

The emphases and overemphases of the various traditions in con-

---

1. See Mitchell, 1988, Chapter 8, and Mitchell, 1993, for an extended
appreciation and critique of developmental approaches.

ceptualizing analytic interaction serve, in some respects, as counter-balances to each other. For example, one of the problems with the Kleinian use of projective identification is that it is often used too concretely. The analyst's experience is interpreted as only the patient's, projected into the analyst. The analyst is portrayed as only a featureless container, and her own participation is denied. This more traditional (one-person) tendency in the Kleinian approach to regard the analyst as merely a vehicle for expressing the patient's dynamics is usefully balanced by the interpersonal emphasis on the actual presence of the analyst and her own issues in the analytic situation.

What I like about the interpersonal approach is its honesty and emotional involvement. By owning his side of the analytic interaction, the interpersonal analyst has a chance to create something new for the patient and to interest the patient in reflecting his own involvement in a more mutual, potentially less defensive atmosphere. This seems very consistent with what Fairbairn (1952) and Loewald (1960) both had in mind when they designated the analyst's emergence as a new object as central to the therapeutic action. "We seem to have arrived at a standstill," the interpersonal analyst might say. "Let's try to understand how we got here."

The complementarity of the two approaches—the interpersonal rationale for expressiveness and openness and the object relations (both developmental and Kleinian versions of object relations theory) rationale for restraint—provides, for me, a rich mix in which the patient and I can learn to appreciate the ways in which, for both of us, internal and external are transformations of each other. There are complex and powerful correspondences between patterns played out in the interpersonal field and the ways in which the suborganizations within the patient's own experience are positioned vis-à-vis each other.

In previous books I have explored the extraordinarily rich array of psychoanalytic ideas about mind, psychological growth, and the analytic process. I have always felt that the most useful way to take advantage of this conceptual cornucopia is to feast on as many different offerings as possible, yet to recontextualize and integrate different notions into one's own, necessarily deep personal vision. Clinical practice works the same way. Good analytic technique concerns not correct actions but hard thinking, in a continual process of reflection and reconsideration. There are no singularly correct clinical actions (although there certainly are some singularly incorrect ones). In this book I have tried to demonstrate that thinking about interaction is one of the most important and, in many respects, a long-neglected area of contemporary psychoanalysis. Each of us is faced with the task and pleasure of exploring the different perspectives on interaction provided by various psychoanalytic traditions, sorting out their advantages and disadvantages, and fashioning a clinical sensibility and style of decisionmaking that is our own. Squarely facing the centrality of interaction in the analytic process, working out its implications with respect to influence and autonomy, and developing new ways of thinking about clinical practice—these are among our greatest challenges today.

REFERENCES

Abend, S. (1986), Countertransference, empathy and the analytic ideal: The impact of life stresses on analytic capability. *Psychoanal. Quart.*, 55:563–575.

_____ (1990), Editors introduction. *Psychoanal. Quart.*, 59:525–526.

Alexander, F. (1925), Review of *The Development of Psychoanalysis*, by S. Ferenczi, O. Rank, *Internat. J. Psycho-Anal.*, 6:484–496.

_____ (1935), The problem of psychoanalytic technique. *In: The Scope of Psychoanalysis: Selected Papers by Franz Alexander*. New York: Basic Books, 1961.

_____ & Frank, T. M. (1946), *Psychoanalytic Therapy: Principles and Applications*. New York: Rounld Press.

Altman, N. (1996), *The Analyst in the Inner City: Race, Class, and Culture Through a Psychoanalytic Lens*. Hillsdale, NJ: The Analytic Press.

Aron, L. (1992), Interpretation as expression of the analyst's subjectivity. *Psychoanal. Dial.*, 2, 4:475–508.

_____ (1995a), Commentary on Mitchell's "Varieties of Interaction" Presented at William Alanson White Institute.

_____ (1995b), The internalized primal scene. *Psychoanal. Dial.*, 5: 195–238.

_____ (1996), *A Meeting of Minds*. Hillsdale, NJ: The Analytic Press.

Bacal, H. (1985), Optimal responsiveness and the therapeutic process. In *Progress in Self Psychology, Vol. 1.*, ed. A. Goldberg. Hillsdale, NJ: The Analytic Press, pp. 202–226.

Bachant, J. L. Lynch, A. A. & Richards, A. D. (1995), Relational models in psychoanalytic theory. *Psychoanal. Psychol.*, 12:71–88.

Basch, M. (1983), How does analysis cure? : An appreciation. *Psychoanal. Inq.*, 6:403–428.

Bass, A. (1996), Holding, holding back, and holding on. *Psychoanal. Dial.*, 6:361–378.

Beebe, B., Lachmann, F. & Jaffe, J. (1997), Mother–Infant interaction structures and presymbolic self- and ego representations. *Psychoanal. Dial.*, 7:133–182.

Benjamin, J. (1988), *The Bonds of Love: Psychoanalysis, Feminism, and the Problem of Domination*. New York: Pantheon.

_____ (1992), Discussion of "The Relational Self" by J. Jordan, *Contemp. Psychother. Rev.*, 7:82–96.

_____ (1995), *Like Subjects, Love Objects*. New Haven, CT: Yale University Press.

_____ (in press), Psychoanalysis as a vocation. *Psychoanal. Dial.*

Bergmann, M. (1988), On the fate of the intrapsychic image of the Psychoanalyst after termination of the analysis. *The Psychoanalytic Study of the Child,* 43:137–153. New Haven, CT: Yale University Press.

Berlin, I. (1996). On political judgement. *The New York Review of Books*, October 3, pp. 26–30.

Bettelheim, B. (1982), *Freud and Man's Soul*. New York: Knopf.

Bion, W. (1962), *Learning from Experience*. London: Heinemann.

_____ (1963), *Elements of Psycho-Analysis*. London: Heinemann.

_____ (1966), *Second Thoughts: Selected Papers on Psycho-Analysis*. New York: Aronson.

_____ (1967), Notes on memory and desire. In *Melanie Klein Today, Vol. 2*, ed. E. B. Spillius. London: Routledge, pp. 17–21.

Blanck, G. & Blanck, R. (1974), *Ego Psychology: Theory and Practice*. New York: Columbia University Press.

Blechner, M. (1992), Working in the countertransference. *Psychoanal. Dial.*, 2:161–179.

_____ (1993), Homophobia in psychoanalytic writing and practice. *Psychoanal. Dial.*, 3:627–638.

Boesky, D. (1990), The psychoanalytic process and its components. *The Psychoanal. Quart.*, 59:550–584.

Bollas, C. (1987), *The Shadow of the Object: Psychoanalysis of the Unthought Known.* New York: Columbia University Press.

_____ (1992), *Being a Character: Psychoanalysis and Self Experience.* New York: Hill & Wang.

Brenner, C. (1969), Some comments on technical precepts in psychoanalysis. *J. Amer. Psychoanal. Assn.*, 17:335–352.

_____ (1996), The nature of knowledge and the limits of authority in psychoanalysis. *Psychoanal. Quart.*, 65:21–31.

Britton, R. & Steiner, J. (1994), Interpretation: Selected fact or overvalued idea? *Internat. J. Psycho-Anal.*, 75:1069–1078.

Bromberg, P. (1988), Interpersonal psychoanalysis and self psychology: A clinical comparison. In: *Self Psychology: Comparisons and Contrasts*, ed. D. Detrick & S. Detrick. Hillsdale, NJ: The Analytic Press.

_____ (1993), Shadow and substance: A relational perspective on clinical process. *Psychoanal. Psychol.*, 10:147–168.

_____ (1994), "Speak, that I may see you": Some reflections on dissociation, reality and psychoanalytic listening. *Psychoanal. Dial.*, 4:517–547.

_____ (1996), Standing in the spaces: The multiplicity of self in the psychoanalytic relationship. *Contemp. Psychoanal.*, 32:509–535.

Brown, L. & Gillgan, C. (1992), *Meeting at the Crossroads.* Cambridge, MA: Harvard University Press.

Busch, F. (1996), The ego and its significance in analytic interventions. *J. Amer. Psychoanal. Assn.*, 44:1073–1099.

Butler, J. (1990), *Gender Trouble: Feminism and the Subversion of Identity.* New York: Routledge..

_____ (1993), *Bodies That Matter.* New York: Routledge.

Calvino, I. (1983), *Mr. Palomar.* New York: Harcourt, Brace.

Chassequet-Smirgel, J. (1988), *Female Sexuality*, Ann Arbor: University of Michigan Press.

Chodorow, N. (1980), Gender, relation, and difference in psychoanalytic perspective. In: *Essential Papers on the Psychology of Women*, ed. C. Zanardi. New York: New York University Press, pp. 420–436, 1990.

_____ (1989), *Feminism and Psychoanalytic Theory.* New Haven, CT: Yale University Press.

_____ (1992), Heterosexuality as a compromise formation: Reflections on the psychoanalytic theory of sexual development. *Psychoanal. Contemp. Thought*, 14:267–304.

Chused, J. (1991), The evocative power of enactments. *J. Amer. Psychoanal. Assn.*, 39:615–639.

Coates S., Friedman, R. & Wolfe, S. (1991), The etiology of boyhood gender disorder: A model for integrating temperament, development and psychodynamics. *Psychoanal. Dial.*, 3:481–524.

Cooper, A. & Witenberg, E. (1983), The stimulation of curiosity in the supervisory process. *Contemp. Psychoanal.*, 19:248–264.

Cooper, S. (1996), Facts all come with a point of view. *Internat. J. Psycho-Anal.*, 77:255–274.

Curtis, R. (1996), The death of Freud and the rebirth of free psychoanalytic inquiry. *Psychoanal. Dial.*, 4:563–589.

Cushman, P. (1995), *Constructing the Self, Constructing America.* New York: Addison-Wesley.

Davies, J. M. (1994), Love in the afternoon. *Psychoanal. Dial.*, 4:153–170.

———— (1996), Linking the "pre-analytic" with the post-classical: Integration, dissociation, and the multiplicity of unconscious process. *Contemp. Psychoanal.*, 32:553–576.

———— & Frawley, M. (1994), *Treating Adult Survivors of Childhood Sexual Abuse: Psychoanalytic Perspectives.* New York: Basic Books.

De Bianchedi, E. T., Antar, R., Fernadez Bravo de Podetti, M. R., Grassano de Piccolo, E., Miravent, I., Pistiner de Cortinas, L., Scalozub de Boschan, L. T. & Waserman, M. (1984), Beyond Freudian metapsychology. *Internat. J. Psycho-Anal.*, 65:389–398.

Dennett, D. (1991), *Consciousness Explained.* Boston: Little, Brown.

Dimen, M. (1991), Deconstructing differences: Gender, splitting and transitional space. *Psychoanal. Dial.*, 1:335–352.

Docherty, R. (1993), Postmodernism: An introduction. In: *Postmodernism: A Reader*, ed. R. Docherty. New York: Columbia University Press, pp. 1–31.

Ehrenberg, D. (1992), *The Intimate Edge.* New York: Norton.

Elliot, A. & Spezzano, C. (1996), Psychoanalysis at its limits: Navigating the postmodern turn. *Psychoanal. Quart.*, 65:52–83.

Epstein, M. (1995), *Thoughts Without a Thinker.* New York: Basic Books.

Fairbairn, W. R. D. (1952), *An Object Relations Theory of the Personality.* New York: Basic Books.

———— (1958), On the nature and aims of psychoanalytic treatment. *Internat. J. Psycho-Anal.*, 39:374–385.

Fast, I. (1984), *Gender Identity: A Differentiation Model.* Hillsdale, NJ: The Analytic Press

Feiner, A. H. (1979), The anxiety of influence and countertransference. In: *Countertransference: The Therapist's Contribution to Treatment*, ed. L. Epstein & A. H. Feiner. New York: Aronson.

_____ & Epstein, L. & Feiner, A. H., ed. (1979), *Countertransference: The Therapist's Contribution to Treatment.* New York: Aronson.

Feldman, M. (1993). The dynamics of reassurance. In: *The Contemporary Kleinians of London*, ed. R. Schafer. New York: International Universities Press, pp. 321–43, 1997.

_____ (1997), Projective identification: The analyst's involvement. *Internat. J. Psycho-Anal.*, 78:227–243.

Ferenczi, S. (1988), *The Clinical Diary of Sandor Ferenczi*, ed. J. Dupont. Cambridge, MA: Harvard University Press.

_____ & Rank, O. (1924), *The Development of Psychoanalysis.* Madison, CT: International Universities Press, 1986.

Festinger, L. A. (1957), *A Theory of Cognitive Dissonance.* Evanston, IL: Row, Peterson.

Fiscalini, J. (1990), On self-actualization and the dynamism of the personal self. *Contemp. Psychoanal.*, 26:635–653.

_____ (1993), The psychoanalysis of narcissism: An interpersonal view. In: *Narcissism and the Interpersonal Self*, ed. J. Fiscalini & A. L. Grey. New York: Columbia University Press, pp. 315–348.

_____ (1994), The uniquely interpersonal and the interpersonally unique. *Contemp. Psychoanal.*, 30:114–134.

Fosshage, J. L. (1992), The self and its vicissitudes within a relational matrix. In: *Relational Perspectives in Psychoanalysis*, ed. N. Skolnick & S. Warshaw. Hillsdale, NJ: The Analytic Press, pp. 21–42.

Fourcher, L. (1996), The authority of logic and the logic of authority. *Psychoanal. Dial.*, 4:515–533.

Freud, S. (1905), On psycho-therapy. *Standard Edition*, 7:257–268. London: Hogarth Press, 1953.

_____ (1907), "Civilized" sexual morality and modern nervous illness. *Standard Edition*, 9:181–204. London: Hogarth Press, 1959.

_____ (1910), "Wild" psycho-analysis. *Standard Edition*, 11:221–227. London: Hogarth Press, 1957.

_____ (1912), The dynamics of transference. *Standard Edition*, 12:99–108. London: Hogarth Press, 1958.

_____ (1913), On beginning the treatment. *Standard Edition*, 12:121–144. London: Hogarth Press, 1958.

_____ (1918), From the history of an infantile neurosis. *Standard Edition*, 17:7–122. London: Hogarth Press, 1955.

_____ (1920), *Beyond the Pleasure Principle. Standard Edition*, 18:3–64. London: Hogarth Press, 1955.

_____ (1921), Group psychology and the analysis of the ego. *Standard Edition*, 18:65–143. London:Hogarth Press, 1964.

_____ (1933), *New Introductory Lectures on Psycho-Analysis. Standard Edition*, 22:1–182. London: Hogarth Press, 1964.

_____ (1937), Analysis terminable and interminable. *Standard Edition*, 23:211–253. London: Hogarth Press, 1964.

Friedman, L., (1988), *The Anatomy of Psychotherapy*. Hillsdale, NJ: The Analytic Press.

_____ (1996), Overview: Knowledge and authority in the psychoanalytic relationship. *Psychoanal. Quart.*, 65:254–265.

Fromm, E. (1947), *Man for Himself.* New York: Fawcett.

_____ (1960), *Crisis in Psychoanalysis.* Greenwich, CT: Fawcett.

Fromm-Reichmann, F. (1950), *Principles of Intensive Psychotherapy.* Chicago: University of Chicago Press.

Gabbard, G. (1994), A response to Davies (but not the last word). *Psychoanal. Dial.*, 4:509–510.

_____ & Lester, E. (1995), *Boundaries and Boundary Violations in Psychoanalysis.* New York:Basic Books.

Gagnon, J. (1991), Commentary. *Psychoanal. Dial.*, 1:373–376.

Gardiner, M., ed. (1971), *The Wolf-Man by the Wolf-Man.* New York: Basic Books.

Gergen, K. (1994), *Realities and Relationships: Soundings in Social Construction.* Cambridge, MA: Harvard University Press.

Ghent, E. (1990), Masochism, submission, surrender. *Contemp. Psychoanal.* 24:108–36.

Gill, M. (1954), Psychoanalysis and exploratory psychotherapy. *S. Amer. Psychoanal. Assn.*, 2:771–797.

_____ (1983a), The interpersonal paradigm and the degree of the therapist's involvement. *Contemp. Psychoanal.*, 19:200–237.

_____ (1983b), *The Analysis of Transference, Vol. 1.* New York: International Universities Press.

_____ (1994), *Psychoanalysis in Transition*, Hillsdale, NJ: The Analytic Press.

Gilligan, C. (1982), *In a Different Voice: Psychological Theory and Women's Development*, Cambridge, MA: Harvard University Press.

_____ (1986), Remapping the moral domain: New images of the self in relationship. In: *Essential Papers on the Psychology of Women*, ed.C. Zanardi. New York: New York University Press, pp. 480–495, 1990.

Goldner, V. (1991), Toward a critical relational theory of gender. *Psychoanal. Dial.*, 1:249–272.

Goodman, N. (1989), "Just the facts, ma'am!" In: *Relativism: Interpretation and Confrontation*, ed. M. Krausz. Notre Dame, IN: University of Notre Dame Press.

Gray, P. (1994), *The Ego and Analysis of Defense*. Northvale, NJ: Aronson.

Greenberg, J. (1987), Of mystery and motive: A review of Levenson's *The Ambiguity of Change. Contemp. Psychoanal.*, 23:689–703.

_____ (1991), *Oedipus and Beyond: A Clinical Theory*. Cambridge, MA: Harvard University Press.

_____ (1995), Psychoanalytic technique and the interactive matrix. *Psychoanal. Quart.*, 64:1–22.

_____ (1996), Psychoanalytic words and psychoanalytic acts: A brief history. *Contemp. Psychoanal.*, 32:195–214.

_____ (1996), Psychoanalytic interaction. *Psychoanal. Inq.*, 16:25–38.

_____ (1997), Analytic authority and analytic restraint. Presented at spring meeting of Division on Psychoanalysis (39), American Psychological Association, Denver, CO.

_____ & Mitchell, S. (1983), *Object Relations in Psychoanalytic Theory*, Cambridge, MA: Harvard University Press.

Greenson, R. (1967), *The Technique and Practice of Psychoanalysis*. New York: International Universities Press.

_____ (1974), Transference: Freud or Klein? In: *Explorations in Psychoanalysis*, ed. R. Greenson. New York: International Universities Press, pp. 519–540, 1978.

Grinberg, L. (1962), On a specific aspect of countertransference due to the patient's projective identification. *Internat. J. Psycho-Anal.*, 31:81–84.

Grosskurth, P. (1986), *Melanie Klein: Her Life and Her Work*. New York: Knopf.

Grossman, W. & Stewart, W. (1976), Penis envy: From childhood wish to developmental metaphor. *J. Amer. Psychoanal. Assn.* 24(Suppl.): 193–212.

Grotstein, J. (1981), *Splitting and Projective Identification*. New York: Aronson.

Grünbaum, A. (1984), *The Foundations of Psychoanalysis*. Berkeley: University of California Press.

Habermas, J. (1968), *Knowledge and Human Interests*. New York: Beacon.

Harris, A. (1991), Gender as contradiction. *Psychoanal. Dial.*, 1:197–224.

_____ (1996), The conceptual power of multiplicity. *Contemp. Psychoanal.*, 32:537–552.

Hartmann, H. (1939), *Ego Psychology and the Problem of Adaptation*. New York: International Universities Press.

_____ (1964), *Essays on Ego Psychology*. New York: International Universities Press.

Havens, L. (1973), *Approaches to the Mind*. Boston: Little, Brown.

_____ (1997), A linguistic contribution. *Psychoanal. Dial.*, 7:523–534.

Heimann, P. (1949), On counter-transference. In: *About Children and Children-no-longer*, ed. M. Tannesmann. London: Routledge, pp. 73–79, 1989.

Hirsch, I. (1987), Of mystery and motive: A review essay on Edgar Levenson's *The Ambiguity of Change. Contemp. Psychoanal.*, 23: 689–704.

Hoffman, I. Z. (1983), The patient as interpreter of the analyst's experience. *Contemp. Psychoanal.*, 19:389–422.

_____ (1990), In the eye of the beholder: A reply to Levenson. *Contemp. Psychoanal.*, 26:291–299.

_____ (1991), Discussion: toward a social-constructivist view of the psychoanalytic situation. *Psychoanal. Dial.*, 1:74–105.

_____ (1992), Some practical implications of a social-constructivist view of the psychoanalyatic situation. *Psychoanal. Dial.*, 2:287–304.

_____ (1994), Dialectic thinking and therapeutic action in the psychoanalytic process. *Psychoanal. Quart.*, Vol 63:187–218.

_____ (1996), The intimate and ironic authority of the psychoanalyst's presence. *Psychoanal. Quart.*, 65:102–136.

Inderbitzin, L. B. & Levy, S. T. (1994), On grist for the mill: External reality as defense. *J. Amer. Psychoanal. Assn.*, 42:763–788.

Irigaray, L. (1977), This sex which is not one. In: *Essential Papers on the Psychology of Women*, ed. C. Zanardi. New York: New York University Press, pp. 344–351, 1990.

Isay, R. (1990), *Being Homosexual: Gay Men and Their Development*. New York: Avon.

Jacobs, T. (1991), *The Use of the Self*. New York: International Universities Press.

_____ (1991), The inner experience of the analyst: their contributions to the analytic process. *Internat. J. Psycho-Anal.*, 74:7–14.

_____ (1997), Analysis, mutual analysis, and self-analysis: On the interplay of minds in the analytic process. Presented at spring meeting of Division on Psychoanalysis (39), American Psychological Association, Denver, CO.

Jacobson, L. (1996), Introduction to symposium on the Grünbaum debate. *Psychoanal. Dial.*, 4:497–502.

Jordan, J. (1992), The relational self: A new perspective for understanding women's development. *Contemp. Psychother. Rev.*, 7:56:71.

Joseph, B. (1989), *Psychic Equilibrium and Psychic Change.* London: Tavistock/Routledge.

Kantrowitz, J. (1996), *The Patient's Impact on the Analyst.* Hillsdale, NJ: The Analytic Press.

Kernberg, O. (1992), *Aggression in Personality Disorders and Perversions.* New Haven, CT: Yale University Press.

_____ (1995), *Love Relations.* New Haven, CT: Yale University Press.

_____ (1996), The analyst's authority in the psychoanalytic situation. *Psychoanal. Quart.*, 65:137–157.

Kerr, J. (1993), *A Most Dangerous Method: The Story of Jung, Freud, and Sabina Spielrein.* New York: Knopf.

King, P. & Steiner, R. (1991), *The Freud-Klein Controversies 1941–45.* London: Routledge.

Klein, M. (1932), *The Psycho-Analysis of Children,* London: Hogarth Press.

_____ (1946), Notes on some schizoid mechanisms. In: *Envy and Gratitude and Other Works.* New York: Delacorte Press, 1975.

_____ (1952), The origins of transference? In: *Envy and Gratitude and Other Works.* New York: Delacorte Press, 1975.

_____ (1975), *Envy and Gratitude and Other Works.* New York: Delacorte Press.

Kohut, H. (1984), *How Does Analysis Cure?* ed. A. Goldberg & P. Stepansky. Chicago: University of Chicago Press.

Kristeva, J. (1981), Women's time. In: *Essential Papers on the Psychology of Women,* ed.C. Zanardi. New York: New York University Press, pp. 374–400, 1990.

Kuhn, T. (1962), *The Structure of Scientific Revolutions.* 2nd ed.. Chicago: University of Chicago Press.

Langs, R. (1979), *The Therapeutic Environment.* New York: Aronson.

Laplanche, J. & Pontalis, J.B. (1973), *The Language of Psychoanalysis.* London: Karnac.

Lear, J. (1990), *Love and Its Place in Nature.* New York: Farrar, Straus & Giroux.

Leider, R. (1983), Analytic neutrality: A historical review. *Psychoanal. Inq.*, 3:665–674.

Levenson, E. (1972), *The Fallacy of Understanding.* New York: Basic Books.

_____ (1983), *The Ambiguity of Change.* New York: Basic Books.

_____ (1991), *The Purloined Self.* New York: William Alanson White Institute.

_____ (1993), Shoot the messenger: Interpersonal aspects of the analyst's interpretations. *Contemp. Psychoanal.*, 29:383–96.

Loewald, H. (1960), On the therapeutic action of psychoanalysis. In: *Papers on Psychoanalysis.* New Haven, CT: Yale University Press, 1980.

_____ (1974), Psychoanalysis as an art and the fantasy character of the psychoanalytic situation. In: *Papers on Psychoanalysis.* New Haven, CT: Yale University Press, 1980.

_____ (1976), Primary process, secondary process and language. In: *Papers on Psychoanalysis.* New Haven CT: Yale University Press, 1980.

_____ (1977), Review Essay of *The Freud/Jung Letters.* In: *Papers on Psychoanalysis.* New Haven, CT: Yale University Press, 1980.

_____ (1978), The waning of the Oedipus complex. In: *Papers on Psychoanalysis.* New Haven, CT: Yale University Press, 1980.

_____ (1988), *Sublimation.* New Haven, CT: Yale University Press.

Malcolm, R. R. (1986), Interpretation: The past in the present. In: *Melanie Klein Today, Vol. 2,* ed. E. B. Spillius. London: Routledge, pp.73–89, 1988.

Marcuse, H. (1955), *Eros and Civilization.* Boston: Beacon Press.

Maroda, K. (1991), *The Power of Countertransference.* Northvale, NJ: Aronson.

Mayer, E. (1985), "Everybody must be just like me": Observations on female castration anxiety. *Internat. J. Psycho-Anal.*, 66:331–47.

_____ (1996), Changes in science and changing ideas about knowledge and authority in psychoanalysis. *Psychoanal. Quart.*, 65:158–200.

McGuire, W., ed. (1975), *The Freud/Jung Letters: The Correspondence Betweeen Sigmund Freud and C.G. Jung.* Princeton, NJ: Princeton University Press.

McLaughlin, J. (1992), Panel: Enactments in psychoanalysis. *J.Amer. Psychoanal. Assn.*, 40:827–841.

Meissner, W. W. (1983), Values in the psychoanalytic situation. *Psychoanal. Inq.*, 3:577–598.

Michels, R. (1996), Gill, Gray, Mitchell and Reed on psychoanalytic technique. *Internat. J. Psycho-Anal.*, 77:615–624.

Miller, J. (1976), *Toward a New Psychology of Women.* Boston, MA: Beacon Press.

Mitchell, S. (1981), The psychoanalytic treatment of homosexuality: Some technical considerations. *Internat. Rev. Psychoanal.*, 8:63–87.

——— (1988), *Relational Concepts in Psychoanalysis.* Cambridge, MA: Harvard University Press.

——— (1993), *Hope and Dread in Psychoanalysis.* New York: Basic Books.

Mitchell, S. & Black, M. (1995), *Freud and Beyond.* New York: Basic Books.

Modell, A. (1991), The therapeutic relationship as a paradoxiical experience. *Psychoanal. Dial.*, 1:13–28.

Money-Kyrle, R. (1956), Normal counter-transference and some of its deviations. *Internat. J. Psycho-Anal.*, 37:360–366.

Nagel, T. (1995), *Other Minds: Critical Essays.* Oxford: Oxford University Press

——— (1986), *The View from Nowhere.* Oxford, UK: Oxford University Press.

Ogden, T. (1982), *Projective Identification and Psychotherapeutic Technique.* New York: Aronson.

——— (1986), *The Matrix of the Mind: Object Relations and the Psychoanalytic Dialogue.* New York: Aronson.

——— (1989), *The Primitive Edge of Experience.* New York: Aronson.

——— (1994), *Subjects of Analysis.* Northvale, NJ: Aronson.

——— (1995), Analysing forms of aliveness and deadness of the transference–countertransference. *Internat. J. Psycho-Anal.*, 76:695–709.

Oliner, M. (1988), *Cultivating Freud's Garden in France.* New York: Aronson.

Oremland, J. (1991), *Interpretation and Interaction: Psychoanalysis or Psychotherapy?* Hillsdale, NJ: The Analytic Press.

Ornstein, A. (1974), The dread to repeat and the new beginning. *The Annual of Psychanalysis*, 2:231–248, New York: International Universities Press.

O'Shaughnessy, E. (1982), Words and working through. In: *Melanie Klein Today, Vol. 2*, ed. E. B. Spillius. London: Routledge, pp. 138–151, 1988.

Ovesy, L. (1969), *Homosexuality and Pseudohomosexuality.* New York: Science House.

Phillips, A. (1993), *On Kissing, Tickling and Being Bored*. Cambridge, MA: Harvard University Press.

_____ (1994), *On Flirtation*. Cambridge, MA: Harvard University Press.

_____ (1995), *Terrors and Experts*, London: Faber & Faber.

Pick, I. (1985), Working through in the counter-transference. In: *Melanie Klein Today, Vol. 2*, ed. E. B. Spillius. London: Routledge, pp. 34–47, 1988.

Pine, F. (1993), A contribution to the analysis of the psychoanalytic process. *Psychoanal. Quart.*, 62:185–205.

Pizer, S. (1992), The negotiation of paradox in the analytic process. *Psychoanal. Dial.*, 2:215–240.

Plato (n.d.), *The Dialogues of Plato*, trans. B. Jowett. New York: Random House, 1982.

Poland, W. (1984), On the analyst's neutrality. *J. Amer. Psychoanal.Assn.*, 32:283–300.

Protter, B. (1996), Classical, modern, and postmodern psychoanalysis. *Psychoanal. Dial.*, 4:533–562.

Racker, H. (1968), *Transference and Countertransference*. New York: International Universities Press.

Rangell, L. (1982), The self in psychoanalytic theory. *J. Amer. Psychoanal. Assn.*, 30:863–92.

Rapaport, D. (1957), The theory of ego autonomy: A generalization. In: *The Collected Papers of David Rapaport*, ed. M. Gill. New York: Basic Books, pp. 722–744, 1967.

Reich, W. (1949), *Character Analysis*. New York: Farrar, Straus, & Giroux.

Renik, O. (1992), Prologue. *Psychoanal. Inq.*, 12:175–181.

_____ (1993), Analytic interaction: Conceptualizing technique in light of the analyst's irreducible subjectivity. *Psychoanal. Quart.*, 62: 553–571.

_____ (1995), The ideal of the anonymous analyst and the problem of self-disclosure. *Psychoanal. Quart.*, 64:466–495.

_____ (1996), The perils of neutrality. *Psychoanal. Quart.*, 65:495–517.

Rorty, R. (1991), *Objectivity, Relativism, and Truth*. New York: Cambridge University Press.

_____ (1996). Sigmund on the couch. Review of *Wittgenstein Reads Freud: The Myth of the Unconscious* by S. J. Bouveresse, trans. C. Cosman. *New York Times Book Review*, September 22.

Rosenfeld, H. (1965), *Psychotic States: A Psychoanalytic Approach*. New York: International Universities Press.

_____ (1987), *Impasse and Interpretation*. London: Tavistock.

Roth, P. & Segal, H. (1990), A Kleinian view. *Psychoanal. Inq.*, 10: 541–549.

Rothstein, A. (1983), *The Structural Hypothesis*, New York: International Universities Press.

Sandler, J. (1987), The concept of projective identification. In: *Projection, Identification, Projective Identification*, ed. J. Sandler. Madison, CT: International Universities Press, pp. 13–26.

_____ & Sandler, A. (1984), The past unconscious, the present unconscious and interpretation of the transference. *Psychoanal. Inq.*, 4:367–400.

Schafer, R. (1966). Authority, evidence and knowledge in the psychoanalytic relationship. *Psychoanal. Quart.*, 65:236–253.

_____ (1968), *Aspects of Internalization*. New York: International Universities Press.

_____ (1976), *A New Language for Psychoanalysis*. New Haven, CT: Yale University Press.

_____ (1983), *The Analytic Attitude*. New York: Basic Books.

_____ (1985), Wild analysis. *J. Amer. Psychoanal. Assn.*, 36:175–300.

_____ (1992), *Retelling a Life: Narration and Dialogue in Psychoanalysis*. New York: Basic Books.

_____ ed. (1997), *The Contemporary Kleinians of London*. New York: International Universities Press.

Schlesinger, H. (1995), Facts is facts—or is they? *Internat. J. Psycho-Anal.*, 76:1167–78.

Schwartz, D. (1993), Heterophilia—The love that dare not speak its name. *Psychoanal. Dial.*, 3:643–52.

_____ (1996), Commentary on Stephen A. Mitchell's "Questioning the Social Construction of Gender and Sexual Orientation." *Gender & Psychoanal.* 1:249–260.

Schwartz, J. (1996), Physics, philosophy, psychoanalysis and ideology. *Psychoanal. Dial.*, 4:503–514.

Searles, H. (1975), The patient as therapist to his analyst. In: *Countertransference and Related Subjects*, New York: International Universities Press, pp. 380–459.

_____ (1979), *Countertransference and Related Subjects*. New York: International Universities Press.

Segal, H. (1990), Some comments on the Alexander technique. *Psychoanal. Inq.*, 10:409–414.

_____ (1994), Phantasy and reality. In: *The Contemporary Kleinians of London*, ed. R. Schafer. New York: International Universities Press, pp. 380–459, 1997.

Seligman, S. & Shanok, R. (1995), Subjectivity, complexity, and the social world: Erikson's identity concept and contemporary relational theories. *Psychoanal. Dial.*, 5:537–566.

Shapiro, T. (1984), On neutrality. *J. Amer. Psychoanal. Assn.*, 32: 269–282.

Silverman, M. (1985), Countertransference and the myth of the perfectly analyzed analyst. *Psychoanal. Quart.*, 54:175–99.

Sinclair, U. (1905), *The Jungle.* New York: Signet.

Slavin, M. D. & Kriegman, D. (in press), *The Adaptive Design of the Human Psyche.* New York: Guilford.

Slochower, J. (1996a), Holding and the fate of the analyst's subjectivity. *Psychoanal. Dial.*, 6:323–354.

_____ (1996b), *Holding and Psychoanalysis: A Relational Perspective.* Hillsdale, NJ: The Analytic Press.

Spezzano, C. (1993), *Affect in Psychoanalytic Theory and Therapy: Toward a New Synthesis.* Hillsdale, NJ: The Analytic Press.

_____ (1995), "Classical" versus "contemporary" theory: The differences that matter clinically. *Contemp. Psychoanal.*, 31:20–46.

_____ (1996), The three faces of two-person psychology: Development, ontology, and epistemology. *Psychoanal. Dial.*, 6:599–622.

_____ (in press), The triangle of clinical judgment. *J. Amer. Psychoanal. Assn.*

Spillius, E. B. (1988), *Melanie Klein Today, Vol. 2.* London: Routledge.

_____ (1993), Varieties of envious experience. In: *The Contemporary Kleinians of London*, ed. R. Schafer. New York: International Universities Press, 1997, pp. 143–170.

Steiner, J. (1993), *Psychic Retreat: Pathological Organizations in Psychotic, Neurotic and Borderline Patients.* London: Routledge.

Stern, D. (1989), The analyst's unformulated experience of the patient. *Contemp. Psychoanal.*, 25:1–33.

_____ (1990), Courting surprise. *Contemp. Psychoanal,* 26:452–476.

_____ (1996), The social construction of therapeutic action. *Psychoanal. Inq.*, 16:265–293.

_____ (1997), *Unformulated Experience: From Dissociation to Imagination.* Hillsdale, NJ: The Analytic Press.

Stern, S. (1994), Needed relationships and repeated relationships: An integrated relational perspective. *Psychoanal. Dial.*, 4:317–346.

Stolorow, R. & Atwood, G. (1992), *Contexts of Being: The Intersubjective Foundations of Psychological Life.* Hillsdale, NJ: The Analytic Press.

———— Brandchaft, B. & Atwood, G. (1987), *Psychoanalytic Treatment: An Intersubjective Approach.* Hillsdale, NJ: The Analytic Press.

Stone, L. (1961), *The Psychoanalytic Situation.* New York: International Universities Press.

Strachey, J. (1934), The nature of the therapeutic action of psychoanalysis. In: *The Evolution of Psychoanalytic Technique*, ed. M. Bergmann & F. Hartman. New York: Basic Books, pp. 331–360, 1976.

Strenger, C. (in press), The desire for self creation. *Psychoanal. Dial.*

Sugarman, A. (1995), Psychoanalysis: Treatment of conflict or deficit? *Psychoanal. Psych.*, 12:55–70.

———— & Wilson, A. (1995), Introduction to the section: Contemporary structural analysts critique relational theories. *Psychoanal. Psych.*, 12:1–8.

Sullivan, H. S. (1936), A note on the implications of psychiatry on the study of interpersonal relations for investigators in the social sciences. In: *The Fusion of Psychiatry and Social Science.* New York: Norton, pp. 15–29, 1964.

———— (1938), The data of psychiatry. In: *The Fusion of Psychiatry and Social Science.* New York: Norton, pp. 32 55, 1964.

———— (1940), *Conceptions of Modern Psychiatry.* New York: Norton.

———— (1950), The illusion of personal individuality. In: *The Fusion of Psychiatry and Social Science.* New York: Norton, pp. 198–226, 1964.

———— (1953), *The Interpersonal Theory of Psychiatry.* New York: Norton.

———— (1954), *The Psychiatric Interview.* New York: Norton.

———— (1956), *Clinical Studies in Psychiatry.* New York: Norton.

———— (1965), *Personal Psychopathology.* New York: Norton.

Symington, N. (1983), The analyst's act of freedom as agent of therapeutic change. *Internat. Rev. Psychoanal.*, 10:283–292.

Tansey, M. & Burke, W. (1989), *Understanding Countertransference: From Projective Identification to Empathy.* Hillsdale, NJ: The Analytic Press.

———— (1995), *Philosophical Arguments.* Cambridge, MA: Harvard University Press.

Taylor, C. (1991), *The Ethics of Authenticity.* Cambridge, MA: Harvard University Press.

Thompson, C. (1942), Cultural pressures in the psychology of women.

In: *Essential Papers on the Psychology of Women*, ed.C. Zanardi. New York: New York University Press, pp. 207–220, 1990.

_____ (1950), *Psychoanalysis: Evolution and Development*, New York: Grove Atlantic Monthly Press.

_____ (1964), *Interpersonal Psychoanalysis*, ed. M. Green. New York: Basic Books.

Wachtel, P. (1987), *Action and Insight*. New York: Guilford.

Wallerstein, R. (1990), The corrective emotional experience: Is reconsideration due? *Psychoanal. Inq.*, 10:288–324.

_____ (1995), Locating Erikson in contemporary psychoanalysis. *Psychoanal. Dial.*, 5:567–578.

Webster's New Universal Unabridged Dictionary (1989). New York: Dilithium Press.

Wilson, A. (1995), Mapping the mind in relational psychoanalysis: some critiques, questions and conjectures. *Psychoanal. Psych.*, 12:9–29.

Winnicott, D. (1960), Ego distortion in terms of true and false self. In: *The Maturational Process and the Facilitating Environment*, New York: International Universities Press, 1965, pp. 140–152.

_____ (1986), *Holding and Interpretation: Fragment of an Analysis*. New York: Grove Press, 1987.

Wolstein, B. (1983), The first person in interpersonal relations. *Contemp. Psychoanal.*, 19:522–535.

_____ (1987), Experience, interpretation, self-knowledge. *Contemp. Psychoanal.*, 23:329–349.

INDEX